KT-156-016

Fundamentals of Production/ Operations Management

FIFTH EDITION

Fundamentals of Production/ Operations Management

FIFTH EDITION

William A. Ruch

Department of Decision and Information Systems
Arizona State University

Harold E. Fearon

Center For Advanced Purchasing Studies
Arizona State University

C. David Wieters

Department of Management
New Mexico State University

West Publishing Company
St. Paul * New York * Los Angeles * San Francisco

Copyediting: Carol Danielson

Composition: Parkwood Composition Services, Inc.

Cover Photo: Pete Turner, The Image Bank

COPYRIGHT © 1979, 1983, 1986,
                 1989   By WEST PUBLISHING COMPANY
COPYRIGHT © 1992   By WEST PUBLISHING COMPANY
                           50 W. Kellogg Boulevard
                           P.O. Box 64526
                           St. Paul, MN 55164-1003

All rights reserved   ∞
Printed in the United States of America
99 98 97 96 95 94 93 92   8 7 6 5 4 3 2 1 0

Library of Congress Cataloging-in-Publication Data

Ruch, William A.
    Fundamental of production/operations management.

    Includes index.
    1. Production management. I. Fearon, Harold E.
II. Wieters, David C. III. Title
TS155.F497   1988   658.5   88-20752
ISBN 0–314–92852-9

Contents

Figures, Exhibits, and Tables   *viii*
Preface   *xi*

CHAPTER 1

The Production Function   1

Products Equals Goods and Services   5
Why Study Production/Operations Management?   6
The Production Function   7
Production/Operations Management
    and Other Business Functions   11
History of Production/Operations Management   13
The Future of Production/Operations Management   16
Productivity and International Competitiveness   19
Functions of Production/Operations Management   21
Types of Manufacturing   26
Types of Services   29
Operations Strategy and Objectives   30
Careers in Production/Operations Management   39
Key Concepts   42
References   42
Discussion Questions   43

CHAPTER 2

Product Design and Development   47

Product Life Cycle   48
Product Strategy   50
Research and Development   52
Product Design   55
Designing Services   62
Product Description   63
Break-Even Analysis   66

Evaluating Research and Development   69
Organizing for Product Development   71
Key Concepts   72
References   73
Discussion Questions   73
Problems   75

CHAPTER 3

Location, Layout, Work Study, and Productivity   79

Facilities Location   80
Facilities Layout   86
Work Study   97
Work Measurement   105
Individual and Organizational Productivity   111
Key Concepts   119
References   119
Discussion Questions   120
Problems   121

CHAPTER 4

Forecasting, Planning, and Scheduling Production   125

Forecasting Demand   125
Planning for Production   136
Scheduling Production   139
Planning and Controlling Projects   150
Key Concepts   156
References   156
Discussion Questions   157
Problems   158

CHAPTER 5

Purchasing/Materials Management   163

Objectives of Purchasing/Materials Management   165
Importance of the Purchasing Function   167
Organization of Purchasing/Materials Management   175
Purchasing Prerogatives   181
The Standard Purchasing System   182
Recognition of Need   184
Description of Need   184
Source Selection   187
Determining Price   192
Preparation of the Purchase Agreement   196

Follow-up and Expediting   196
Receipt and Inspection   197
Invoice Clearance and Payment   198
Maintenance of Records   198
Current and Future Developments   199
Key Concepts   205
References   205
Discussion Questions   206
Problems   207

CHAPTER 6

Inventory Management   **209**

The Functions of Inventories   210
Economics of Inventory Management   212
Economic Order Quantity Model   215
Safety Stocks and Uncertainty   221
MRP and Inventory Management   224
JIT: Just-In-Time Management System   229
Physical Care of Inventories   234
Key Concepts   236
References   236
Discussion Questions   237
Problems   237

CHAPTER 7

Quality Management   **241**

Product Quality   242
The Meaning of Quality   243
Total Quality Management   246
Factors Affecting Quality   250
Quality Costs   253
Statistical Quality Control   258
Process Capability   270
The Growing Importance of Quality   275
Key Concepts   276
References   276
Discussion Questions   277
Problems   279

GLOSSARY   281

INDEX   299

Figures, Exhibits, and Tables

Figures

1-1	The Production Function	9
1-2	U.S. Labor Productivity Growth	20
1-3	International Labor Productivity	21
1-4	A Typology of Services	30
2-1	Stages of the Product Life Cycle	49
2-2	Bill of Materials for a Yo-Yo	64
2-3	Bill of Materials for a Car Wash	65
2-4	Route Sheet for a Yo-Yo	66
2-5	Break-Even Chart	67
2-6	Break-Even Time Model	70
3-1	Total Costs for Alternative Locations A, B, C, and D Compared to Volume	85
3-2	Matrix for Transportation Method of Linear Programming	86
3-3	Solution Matrix for Proposed Site A	87
3-4	Solution Matrix for Proposed Site B	87
3-5	Process Layout Showing Movement of Two Different Products	89
3-6	Product or Line Layout Showing Movement of Two Different Products	90
3-7	Layout by Process Versus Cellular Layout	91
3-8	Process Chart	100
3-9	Flow Diagram	102
3-10	Assembly Chart (Garden Hoe)	103
3-11	Multiple Activity Chart	104
3-12	Operation Chart	106
3-13	Calculation of Standard Time	108
3-14	Calculation of a Performance Rating	110
3-15	Partial Productivity Measures	113
3-16	Nine-Box Model of Productivity	116
3-17	First Quarter to Second Quarter Comparisons	117

4-1	Illustrations of Seasonal, Trend, Cycle, and Random Time-Series Fluctuations Cycles	129
4-2	Multiplicative Model for Trend and Seasonals	134
4-3	Transforming Strategic Planning into Actions Plans	137
4-4	The Detailed Schedule	140
4-5	Frame Bill of Materials	142
4-6	MRP Time-Phased Inventory Records	144
4-7	Gantt Chart	149
4-8	PERT Network	154
5-1	Return-on-Assets Factors	174
5-2	Multidivision Organization Structure for Purchasing	178
5-3	Organization Strucutre for Materials Management	180
6-1	Inventory Levels over Time	216
6-2	Inventory Costs With and Without Quantity Discounts	218
6-3	Inventory Levels with Replenishment Spread over Time	220
6-4	Contrast Between Uniform and Lumpy Demands on Inventory	225
6-5	Different Lot-Sizing Techniques	227
7-1	Fishbone Diagram	245
7-2	Behavioral and Technical Factors Affecting Quality	251
7-3	Quality-Cost Relationships	258
7-4	Sampling Errors	261
7-5	Operating-Characteristics Curve	262
7-6	Effect of Changing the Acceptance Number	263
7-7	Effect of Changing the Sample Size	264
7-8	P-Chart	266
7-9	$\bar{X}$ and R-Chart	267
7-10	Control Chart Patterns	271
7-11	Process Capabililty Index	273

Exhibits

4-1	Forecast Model Selection Criteria	128
4-2	Job-Shop Priority Scheduling Rules	147
7-1	Costs of Quality	254

Tables

1-1	Production Function for Selected Firms	3
1-2	Characteristics of Process-Focused and Process-Focused Firms	32
1-3	Elements of Operations Strategy	34
1-4	Career Tracks in Productions/Operations Managment	40

3-1	Weighted Factors Analysis of Locations	84
4-1	Methods of Smoothing Random Variations	131
4-2	The Multiplicative Model	132
4-3	PERT Data on Activities: Precedence and Time Estimates	153
5-1	Cost of Materials—Value of Industry Shipments Ratios for Manufacturing Firms, 1988	170
7-1	Factors for Determining Control Chart Limits	268

Preface

As we rapidly approach the twenty-first century, the need for understanding fundamentals of production/operations management has never been greater. The success of our economic system and the organizations in it depend on our ability to productively employ resources–human and physical–in the creation of goods and services. Our standard of living and quality of life will be determined, to a great extent, by the effectiveness of our production systems and their competitiveness in world markets.

This book was written with the belief that an understanding of the managerial issues involved in organizational operations can help prepare both college students and business executives to cope with the challenges of designing and managing production systems. The teachings of POM need not use a highly mathematical approach; such an approach tends to distance students and managers from the problems they generally face. For those that need them, advanced texts and specialized courses delve more deeply into this field.

Nor should POM be limited to applications in manufacturing. With each new edition, we have broadened the coverage of service producing systems, and this edition is no exception. Where appropriate, we have included service applications or special sections to indicate how service firms differ from manufacturing organizations.

We have tried to make the book more "teachable" for the instructor, more readable for the student, and more relevant to the problems that manufacturing and service organizations face today. New sections on operations strategy, productivity, and Just-In-Time (JIT) management systems have been added, and substantial revisions have been made to the coverage of quality, project management, and inventory management to reflect current developments. More end-of-chapter problems and an expanded glossary make the book more useful in the classroom.

Our purpose is twofold: to impart a broad understanding of production/operations management for students majoring in other areas, and to build a solid foundation for those who have chosen this field as their primary area of study. Because the book is compact, supplements of cases, current readings, computer simulations, or specialized books can be added to fit the preferred focus and teaching methodology of the instructor.

In this edition, the fifth, we are again indebted to our colleagues in the academic and business communities who have provided constructive advice. We thank the faculty, staff, and graduate students in the Department of Decision and Information Systems and in the Center for Advanced Purchasing Studies at Arizona State University and in the Department of Management at the New Mexico State University. The authors take full responsibility for the content of the book.

We express our gratitude to the following professors for their helpful comments:

Billy Ng
Arizona State University

Emil Rau
Hofstra University

Steve Faulkner
Spartanburg Technical College

Steve Redmer
Lakeshore Technical College

Robert Smith
California State–Long Beach

Mary S. Thibodeaux
University of North Texas

Kirk R. Karwan
University of South Carolina

The Authors

Fundamentals of Production/ Operations Management

FIFTH EDITION

C H A P T E R

1

The Production Function

Production/operations management is the art and science of producing things for consumption. The creation of manufactured goods and services–which we refer to collectively as products–is fundamental to the survival and success of any business organization. It follows, therefore, that the concepts of production/operations management (POM) are fundamental to the education of business managers and students alike.

Two disturbing trends have emerged in recent years to cause concern in business firms as well as in business schools. First, the manufacturing superiority that once clearly resided in the United States has begun to migrate to other parts of the globe. A large part of the automobile industry, most of the steel industry, all production of television sets, VCRs, and stereos, and a significant portion of the textile industry are now located in Europe and the Pacific Rim countries. Many analysts attribute this phenomenon of the "hollowing" of American industry to the inability to manage the production function in the organization to produce products that can compete in quality, cost, availability, and performance with foreign-made items. American managers are accused of forgetting that the primary purpose of a manufacturing organization is to produce a product that satisfies customer needs.

The second major trend is the rapid growth of the service sector combined with a corresponding increase in complaints about "poor service." Everyone has stories about ineffective and inefficient services; about waiting in line, errors in orders or paperwork, and return calls to correct improperly performed services. In the medical field, for example, malpractice insurance rates are skyrocketing because customers are demanding that doctors and other medical professionals be held accountable for delivering the proper high-quality services the first time. Services, like manufacturing, are not immune to foreign competition. In banking, for example, the once dominant U.S. position has eroded to the point where the largest U.S. bank is now twenty-eighth on the list of world banks.

Yet, examples of superior American-made products abound and many U.S. firms are counted among the world-class leaders that set the standards for effectiveness, efficiency, productivity, quality, and innovation. Some U.S. companies produce steel that is sold in Japan. McDonald's, Disney, American Express, and many others are unequaled in the goods and services they provide, and they can compete on a worldwide basis. The capability is there if it can be properly managed.

A part of the answer to becoming a world-class organization is to return to the basic premise of designing and producing products that meet international standards. That means placing the production/operations function in a high priority and employing the latest tools, techniques, theories, and ideas in the design and control of the processes and systems within the organization. Concepts that made perfect sense in the 1950 environment could spell disaster for a firm today. Old ideas have been replaced with new ways of thinking that respond to the changing needs and constraints of the 1990s and beyond. The study of production/operations management–and the continual study of the changes that are taking place in the field–is essential for the survival of the firm.

In simplest terms, production/operations management (POM) is the study of the conversion of inputs into outputs in any organization. It deals with manufactured goods and with services. It includes large and small firms, profit and nonprofit organizations. With some modifications it applies to all government functions, bureaus, and agencies. Table 1-1 provides a sampling of organizations from different industries and lists the inputs, demand, conversion process, and outputs for each. Each of these terms and their interrelationships are explored in greater depth in the remainder of this chapter.

This book describes the fundamentals of those areas that make up production/operations management. It discusses the importance of each area and shows how the various functions fit together to create an effective, efficient production system. It provides the key elements of each subfunction but does not attempt to explore all the details and

Table 1-1
Production Function for Selected Firms

Organization	Basic Inputs	Demand	Conversion	Products
Automobile manufacturer	Labor, capital, material, energy	Forecasts	Fabrication and assembly	Autos and other vehicles; services such as financing and warranties
Fast-food restaurant	Labor, capital, material, energy	Counter customer	Cooking and preparation	Sandwiches, fries, drinks; friendly, efficient service
Hospital	Labor, capital, material, energy	Ill or injured people	Health care	Healthy people
University	Labor, capital, material, energy	Applications for enrollment	Teaching and research	Graduates and new knowledge (articles, books, papers, etc.)

Table 1-1 (Continued)

Organization	Basic Inputs	Demand	Conversion	Products
Bank	Labor, capital, material, energy	Customer requests	Financial analysis, decision making, record keeping	Loans, checking accounts, savings plans
City Parks and Recreation Department	Labor, capital, material, energy	Voter preferences, enrollments, visitations	Construction and maintenance of parks; operation of programs	Softball leagues; special events, park facilities
Home builder	Labor, capital, material, energy	Customer order	Construction activities	Houses
Airline	Labor, capital, material, energy	Ticket sales, shipping requests	Aircraft scheduling, operation, and maintenance	Transported freight and passengers; friendly service

nuances of each area. In-depth discussions of the tools, techniques, and issues in POM can be found in more advanced texts, some of which are listed at the end of each chapter.

Products Equals Goods and Services

Production and operations management often is mistakenly associated only with manufactured goods. Indeed, today's instruction in POM traces its roots to college courses titled "Production Management," "Manufacturing Management," and "Factory Management." Yet the addition of the word *operations* signifies that many of the concepts originally developed in and for the factory apply equally well to service firms, not-for-profit organizations, and government agencies. Manufacturing companies generally have a Production or Manufacturing Department responsible for the creation of the product. In service firms, such as airlines and financial institutions, the comparable department is usually called "Operations."

All nonmanufacturing organizations perform the same basic functions as manufacturing firms. They acquire inputs of people, materials, and equipment, convert them into outputs (in this case, services), and deliver them to their customers. This is true for banks, hospitals, public utilities, restaurants, counseling services, state parks, military bases, barber shops, bookstores, trucking firms, libraries, health clubs, and, of course, universities.

Each firm must respond to a demand or customer order in some form. In many firms, especially large manufacturers, products are produced to meet forecasts of anticipated customer needs. In other cases, notably most services, the firm must wait for the customer order before the product can be completed. Consider three examples: buying a bicycle, contracting for landscaping services, and using a hospital emergency room. The bicycle manufacturer determines the design, color, and other features of the unit, produces the bicycle months in advance, and then offers it for sale. The landscaping service, in spite of its title, deals with physical products that can be held in inventory until a customer order allows the trees and plants to be arranged at a particular site. The hospital emergency room must be prepared to respond quickly and effectively to any medical emergency that arises at any time.

The nature of the demands in these three situations is different. In one case, the customer must be present for the product to be completed. In the other two cases, the action can be done by phone or through an agent. Similar contrasts can be drawn among these three in terms of timing, control over the specifications of the product, and other aspects of demand. As we will see later in the book, these situations differ also in the relative mix and importance of POM areas such as quality, scheduling, and inventory control.

Up to this point and throughout the book, we use the term **product** to refer to a manufactured good or to a service. Bicycles, automobiles, furniture, processed food, and books are all products. So too are checking accounts, haircuts, counseling sessions, health-club packages, sporting events, and career training programs. The term **product** is a more efficient way of saying the cumbersome phrase *goods and services*. More importantly, it helps us deal with manufacturing and service firms within the same framework.

With services accounting for a larger and larger portion of business activity, it is important that principles and practices proven beneficial in manufacturing be used to make the provision of services more effective and efficient. Scheduling patients in the hospital emergency room example can be accomplished using waiting-line methods (queueing theory) just as these methods are used to schedule jobs in a machine shop. Assigning costs to waiting patients is more difficult than for batches of materials, but it can be done. The challenges may be greater because of the less tangible nature of the services, but the potential rewards make the effort worthwhile.

Why Study Production/Operations Management?

The study of production/operations management has sometimes suffered from a bad reputation among college students. The operations part of any organization is neither as obvious nor as well understood as marketing, advertising, personnel, and finance. Operations management has been mistakenly believed to be a highly quantitive field that applies only to the running of factories. In part, this erroneous view of operations as a technical field rather than as a key part of the management of any firm accounts for the competitive problems the United States is experiencing in international product markets. In this text, the emphasis is on the **management** of operations. Well-managed organizations are more competitive than poorly managed ones.

The first reason to study POM, therefore, is to develop a level of expertise in operations management graduates. The success of all types of organizations depends on the knowledge and talent of its managers.

Second, many students find that the field of production/operations management can be more intriguing and exciting than their initial impressions led them to believe. Production is where the action is in most business firms. The operation and control of the production process–

whether producing hamburgers, automobiles, or insurance policies–is demanding work, requiring talent, skill, and a desire to get the job done right and on time. The people who manage the direct work process derive great satisfaction from seeing the results of their efforts in terms of goods shipped and services delivered.

A third reason for studying production/operations management relates to the laws of supply and demand. At present, more opportunities than graduates exist in this field. As the need continues to grow in service industries for people who can plan, schedule, and control, the market for POM graduates will remain stable. In many universities, POM graduates receive more job offers at higher salaries than any of their peers.

Not everyone should become a POM major, but all business students should be aware of the nature of each of the major subfunctions of business. The fourth reason for studying POM, then, is to complete an education that would be seriously lacking without it. Knowledge of the special problems and issues in POM enhances the effectiveness of the accountant, the marketing manager, the financial analyst, or the personnel specialist. An integrated-systems approach based upon an understanding and appreciation of all business functions is the goal of every organization.

The Production Function

Every organization has a production function, just as it has a finance function and a marketing function. Finance is concerned with the acquisition and use of funds, while marketing is focused on selling and distributing products. The production function is the third side of this triangle, for it uses the funds acquired by finance to buy raw materials, machines, and labor, and converts these into products that marketing can sell.

Inputs

Part of the production function concerns the acquisition of inputs, as illustrated in figure 1-1. Any product or service that is created requires some combination of materials, machines, and people. General Motors employs hundreds of thousands of people, ranging from unskilled or semiskilled workers to top executives. GM uses billions of dollars worth of plants, machines, and tools and purchases materials (steel, glass, fabric, plastic, etc.) at the rate of more than 100 million dollars a day to produce the millions of cars the world wants. One of their suppliers,

Small Parts, Inc., employs about fifty workers and a dozen machines to make tiny metal parts out of strip steel. The two firms are vastly different in size and scope, yet each draws from the same basic categories of inputs to produce its unique outputs.

The list of inputs is almost endless. The people category includes unskilled, semiskilled, and skilled workers; clerical personnel; secretaries; technicians; supervisors; professionals (doctors, teachers, etc.); part-time students; supervisors; engineers; artists; accountants; and executives.

Similarly, materials and equipment come in all forms, sizes, and shapes. A critical part of the production function is the acquisition of the proper raw materials, tools, machines, and other supplies and equipment to permit the efficient and effective operation of the firm. The lack of even low-cost parts can idle hundreds of workers and their equipment.

Acquisition of capital inputs (land, buildings, and machinery) is generally done at high levels in the organization. A firm frequently enlists specialists in real estate, finance, law, and capital budgeting to work as a team to decide on locations and equipment for new facilities. Large motel chains, fast-food firms, and many retail houses illustrate this situation. Where these acquisitions are less frequent, a firm may designate key executives to act as an ad hoc committee to work with outside consultants in reaching a decision.

Acquisition of people is the primary responsibility of the personnel or human resources department. Recruiting, interviewing, testing, selecting, hiring, placing, evaluating, compensating, and terminating are subfunctions of this activity. The personnel department provides a service to the rest of the firm by arranging for the proper workers when and where they are needed. Trained personnel specialists can perform this task more effectively and efficiently than could each department duplicating these functions.

Both manufacturing firms and service organizations (including government) rely on purchasing managers to obtain material inputs, including raw materials, purchased parts, and supplies. Purchasing managers, skilled in the techniques of buying and knowledgeable about the products for which they are responsible, buy the proper raw materials for a hospital or a restaurant; this task is no less important than in a manufacturing firm.

The purchasing department staff may constitute a small percentage of the organization's personnel, yet, because of the dollars involved, it exerts a major influence on the profit-making ability of the firm. Chapter 5 examines this purchasing function in greater depth.

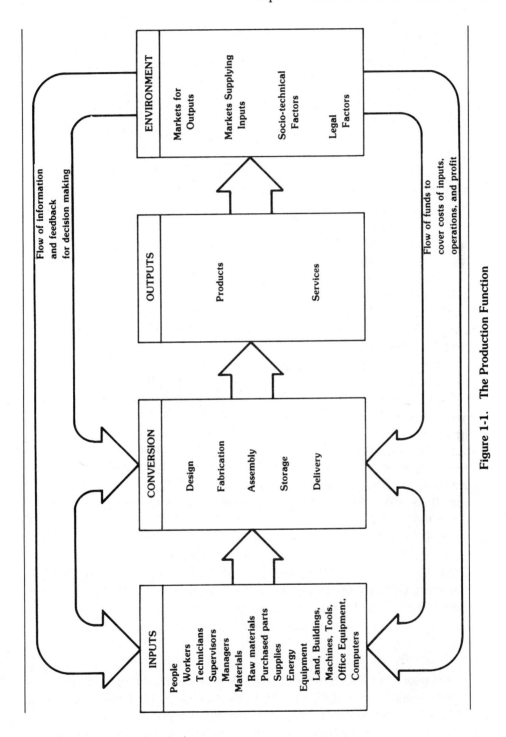

Figure 1-1. The Production Function

Conversion

The conversion process is the merging of time and place and the transformation of inputs to make them more usable and accessible to customers. The customers may be the final consumers, or they may be other business firms in the chain between natural resources and final users. Because decisions of time and place are handled primarily by the marketing and distribution functions of the firm, the emphasis in conversion is on form of the output—that is, the creation and production of products.

A useful distinction can be made between the *technology* of transformation and the *methodology* of transformation. Technology refers to the scientific principles applied to convert inputs to outputs; often, this is unique within an industry. For example, the petroleum industry applies its technology—derived from chemistry, physics, hydraulics, and other sciences—to convert crude oil into gasoline, aviation fuel, asphalt, tar, paint, and many other salable products. No other industry uses exactly the same technology.

A dairy, on the other hand, begins with raw milk and produces whole milk, skim milk, butter, cheese, ice cream, and other products. The technology in a dairy is quite different from that of an oil company, yet the processes are similar enough to allow much of the same methodology to be applied. The problems of scheduling, controlling, storing, shipping, and generally *managing* the two processes are similar.

This text will concentrate on the methodology of transformation and will draw examples from specific technologies. Principles of scheduling can be discussed and then applied to either a machine shop or the receiving ward of a hospital. Techniques of inventory control apply equally well to inventories of fresh vegetables or auto parts. Although the examples vary, the reader is encouraged to apply the principles and techniques in each chapter to as many organizations or processes as possible. Laundries, libraries, fraternities, bicycle-repair shops, government bureaus, real estate agencies, and even universities have transformation processes to which the tools and techniques of POM can be applied.

Outputs

It is easy to recognize that the output of an automobile manufacturer is automobiles, the output of a restaurant is meals, and the output of a university is graduates. Very few firms, however, produce only one output. As noted earlier, the auto manufacturer produces cars with an array of body styles, colors, and optional equipment. It also may produce trucks, industrial vehicles, refrigerators, and railroad engines. In addition to the physical products, the firm also may provide many services, such as repairs, delivery, setup, and financing.

Two outputs in the firm's array may complement or supplement each other to the firm's advantage. In other cases, outputs may conflict, to the detriment of profitability and effectiveness. For example, a firm that produces razor blades may benefit if it also produces razors, but a travel agency probably would not benefit from also selling TV sets.

When manufacturing a product, the firm begins with raw materials, feeds them through a conversion process, and ends up with a finished product ready to sell. In the decision-making process, however, the time sequence of the steps is reversed. The firm begins with the design of the output, forecasts sales, and then uses the specifications and projections it obtains to set up the conversion process and acquire inputs. Thus, the desired output is the goal from which all other decisions are derived.

Environment

Every business operates in an environment that provides markets for the products it produces, as well as markets from which the firm buys inputs. In addition, the environment provides sociotechnical and legal constraints and guidelines within which the firm must operate if it is to be law abiding, socially responsible, and successful.

To make the model complete, two feedback loops are necessary. First, the sale of goods and services produces the flow of dollars back to the firm so it can purchase additional inputs, pay operating costs, and generate profits for owners. Second, a constant flow of information from the environment to the firm allows management to employ new technology and respond to changing needs and desires of customers.

Production/Operations Management and Other Business Functions

The production/operations function of any business interacts closely with each of the other key functions of the organization. In concert, these functions—and their interactions—determine the success or failure of an organization. One company may be called a "marketing organization," another an "accounting firm"; yet each must integrate the functions of finance and accounting, human resources (personnel), marketing, and production/operations. Although often treated separately for purposes of analysis and study, the functions are merged into a total system in an organization; dividing lines between functions are not easy to see in the real world. It is important, therefore, not only to examine the production/operations function but to keep in mind critical interactions with other functions.

Production/operations employs the capital resources acquired by the finance function. It converts funds into equipment, tools, facilities, and inventories to produce products. The decision to replace an old machine with a new one is not solely a technical decision, nor is it solely a financial one; it is a combination of the two. The decision is made using capital budgeting analysis based on information concerning the capacity of the machine and its relationship to other phases of the production process. For example, the new machine may produce at a higher speed, but it may also require more maintenance, produce more scrap, or use more energy.

Accounting data are needed to make this equipment decision as well as most other decisions in the production/operations function. Inventory policies, for example, depend upon the value of the item in stock. The knotty problem of determining the value of the in-stock unit, either purchased or manufactured internally, depends on sound accounting principles applied through an accurate, timely management-information system to evaluate the effects of past production/operations decisions and to provide input to future decisions.

Production/operations cannot function without people. The human resources function is to recruit and train workers to fill positions within the production process according to the job design and skill assessments performed by work-study analysts. As changes–such as overtime, adding a shift, employing newer technologies, or redesigning the product–are made in the production process, they must be coordinated with the human resources function. To ensure a smooth transition as the change takes place, this coordination should occur during the planning phase.

The interaction between production/operations and the marketing function is both complex and critical. It is simplistic to say that marketing sells what production produces, or vice versa. Actually, marketing research gathers information that guides the design or redesign of products. A marketing forecast of sales potential must be integrated with a production forecast of capacity to provide a realistic production schedule. Marketing promotes and sells, production produces and delivers. If any link of that chain is weak, the entire organization suffers. Many cases can be found of firms with good production *and* good marketing functions that have failed because of a lack of coordination between the two.

History of Production/Operations Management

Production/operations management began when the first crude tool was produced. In the ensuing years, we have reached the point where nearly everything we touch is a manufactured or processed product. Improvement in *performing* manufacturing tasks has been a gradual, if not a consistent, trend. But the systematic *study* of production is a relatively recent phenomenon, confined mainly to the last two hundred years and concentrated in the last ninety.

We think of mass production as a twentieth-century concept, yet assembly lines were in use in the early fifteenth century. Venetian shipbuilders equipped their fighting galleys by towing them through a water channel between warehouses where the provisions and equipment were stored. They eventually reached a production level of equipping a ship every thirty-six minutes.

In the fifteenth century, no mass markets existed, nor were there advertising, distribution networks, or other support services. Measurement technology and manufacturing methods were not yet sufficiently precise to produce interchangeable parts. Mass production, therefore, was found only in rare, isolated instances; manufacturing at this time was performed predominantly by independent artisans.

Factories began to appear in the early eighteenth century in the textile industry. Later, factories were built to accommodate other types of manufacturing. In 1776, Adam Smith described, in *The Wealth of Nations*, the subdivision of labor employed in manufacturing straight pins. Later scholars, such as Charles Babbage, developed and refined Smith's theories of work organization. From 1700 to 1900, the industrial revolution flourished, and students of this field attempted to describe the new developments and provide theoretical foundations for existing practices. Not until the twentieth century were scholars able to develop theories based upon research and experimentation and then to implement them in business.

Frederick W. Taylor was one of the first people to study business using a scientific approach. In the early 1900s, business knowledge was not yet organized into principles. Taylor studied business by beginning with basics, experimenting and adding building blocks to form a cogent body of knowledge. Many of the principles of management he developed are still being taught and used today.

Other pioneering scholars such as Frank and Lillian Gilbreth advanced Taylor's work in their motion and time study. Industrialists like Henry Ford applied these principles to mass production and built empires from which flowed manufactured goods that many could afford.

The early twentieth century was a period of rapid growth and change in business. Factories were becoming more efficient, even though working conditions in many of them were not yet entirely humane. Upton Sinclair described the evils of this capitalistic system in his exposé of the meat-packing industry, *The Jungle*. The working conditions he described were horrifying, but rather than repelling people from capitalism, his writing led to government regulations (such as the Pure Food and Drug Act) and fueled the labor movement to develop powerful industrial unions to protect workers' rights. Before the middle of the twentieth century, human-relations research had begun to develop principles of effective utilization, rather than exploitation, of workers.

Many tools and techniques developed in the first half of this century have enhanced the efficiency and effectiveness of business organizations. In 1915, F. W. Harris developed the economic order quantity formula that now is a fundamental concept in inventory control. A decade later, several individuals, including H. F. Dodge, H. G. Romig, and W. A. Shewhart, applied probability theory to quality control and introduced the concept of assessing quality based on a random sample. Waiting-line theory was born, and work sampling was first applied. On other fronts, the first experiments in work-group behavior were laying foundations for human-relations and organization behavior theories.

The decade of the 1940s and World War II produced the most concentrated manufacturing effort yet known. Operations research (OR) teams found ways to better utilize severely limited resources to fill the greatly expanded needs caused by the war. When the war ended, the military outputs were changed, but the new OR techniques had found a permanent place in industry.

Perhaps the single most important technological advancement in the recent history of business is the computer. Computer applications in accounting, finance, marketing, and personnel abound, as they do in POM. The various tasks of scheduling and control always have been performed in business, but the computer now permits complex algorithms to be applied routinely in situations where judgment and guessing previously prevailed. Material requirements planning (MRP), a technique that determines when and how much material to order, is becoming an invaluable managerial tool, but it cannot be employed effectively without a computer because it involves a vast number of calculations.

Just-in-time (JIT) production systems, popularized in Japanese manufacturing firms, rely on computerized scheduling of raw materials to arrive just as they are needed in production, thus eliminating costly levels of inventory. (MRP, JIT, and other systems are described in more detail in chapters 4 and 6).

Recent developments in minicomputers are making it possible for many small manufacturing companies to take advantage of computer control techniques in manufacturing. In fact, the elements that constitute a minicomputer are becoming difficult to determine. Minicomputers originally were classified as small computer systems with limited storage capacity and functional capability; they often were used to support only a single application. With the explosive growth in computer technology, however, these so-called minicomputers have capacities and functions that equal or surpass the larger data-processing equipment of just a few years ago, and a wide assortment of manufacturing software support for the minicomputer user now is available.

The microprocessor–a computer on a chip–is another modern technological development that has far-reaching implications for the management of production systems. Microprocessors are designed to perform a single application but are inexpensive and can be preprogrammed to perform a wide variety of logic functions; consider, for example, the capabilities found in video games and hand-held calculators. The major difference between a microprocessor and a small computer is that there is limited ability to reprogram a microprocessor: All the programmed logic is predetermined and actually designed into the physical circuitry itself. Microprocessors are being developed to support new applications of industrial robots and many of the functions performed in computer-aided design and computer-aided manufacturing (CAD/CAM) systems.

As more and more elements of the production process become automated and computerized, operations managers have recognized the need to tie together these "islands of automation" into an integrated system to avoid problems of coordination and suboptimization. Computer-integrated manufacturing (CIM) is the new term for the systems that seek this objective. Still in its infancy, CIM promises to be the key link in advancing manufacturing into the flexible, responsive, efficient "factory of the future."

Technologies related to minicomputers and microprocessors also may affect production planning and control systems. These include magnetics (i.e., the magnetic strip used on the back of bank cards); optical reading of numeric and alphabetic printed data; and light scanning or laser sensing devices like those used in supermarket checkout systems and department store point-of-sale terminals. In an operations environment, such devices may be used for data collection in receiving, storeroom, and shipping operations.

The Future of Production/Operations Management

Until recently, factories have become more efficient by employing mass-production technology that involved moving identical product units along a transfer line (as in the automobile assembly plant). The gains in efficiency were often offset by losses in flexibility. The factory of the past, for all of its advantages, could be characterized as rigid, inflexible, and unresponsive to rapid change. The factory of the future seeks to remove these disadvantages while retaining the cost efficiency of large-scale production.

Some describe the factory of the future as a design engineer working with a CAD system to design and test a product without having to build a prototype. Release of the design in this ideal environment would trigger the ordering of necessary materials and the programming of automated equipment from the design engineer's data. Flexible machines would produce one or many units of the product to the customer's order and quickly change over to produce other products. The CIM system would allow coordination of all aspects of ordering, processing, and distribution, with rapid response time to any changes.

Few factories have achieved this level of sophistication, but some are approaching it and many will achieve it in the near future. Flexible manufacturing systems (FMS) have the goal of producing as few as one unit at a time with the speed and efficiency of an assembly line. At Motorola, for example, pagers are produced in a standard case, but with special features and programming that includes a unique frequency for the customer. When first set up, the cycle time from the receipt of an order to the shipping of the product was twenty-nine days. Today, by using highly automated programmable equipment (robots) and sophisticated order-entry and information processing, they can ship a unit one hour and fifteen minutes after the order is received!

As systems like this continue to be developed, more engineers, technicians, and managers will displace production workers, and we will reach capital-to-labor ratios previously thought impossible. The "lights out" factory, where machines run unattended producing products used to be a fantasy. Today one factory in Japan runs three shifts of production with only two shifts of employees. The third shift is run entirely by computer controlled machines.

Old services are being revamped and new ones are being created at a fantastic rate. The United States became a service economy in the early 1970s, when people began to have the money and leisure time to demand more services. This trend is bound to continue. Service firms will grow in absolute numbers, and the value of their output will grow as a percentage of the gross national product.

These new businesses provide services, primarily, but they still must convert inputs into outputs. They must make forecasts and purchase materials. Their activities must be planned, scheduled, and controlled. It may be more difficult to measure the quality of an intangible service than that of a manufactured item, but the quality is no less important. As services grow relative to manufactured goods, the emphasis of operations management will evolve into new applications of existing principles and the development of new techniques of measurement and control.

The similarities between manufacturing and service industries are closer than one might imagine. Just as the factory of the future will attempt to become more responsive while maintaining its efficiency through computerization and automation, we can see similar trends beginning to creep into service businesses. Fast-food restaurants, for example, are expanding their product lines (menus), becoming more flexible ("Have it your way"), adding more automated equipment such as soft drink-filling machines and automatic friers, while attempting to retain their cost effectiveness, quality of product, and level of service. With some creative thinking, we can imagine a totally automated fast-food facility in which the customer uses a debit card to place an order and watches as a hamburger and fries are prepared entirely by machines.

Although predicting the future is risky, another trend in operations management that is likely to continue in the foreseeable future is the increasing sophistication of technology in products and in the processes used to create them. Plastics and other synthetic substances have replaced many natural products such as leather and cotton. As a new basic product is created, existing industries change and new industries emerge. Oil companies become petro-chemical firms, and electronics companies drop radios and televisions to produce medical instruments, calculators, and even watches. And we are standing on the threshold of an entirely new industry in biogenetics.

Just as bulldozers now substitute for a pick and shovel, lasers will be commonly employed in the future in such diverse industries as mining and medicine. Solar-powered equipment will alleviate demands and restraints on other energy-distribution networks. And the revolution that has begun in information processing, storage, and retrieval will cause many changes in communications within the business community. Evidence of this is the fact that cellular phones are now as common as pagers were a few years ago.

Another trend representing a challenge for the future is production of products on a worldwide scale. Many firms market their outputs in many countries, and, in some, the manufacturing process transcends national boundaries. Cotton grown in the United States is processed into printed cloth and cut into patterns; the pieces then are shipped to the other side of the globe (Taiwan, Korea, or Hong Kong), where they are sewn into shirts; finally, the shirts are transported back to the United States to be sold. Some of our "American" cars are assembled in one European country from parts made in half a dozen other countries. In some cases, we have seen entire product lines (radios and TVs, for example) migrate to other countries where wage rates, natural resources, or some other factors permit sufficient manufacturing economies to outweigh increased transportation costs.

Recent developments in Europe and Asia have created new challenges for American industry. The European Common Market, slated to be substantially revised in 1992, will operate more like a single country in terms of its production, labor market, consumer market, and financial community than it has in the past. The democratization of Eastern Europe is progressing, but its ultimate outcome is still unknown. And one of the largest markets in the world, China, is still very much in doubt as to whether it will become a major economy with corresponding production and consumption of international products. Finally, the entire southern hemisphere–Africa, South America, and Australia–are poised to enter the world market if social and political problems can be resolved. Whether these developments are advantages (new markets) or disadvantages (new competitors) to American industry depends on our ability to remain competitive in the production of products for global markets.

Services, too, are becoming international. Telephone service, credit cards, hotels, restaurants, and many other services can handle our needs in almost any part of the globe.

The trend toward increased internationalization will be enhanced by less expensive and faster transportation methods for physical goods and more efficient communication technologies for most services. The deterrents, however, include a lack of standardization of technologies, differences among common business practices, and conflicts among governments. In spite of these disadvantages, world trade is likely to increase in the future and carry with it greater challenges for operations management. When territorial boundaries are crossed, we enter new political and cultural ideologies and may find that our assumptions about designing jobs, scheduling work, and controlling operations must be replaced with new, creative solutions.

As economies become international, we become increasingly aware of the effects of industrialization on the ecology of the planet. The production function of the future, therefore, must bear its responsibility for producing products that are environmentally consonant and for assuring that the byproducts of production are properly managed and controlled to preserve the environment.

Productivity and International Competitiveness

Productivity, in simplest terms, is a ratio of outputs to inputs. It describes how well an individual worker, a business firm, or a national economy utilizes resources to produce valued outputs of goods and services. Unfortunately, the term is often misunderstood. Productivity frequently is limited only to the labor input, individual workers are commonly blamed for poor productivity performance, and the road to productivity improvement is often seen as working faster and harder. Generally, none of these conceptions is true.

To put productivity in perspective, consider the history of agriculture in the U.S. In 1840, over seventy percent of the workforce was on the farm; all other goods and services were produced by the remaining thirty percent. Today we produce much more food with less than four percent of the workforce. Farmers are not working harder or faster (nor are their oxen) but they do have (1) much more advanced capital equipment (such as tractors and combines), (2) a greater level of technical knowledge (such as rotation of crops and irrigation methods, (3) better raw materials (such as hybrid seeds, chemical fertilizers, and herbicides), (4) better managerial knowledge (such as economics of farming), and (5) better systems (such as co-ops, larger farms, shared resources, and subcontracted harvesting). The relatively poor productivity of the 1840s was not the farmer's fault; the road to productivity improvement involved the integration and application of technology and knowledge to reach the level we have today. The same can be said of any industry.

Productivity–how well we use our resources to produce goods and services–is a prime determinant of our standard of living and, to some extent, our level of civilization. We have more goods, more services, more leisure time, more fine arts, more cancer research, and more space exploration this century than we have in the past because we have learned to be more productive in the production of necessities. Without productivity improvement, we can have more of one thing only by having less of another.

Productivity also affects our international competitiveness as a nation. Our ability to produce high-quality products with a minimum of resources affects our trade balance, relative inflation rate, unemployment levels and many other factors. When our productivity growth rate falls

Annual Percent Growth
Output per Hour

Period	Non-Farm Private Business	Manufacturing	Estimated Non-Farm Non-Manufacturing
1968-78	1.3%	2.6%	0.9%
1978-82	(0.4)	1.2	(0.9)
1982-86	2.1	4.7	1.3
1986-89	1.0	2.7	0.4
Last 12 Months Oct. 89- Sept. 90	(0.5)	4.0	(2.0)

Source: Bureau of Labor Statistics, American Productivity and Quality Center

Figure 1-2. U.S. Labor Productivity Growth

below that of other industrialized nations, our ability to compete in world markets is lessened.

Productivity in the United States, measured as non-farm output in the private sector per employee hour, grew at a steady rate of about 3.2 percent from the end of World War II to the early 1970s. Our growth since then, detailed in figure 1-2, has not been as good. In fact, in the 1978-82 period, average productivity growth was negative, meaning that it took more labor to produce a unit of product than it had previously. (If this were an international horse race, it would mean our horse was backing up!) The manufacturing sector has displayed positive growth over these periods; we should continue this trend but the real challenge in the decade ahead is to improve the productivity of services.

With all the talk about productivity slowdown, it may surprise some to learn that the U.S. is still the most productive nation. Figure 1-3 shows international comparisons, this time measured as gross domestic product (GDP) per employee. Japan, with whom we are so often compared, has a much lower level of productivity but a much higher growth rate. And Korea may well be the Japan of the 1990s. To use the horse race example again, the lead horses are the slowest, the trailing horses are the fastest. The hypothetical relative levels in figure 1-3 indicate what will happen if these trends continue.

(GDP/Employee, Purchasing Power Parity)

Country	1989 Level (U.S.=100)	Average % Growth 1979-89	Hypothetical Relative Levels*	
			2000	2010
United States	100.0	1.1	100	100
Canada	94.0	1.3	96	98
France	85.9	2.0	95	103
Italy	87.3	1.9	95	103
West Germany	82.0	1.7	87	93
United Kingdom	71.5	1.8	77	83
Japan	72.7	3.0	89	107
Korea	39.8	5.2	62	92

*Using 1979-89 Growth Rates
Source: Bureau of Labor Statistics, American Productivity and Quality Center
Purchasing power parity uses a common set of commodities and services in each country for comparing dollar aggregates, such as outputs, rather than using volatile market exchange rates.

Figure 1-3. International Labor Productivity

Many analysts have developed theories and proposed reasons for the productivity slowdown including lower rates of saving, investment, and research; changing workforce demographics; governmental regulations; environmental clean-ups; the attitudes of workers; and the skill of managers in operating our organizational systems. Undoubtedly there is some causative influence in each of these factors, but ultimately the economy is composed of individual business firms contributing to national productivity. If each firm becomes more productive, U.S. productivity will grow. The majority of the concepts in this book are aimed, one way or another, at improving productivity in organizational systems.

Functions of Production/Operations Management

The process of converting inputs into outputs requires certain functions to be performed. Some are design functions, which receive the most attention when the business is formed and at periodic intervals when major changes are made. Others are control functions, which must be performed continuously if an organization is to operate successfully.

Product Design and Development

Business organizations, research laboratories, and independent inventors are continuously developing new products. Yet few products are truly new. The Hula-Hoop, so successful in the 1950s, was a plastic adaptation of the cane hoops used by children in the late nineteenth century. The yo-yo traces its history to ancient Egypt, although many refinements have since been made in its design and materials. Most new products are variations and improvements on already-existing products.

Innovations in complete detail, ready for manufacture, seldom spring into the mind of an inventor. Usually an idea is developed, refined, and tested over many months before a working prototype is produced. The original idea may be creative, but the development of that idea into a marketable product requires a systematic, scientific study involving diligent work and attention to detail. Product specifications must be developed to assure that the item can be produced at a reasonable cost and be of the desired quality.

Most large organizations, and many small ones, have research and development departments that study new products and new processes to produce them. Few companies can afford to produce the same product in the same way, year after year; nor can they rely on copying the innovations of others.

In service industries, product development means determining the specifications of the service and how it is to be delivered. Services should be specified in terms of level of service, line of service, hours of availability, and many other, more detailed characteristics if the organization is to be competitive.

Facilities Location

The proper location for the organization's facilities can be a one-time decision when the business is formed, or it may be a frequently recurring question. The location decision may be critical to some firms and inconsequential to others. For example, the management of a small firm that makes garden tools for a major retailer may have to decide only on the original location, which may be anywhere within a 50-mile radius of the customer. A large fast-food chain, however, may be opening a new outlet every week, and the specific locations chosen for the outlets may be the most critical factor in determining their success.

The location decision must combine land and building costs, tax rates, distribution availability, customer access, growth potential, competitors' locations, suppliers' locations, energy sources, community acceptance, and a host of other factors. Depending on the importance and frequency of the decision, decision-making methods can range from simple rules of thumb and judgment to complex computer algorithms.

Capital Equipment

Included in capital equipment are the functions of determining the capital equipment needed, acquiring it at a reasonable cost, installing it, providing for both routine maintenance and emergency repair, and eventually replacing it. As with the location decision, capital-equipment decisions can be simple or complex. Large manufacturing firms succeed or fail on the basis of the management of their capital assets. Service firms often have minimal material inventories but huge investments in capital. One obvious example is a dentist's office; but airlines, trucking companies, and rental firms also fall into this category.

The small firm making only occasional capital acquisitions often can rely on the equipment supplier to provide much of the cost and performance analysis. For example, a lumber yard needing a forklift can get need assessments and competitive bids from two suppliers and then simply pick the best deal.

Facilities Layout

The layout of physical facilities has an important influence on the efficiency of a firm. Layout for a manufacturing plant should follow a logical sequence so that materials can flow smoothly through the process with minimal handling. For service functions, such as those performed by a bank teller, equipment and materials should be arranged to provide easy access and minimal delay. When several service functions interact, they should be arranged in sequence according to the main stream of customer flow through the process.

Unfortunately, many manufacturing and service operations are not laid out efficiently. This may be because they were never carefully laid out in the beginning, but it is more likely because the layout has grown inefficient as products and processes have changed. New machines have been added, old ones replaced, different products now are being produced, or space originally designated for material storage has been converted to office space for clerical workers. Few layouts are perfect, yet it is difficult to determine when a layout is bad enough to justify the costs of disrupting production to move equipment and rearrange facilities.

Work Design and Measurement

Individual tasks within the production process must be designed to achieve goals of efficiency and cost. The higher the volume, the more critical the design. When even a few seconds of unnecessary activity are eliminated from routine, repetitive jobs with short cycle times, thousands of dollars can be saved.

Work design and measurement are necessary for worker control. The price of the output is largely a function of the labor and material it contains. If material usage, including scrap and waste, must be accurately measured and controlled, so, too, should the labor component. The problems associated with measuring labor efficiency are more difficult than with material, but they are surmountable.

Work design and measurement are not as widespread in services as in manufacturing, because services are less repetitive. Since services generally are more labor intensive, however, the need for more accurate labor measurement and control is critical, and the potential payoff is great.

Production Forecasting

Forecasting is necessary if a business firm is to anticipate the demand for its products. Sufficient time must be allowed to acquire inputs and transform them into outputs at the time and place needed. Forecasts can be based on analysis of past data, consideration of current events, and educated guesses about future developments.

Both simple and complex statistical techniques are available to help the decision maker form a reasonable and accurate prediction of needs. These forecasts then become the basis of the plans and schedules for the buying, manufacturing, and other activities of the firm.

Production Planning and Scheduling

To coordinate the many diverse yet dependent operations of an organization, a master plan of activities and a schedule of their timing are needed. Each operating unit should then derive from the master plan the information necessary to coordinate the activities for which it is responsible. Careful planning anticipates the needs for people, materials, and equipment so that sufficient lead time is available to make any changes that may be necessary.

Planning and scheduling are dynamic activities. No matter how carefully initial plans are formed, unanticipated events will occur and rescheduling will be necessary. Some activities may need to be expedited; others may need to be delayed. The planners and schedulers of the firm perform a juggling act with resources and available time in attempting to best utilize the firm's capacity to produce.

Purchasing/Materials Management

All organizations use materials. The material input may account for as much as 80 percent of the value of the output or for as little as 1 percent. The effort devoted to purchasing and materials management should reflect this relative importance; most firms place too little, rather than too much, emphasis on this activity.

The purchasing function includes researching, analyzing, and selecting vendors. Negotiation of contracts or other buying agreements are made to assure that the firm obtains the right quality, at the right time, in the right quantity, in the right place, and at the right price. The purchasing manager is responsible for vast amounts of the company's money, and failure to achieve any of these objectives will result in a less profitable operation.

Inventory Management

One of the major changes in POM in recent years is the treatment of inventories. At one time, large inventories were considered a necessary part of doing business. But we now know that inventories can cover many inefficiencies in the business. If we have sufficient inventory, we have little motivation to reduce set-up times, to streamline maintenance procedures, or to tightly schedule the receipt of raw materials and production activities. We were paying for the inefficiencies as well as paying the costs associated with having large inventories of raw materials, work in process, and finished goods.

Today, we make every effort to reduce inventories to a minimum. Better relationships ("partnerships") with suppliers, more efficient production systems (such as FMS and JIT), and vastly improved information processing systems have greatly reduced the average inventory levels in most firms. Some inventory is inevitable, but the proper balance between too much and too little inventory is much lower today than it has ever been, and it is likely to be even lower in the future.

Quality Management

Production planning and scheduling are responsible for the *quantity* and timing of production; quality management is responsible for its *quality*. No amount of inspection can make a bad product a good one. Quality must be designed and produced into the product. It is essential, however, that the company monitor the quality of incoming materials, goods-in-process, and finished items to assure that quality goals are being met or that necessary corrective action is taken.

In recent years, quality has become a major basis for competition, particularly in international markets. New research into the costs of poor quality to an organization have caused operations managers to raise the issue of quality to a higher priority. Rather than accepting low levels of quality as an inescapable fact, new approaches are being developed in the pursuit of quality improvement in materials, craftsmanship, processes, and systems.

Quality is no less important to service industries, although it may be more difficult to define and measure. Many advances are being made, but much work remains to be done on the application of existing principles and the development of new techniques to manage the quality of services.

The functional areas outlined in this section form a plan for the remainder of the book. Chapter 2 deals with product design and development. The related functions of work design and location and the layout of facilities and equipment are combined in chapter 3. Forecasting, planning, and scheduling for production are the subjects of chapter 4. Chapter 5 details the fundamental principles and techniques of purchasing and materials management. Inventory control is the subject of chapter 6. And managing the quality of output is addressed in chapter 7.

Before exploring each of these areas, however, several basic concepts of POM should be understood. The first of these is a classification format for manufacturing and service firms.

Types of Manufacturing

Manufacturing firms can be classified according to size, type of product, location and many other variables. A classification more useful to the study of POM concepts, however, is a subdivision based on the type of process employed. This typology is based on the size or length of the production run and ranges from a lot size of one large complex unit to a continuous flow of product that operated 24 hours a day, seven days a week.

Project Production

A project is typified by building construction, missile programs, shipbuilding, and research activities. Completion may take weeks, months, or even years and involve many different firms or business units coordinated under a project manager. Since there is generally only one large, complex unit being produced, but myriad interrelated activities, the functions of planning, scheduling, quality control, and other POM functions assume a different meaning. In scheduling, for example, special techniques such as PERT and CPM (see chapter 4) have been developed to apply directly to the unique requirements of this type of manufacturing.

Job-Shop Production

Job shops do work on many different products in small lot sizes, generally to the customer's unique specifications. In a print ship, for example, many different jobs go on at any one time. The press is set up to run one job; when that is completed, the press is set up to run the next job. In the meantime, the first job is routed to other areas, where it is folded, collated, stapled, trimmed, packaged, and shipped. Each work area in the job shop performs its function on each job as it arrives. When, for example, packaging jobs arrive in rapid succession from other work areas, a waiting line of jobs develops; at other times, when no jobs are ready to be packaged, the packaging facilities are idle. One of the major problems in a job shop is scheduling the work in the proper amount and sequence to balance the costs of idle time against the costs of having jobs waiting.

The resources in a job shop are general rather than specialized. Basic materials can be used in many different jobs with different specifications. Equipment should be adaptable to different uses. Similarly, the skills of the employees should be broad enough to allow them to work on any job within their area.

Batch Production

Batch production is appropriate for the firm that produces many standard products but none in sufficient quantity to justify the set up of an assembly line devoted to the continuous production of one item. For example, a furniture manufacturer may make everything from dining sets to computer desks. It may set up a line or a production area to produce a two-months supply (a batch) of computer desks and place them in finished goods inventory to be used as needed while it then sets up to run a batch of kitchen tables. In some cases, the batches may be intermediate products such as chair legs or table tops which are stored and then assembled to customer order.

Businesses that face highly seasonal demand often use batch production. A clothing manufacturer may make ski caps and scarves in the summer and bathing suits in the winter months. Toy manufacturers are frequently batch producers.

The size and number of batches is determined by the volume of demand the firm faces and the technology of producing the product. In a batch production firm, the emphasis is on forecasting and scheduling production so that sufficient product is available when needed and on reducing the changeover time from one batch to the next.

Repetitive Production

Repetitive production is often associated with a moving assembly line. It involves high-volume production of discrete units such as automobiles, pencils, chairs, or bicycles. When the volume for one item is high enough, repetitive manufacture is more economical than the job-shop method. Specialized materials, equipment, and skills are employed to produce this one item and are not used on anything else.

The automobile industry is a good example of repetitive manufacturing. The lot size for a given model may be in the hundreds of thousands, and the production run will be almost one year. Specialized equipment is built to perform a task on this particular model, the workers are trained to be responsible for only one job. The critical problem in repetitive production is not daily scheduling, but setting up and balancing the jobs so the process will run smoothly and efficiently.

Flow-Process Production

The flow-process method is characterized by the continuous flow required by production technology. The petroleum industry, for example, does not produce discrete units; it transforms crude oil into various end products through a process that rarely stops. Individual operations do not exist; the input gradually is converted to outputs. Because of these special characteristics, a strong emphasis is placed on design and planning. Once the process begins, replanning is seldom possible, so the process is carefully monitored and controlled to adhere to the original plan.

Types of Services

The above classification of production methods applies to manufacturing firms, but, to some extent, it can apply to services. For example, some aspects of food service resemble an assembly line in repetitive production (such as preparing identical plates for airline meals), while others more nearly resemble a job shop (as in preparing a special salad or dessert in a restaurant).   Similarly, a wedding banquet for 250 people could be considered a "project" and employ many of the planning and scheduling techniques of project management. To the extent that a service firm approximates the characteristics and shares the problems of a given type of manufacturing firm, it probably can employ the problem-solving methodology already used in the other firms in that category. A more useful classification of services, however, is based on a typology with two dimensions: (1) the degree to which a tangible product is produced as part of the service and (2) the requirement of the presence of the customer for the service to be delivered. Figure 1-4 depicts this typology.

At one extreme in the array of services, the firm produces a physical product (such as a hamburger) and delivers it to the customer. Moving along the tangibility continuum, we find a physical manifestation of the product, which is often treated as the product itself. An example is an insurance policy, which is a recording and description of the true service: payment in the event of some specified outcome. Further down the continuum is the instance of physical evidence that the service has been performed, such as a haircut, but, unlike the insurance policy, the haircut cannot be changed after it is delivered. Finally, at the end of the continuum are the "pure" services such as counseling, in which no physical product is evident.

The customer contact dimension is also a matter of degree. For haircuts and dental work, the customer must be present while the service is being performed. The middle range of this scale covers instances in which the customer is usually present or, at least, involved, as with most retailing and many financial services such as cashing a check or applying for a loan. At the far end are the "automatic" services such as having a paycheck deposited directly into a bank account, or contracting for a lawn-care service while you are at work.

Labels for the four major categories of services and examples of each kind are presented in figure 1-4. It should be noted, however, that some services are on the borderline between major categories, and some industries may span two or more categories. The entertainment industry, for example, covers the range from the production of compact discs and videotapes (pseudomanufacturing) to the production of Broadway plays

CUSTOMER CONTACT

	Present	Not Present
	PSEUDO-MANUFACTURING	**PRODUCT DELIVERY**
Physical product	Food Service Retailing Publishing Rentals	Mail-order catalogs Transportation/Shipping Stockbrokering Insurance
TANGIBILITY		
	PERSONAL SERVICE	**ABSENTEE SERVICE**
No physical product	Counseling Health care Education Physical fitness	Lawn care Auto repair Security protection Custodial service

Figure 1-4. A Typology of Services

(personal service). Similarly, utility companies (gas, electric, and phones) have parts of their operations in all four categories.

Generally, the concepts of operations management apply most directly to the category of pseudomanufacturing. Adaptations of POM concepts can be made in many product delivery and absentee service firms, but the real challenge lies in adapting or developing new concepts, tools, and methods for the operations of firms producing personal services. Throughout this text, examples of services are used where applicable.

Operations Strategy And Objectives

A well-managed business has a mission statement, a general business strategy, functional strategies to cover major business activities, objectives to guide the firm, and specific goals to monitor its progress.

The mission statement answers the question "What business are we in?" as well as how we are positioned in the industry. If we define ourselves as "a railroad" it confines our operations to transporting goods by rail and interfacing with other modes of transportation. On the other hand, if we are a "transportation company" we can integrate into owning trucking companies, steamship lines, and air transport firms. Until the mission is clearly defined, the firm is operating without a unified sense of direction.

A general business strategy follows from the mission statement. It specified the markets in which the firm will compete, the level and breadth of product offerings, and the size and scope of the firm's activities. Coors beer, for example, followed a strategy of being a regional producer for many years before it finally decided to yield to the eastern pressure to go national.

Product vs. Process Focus

Manufacturing firms and, to some extent, service firms can be divided into a product focus or a process focus in terms of their strategies, organization, and activities. **Process focused firms** generally deal in low-volume customized products and utilize a job shop or batch methodology. They are organized by process; that is, the departments carry titles like cutting, sanding, assembly, painting, and packaging and the layout of the process follows this breakdown. Individual jobs are routed through different departments depending on the operations needed to manufacture the item.

By contrast, a **product-focused firm** produces high-volume standardized products using repetitive or continuous flow processes. The organization chart and the physical layout reflect the fact that groups of employees and equipment are dedicated to the continuous production of one product. Thus you would find a department for product A (cabinets), product B (tables), and product C (chairs). Each department contains the proper tools and equipment arrayed in the proper order to produce the product from beginning to end. (See chapter 3 for more detail on product- and process-focused layouts).

The strategic choice of a product or process focus for the firm has many implications in terms of the markets in which it competes, the types of resources it uses, and the way in which it is organized. Some of the more important differences are outlined in Table 1-2. Although a few firms can be classified as a "pure" product focus or process focus, most firms really fall on the continuum somewhere in between. Sometimes called "jumbled shops," they contain a mix of the two extremes.

Service firms display many of the characteristics of process or product focus, but the differences are not always as clear. A flower shop, for example, may be classified as primarily process focused since its output is generally small batches of customized products. An automatic car wash, on the other hand, is set up much like an assembly line in repetitive

Table 1-2
Characteristics of Process-Focused and Product-Focused Firms

Factor	Process Focus	Product Focus
Market	Individual customers	Mass market
Product	Customized high variety	Standardized low variety
Volume	High	Low
Sales	Make to order	Make to stock
Distribution	To the customer	Distribution channels
Organization	Departments by process (e.g. Cutting Department)	Departments by product (e.g. Chair Department)
Layout	By process (e.g. Cutting Area)	By product (e.g. Chair Assembly)
Employees	Generalized skills	Specialized skills
Equipment	General purpose	Special purpose
Capital/Labor ratio	High	Low
Unit cost	High	Low
Quality	Customer specs	Company specs
Inventory	High work in process	High finished goods
Major Problem	Scheduling jobs through the process	Process planning, design and control
Firm size	Generally small	Generally large

production with each employee and each piece of equipment doing one job on the standardized unit as it passes through the process.

Operations Strategy

From the general business strategy, the more specific functional strategies for marketing, finance and production/operations are developed. For POM, the operations strategy of the firm covers key decisions related to product development, raw material acquisition, production processes, quality levels, and many more (see Table 1-3). Of course, the elements of the operations strategy are closely linked to the elements of other functional strategies. The quality level selected, for example, must fit with the target markets, channels of distribution, and methods by which the product is sold.

From the operations strategy, general objectives are derived to provide a sense of direction for the firm and to form a base for the evaluation of the firm's activities. Each company will develop its own objectives and specific time-based goals, but in today's competitive global markets, several general objectives are universal.

Effectiveness

Effectiveness is the degree to which the purpose of an organization is achieved. The purpose of a firm in the transportation industry is to move materials, people, or both; the more it moves, the more effective it is. Effectiveness requires eliminating unnecessary activities and outputs that fail to meet standards of performance. It is a combination, therefore, of how much and how well the output of the firm conforms to the purpose of the organization. Effectiveness can be measured by sales, market share, consumer opinion, and other global measures, as well as by comparing specific results to specific company goals.

Efficiency

Efficiency refers to how fast the output is produced and how many resources are consumed. Efficiency generally relates to reducing waste— of time, effort, and materials. Greater efficiency can result through technical changes, such as better, faster machines; through managerial changes, such as better planning, scheduling, and control activities; or through behavioral changes in workers, such as working smarter or working harder. Improved efficiency means greater output for a given amount of resources, which leads to greater benefits for all concerned.

Table 1-3
Elements of Operations Strategy

Category	Strategy	Range of Options
General	Focus	Product . . . process
	Innovation	Leader . . . follower
	Process flexibility	Quick changeover . . . long production runs
	Technology	Adopt latest innovations . . . maintain proven technologies
	Process	Job shop . . . batch . . . repetitive. . .
	Priorities	Cost, quality, time, service . . .
	Capital/labor ratio	High (automated) . . . low (manual)
	Production planning	Make to customer order . . . make to stock (forecasted demand)
	Integration	Highly integrated with engineering and marketing . . . highly autonomous (silos)
	Response time	Quick response to changes in demand . . . slow response
	Cycle time	Short . . . long
Product	Design	Innovator . . . copier
	Stability	Frequent changes . . . infrequent changes
	Line	Limited product line . . . complete product line
	Service	Limited service (e.g. delivery, installation and repair) . . . full service
Physical Facilities	Plant size	One large plant . . . several small ones
	Plant location	Near product markets . . . near resource markets
	Equipment	General purpose . . . special purpose
	Span of process	Make . . . buy
	Capacity	Meet peak demand . . . meet average demand

Table 1-3 (Continued)

Category	Strategy	Range of Options
	Maintenance	Preventive . . . on-demand
	Layout	By product . . . by process
Human Resources	Skills	Generalized . . . specialized
	Compensation	Hourly or salary; incentives or not
	Supervision	Technical orientation . . . managerial orientation
	Style	Participative . . . autocratic
	Job specification	Highly structured . . . highly discretionary
	Job design	Narrow, repetitive . . . broad, varied
Organization	Structure	Tall (many levels) . . . flat (few levels)
	Type	Functional, product focused, geographical or . . .
	Decision making	Centralized . . . decentralized
Quality	Level	High end (luxury) . . . low end (basic)
	Scope	Total quality management . . . control by inspection
	Reliability	Highest reliability . . . planned obsolescence
	Locus of control	Every worker . . . quality control department
	Raw material	Supplier partnership . . . incoming inspection
	Responsibility	Unlimited warranties . . . caveat emptor
	Philosophy	Zero defects . . . acceptable quality level
Inventory	Purpose	Buffers (push) . . . Kanban (pull)
	Level	High levels (safety stock) . . . low levels

Table 1-3 (Continued)

Category	Strategy	Range of Options
Inventory (con't)	Location	Majority in raw material, work in process, or finished goods
	Control	Tight . . . loose
	Velocity	High turnover . . . low turnover
Scheduling	Scheduling objective	Schedule to fill capacity . . . chase demand
	Sequence priority	Due dates or job length or first in or . . .
	Horizon	Short (days or weeks) . . . long (months or years)
Purchasing	Supplier selection	Most qualified . . . most convenient
	Supplier relationship	Partnership . . . competitive bidding
	Sourcing	Many suppliers . . . sole source
	Supplier evaluation	Supplier qualifications . . . informal monitoring
	Tradeoffs	Quality vs. cost vs. service vs. . . .

The notation . . . between two factors indicates a continuum with many degrees in between; at the end of a list of factors, it indicates other factors could be added to the list.

Unit Cost

One of the best "how are we doing?" measures available to a production manager is unit cost. If the production manager is doing a good job of controlling the quantity, quality, and price of the inputs and is carefully planning, scheduling, and controlling the process, those efforts will be reflected in a favorable unit cost. One must be wary, however, because many different accounting methods exist to determine unit cost. In making comparisons between firms or divisions or from year to year, one should use comparable accounting procedures. Currently, the accounting profession is exploring new methods, such as activity based accounting, to more realistically assign costs to production activities and provide a better basis for operations decision making.

Contribution to Profit

Because profit is one of the major objectives of the firm, contributions to profit should be recognized. When comparing one product line with another or one division with another, measures of unit cost, efficiency, or effectiveness may not be meaningful. Contribution to profit–the excess of revenue over costs–can determine whether a product line should be expanded or discontinued. Contribution to profit also can be a factor in decisions regarding new capital equipment, plant location, research and development activities, and other areas in which efficiency measures are incomplete or inappropriate.

Quality

Increasingly, quality is becoming a competitive factor in domestic and international markets. Traditional "low-cost producers" that achieve savings by cutting quality find their markets disappearing. Firms that produce products that meet customer expectations for reliability, fit, and function discover that their products have greater value in the market even at a slightly higher price. And they are learning that, contrary to popular belief, improved quality leads to lower overall production costs by eliminating or reducing scrap, rework, warranty service, and liability. Managing quality in the organization has become a top priority for modern manufacturing and service organizations.

Productivity

Perhaps the most often misunderstood objective of POM is productivity. Productivity frequently is used to mean output per hour, but it really means any ratio of output to input. The total productivity of the firm is the total of all output divided by the total of all inputs. When measuring individual jobs, we usually deal with partial measures, such as labor productivity, capital productivity, or material productivity.

Productivity differs from efficiency in that efficiency seeks the maximum output from a *given* amount of resources. Productivity looks for the maximum ratio between the two and, thus, can involve a change in the output, the input, or both.

Productivity is critically important to individual business firms as it is to the economy as a whole; to remain successful, a firm must maintain or improve its productivity.

Responsiveness, Flexibility, and Innovation

Success in the world of fast-changing technology and intense international competition requires a rapid response rate. Firms must develop new products and get those products to market quickly. Being late in the market for a highly competitive new product might be much more costly to the manufacturing firm than even a significant overrun in research and development costs would be.

Efficiency, effectiveness, unit cost, and all the other criteria depend in part on the flexibility of the firm and its ability to respond quickly. "Time-based competition" is the term used to describe the many efforts of the firm to increase innovation, decrease development time, shorten manufacturing or service delivery cycle times, and respond to the individual needs of the customer.

Environmental Responsibility

Every business firm operates within five environments: legal, social, economic, technological, and physical. The responsibility of the firm spans all of these. It is obligated to obey laws and regulations, operate in an ethical and socially responsible manner, and to help protect the physical environment upon which we all depend. Unfortunately, we read too often of a firm caught in the act of deceit, unfair trade practice, improper pricing policies, or suppressing of technological advancements in the hope of protecting their competitive advantage. In the long run, however, illegal and unethical practices are costly for the firm and for individual managers within it. Firms that operate within high standards of ethical conduct prove that success can be achieved within the bounds of social responsibility.

Virtually every subfunction of operations management has implications for the environment and for the constituencies that the firm serves. Product design, for example, must consider safety features such as guards on power tools, regardless of whether they are required by law. Scheduling decisions can enhance or disrupt the personal lives of employees, and quality control decisions can affect the health and safety of both employees and customers. And consumer groups can make a difference. Recently, McDonalds responded to the growing concern for the environment by completely changing the packaging materials for most of its products.

Careers in Production/Operations Management

Positions in operations management span the organization from lowest to the highest levels. Many opportunities are available for the college graduate, and it is possible to spend an entire career in various areas of the production/operations function while progressing from an entry-level position to upper management. Assignments in POM also provide a good background for entry into other areas of the organization.

The chart in Table 1-4 indicates some of the common position titles at the entry, department head, and division or corporate levels of the organization. One problem in compiling such a list is that different organizations use different terminology. For example, in one company the title "planner" may refer to a very senior position, while in another firm, it may be an entry-level job.

In the area of forecasting, planning, and scheduling, a junior planner or scheduler could be responsible for compiling the machine, material, and workforce schedules for one or more of the manufacturing departments. The department manager is responsible for organizing all schedules and forecasts into a realistic master production schedule and for seeing that the plans are being carried out and taking corrective action where necessary. Although the department head is responsible for these activities, this position involves more supervision of the people performing the activities than actually doing the day-to-day work. At the corporate level, the vice president of planning is concerned with a longer time span and more critical decisions, such as five-year forecasts, capacity additions, and major production changeovers.

Each of the other functions follows a similar pattern: entry-level jobs are more involved with *doing*, while upper-level jobs involve supervision of the activities and long-range planning. Methods analysts redesign jobs, buyers purchase materials, and inventory-control specialists make decisions about inventory levels, storage, and handling of materials.

Concern for professionalism within POM areas is reflected in the increased number of certification programs that have developed over the last decade. Organized mainly by professional associations, these programs establish criteria for knowledge, skill, and experience required to successfully perform the responsibilities of some POM jobs. Procedures then are developed to certify an individual as qualified; often the certification process requires individuals to pass a rigorous test and also may include education, experience, or other requirements. Although not required by law, certification can be a deciding factor for the firm when choosing among candidates for a POM position.

Table 1-4

Career Tracks in Production/Operations Management

FUNCTION AND TITLE

Level	Forecasting, Planning, & Scheduling	Work Design, Location, & Layout	Purchasing	Inventory Control	Quality Control	Product Design & Development	Line
Division or corporate	VP (or Director), Planning	VP, Plant Engineering	VP, Purchasing	VP, Materials Management	VP, Product Quality	VP, R & D	VP, Manufacturing
Department	Manager, Production Control	Manager, Industrial Engineering	Purchasing Manager	Inventory Manager	Quality-Control Manager	Manager, Product Development	Department Manager
Entry level	Scheduler/ Planner	Methods Analyst	Buyer	Inventory Control Specialist	Inspector	Product Engineer	Supervisor or Management Trainee

Many certification programs are now in operation, and more are being planned. For example, the American Production and Inventory Control Society (APICS) conducts a series of tests leading to the designation "Certified in Production and Inventory Management," allowing Bill Jones for instance, to write his name as William Jones, CPIM. The National Association of Purchasing Management (NAPM) awards a C.P.M. (Certified Purchasing Manager) designation based on educational and experiential requirements and test results. Through the American Society for Quality Control (ASQC), an individual can earn a CQE (Certified Quality Engineer), CQT (Certified Quality Technician), or CRE (Certified Reliability Engineer).

While the certification programs promote professionalism in specialized POM functions, the performance of the functions at the entry level often requires a close relationship between managers and engineers or other specialists. In the government, for example, management analysts and industrial engineers work jointly on problems of layout, equipment selection, and job design. Under the supervision of the manager of industrial engineering, each contributes special expertise to the problem.

While it is possible to take a straight track to the top, advancing from inspector to manager of quality control to vice president of product quality, diagonal tracks involving lateral transfers are more common. Many firms prefer–and some insist–that a corporate-level director have some experience in each of the areas under his or her control. A vice president of materials management, therefore, could have started as a scheduler, then worked as a senior buyer, and progressed through other positions in several related areas.

One track deserves special mention. In virtually every business, whether manufacturing or service, there is a manufacturing or operations department. Beginning with the workers who create the product, the advancement track progresses through supervisor to department manager, plant manager, vice president of manufacturing, and president. These are the "line" positions, and in many organizations this is the shortest and surest route to the top. Automobile companies, for example, seldom have a top-level executive who has not had some line experience.

Service firms differ considerably from manufacturing firms (and from each other) in the way they organize these operations functions and the position titles they attach to them. These same functions must be performed, however, and the same general principles apply. An airline, for example, must carry an inventory of parts and supplies, and maintenance jobs must be carefully scheduled. In a hospital, purchasing obviously is a critical function; and, although job-design principles are being applied to health-care facilities, few have an industrial engineering department in their organization. Many POM positions in service industries are yet to be established, even though they are critically needed. Obviously, there is considerable opportunity for people to build careers in many service organizations.

Key Concepts

Definitions of most key concepts are found in the Glossary

Products	**Project Production**
The Production Function	**Job Shop**
Methodology/Technology of Transformation	**Batch Production**
Factory of the Future	**Repetitive Production**
Flexible Manufacturing Systems (FMS)	**Flow-Process Production**
Computer Integrated Manufacturing (CIM)	**Types of Services**
Operations Strategy	**Effectiveness/Efficiency**
Process and Product Focus	**Productivity**
Subfunctions of POM	**Responsiveness**

References

Adam, Everett E., Jr., and Ebert, Ronald J. *Production and Operations Management.* 4th ed. Englewood Cliffs, NJ: Prentice-Hall, 1989.

Chase, Richard B., and Aquilano, Nicholas, J. *Production and Operations Management.* 5th ed. Homewood, IL: Richard D. Irwin, 1989.

Fitzsimmons, James A., and Sullivan, Robert S. *Service Operations Management.* New York: McGraw-Hill Book Company, 1982.

George, Clause S., Jr. *The History of Management Thought.* 2nd ed. Englewood Cliffs, NJ: Prentice-Hall, 1972.

Hall, Robert W., *Attaining Manufacturing Excellence.* Homewood, IL: Dow Jones-Irwin, 1987.

Hayes, Robert H., and Wheelwright, Steven C.   *Restoring Our Competitive Edge.* New York: John Wiley & Sons, 1984.

Hayes, Robert H., Wheelwright, Steven C., and Clark, Kim B. *Dynamic Manufacturing.* New York: The Free Press, 1988.

Schonberger, Richard J. *World Class Manufacturing.* New York: The Free Press, 1986.

Skinner, Wickham.   *Manufacturing: The Formidable Competitive Weapon.* New York: John Wiley & Sons, 1985.

Taylor, Frederick W. *The Principles of Scientific Management.* New York: Harper & Bros., 1911.

Discussion Questions

1. For each of the organizations listed below, (a) list the major inputs needed; (b) explain the nature of the conversion process; and (c) list the major outputs of goods, services, or both.

   a. Boeing Aircraft

   b. American Airlines

   c. Bechtel Construction Company

   d. The Village Delicatessen

   e. Sears

   f. U.S. Bureau of Engraving and Printing

2. List and explain three examples of real companies for each category of manufacturing: project, job shop, batch, repetitive, and flow process. Give two examples of companies that contain two or more of these categories within the same firm.

3. In what categories of the service typology (figure 1-4) would you place AT&T before divestiture? Give specific examples of different divisions such as Long Lines, Bell Labs, Western Electric, or the local repair service. Where would you place your local telephone company after divestiture? Where would you place long-distance competitors such as MCI?

4. Consider the ten functions of operations management discussed in this chapter. Lay them out in time sequence; that is, which functions must be (can be) performed before another is begun?

5. Is it possible for a business firm to be effective but not efficient? Efficient but not effective? Effective and efficient but not productive? Discuss.

6. "Students are processed (educated) in 'lots' (classes). In that respect, a university is a giant job shop."

   a. Indicate whether you agree or disagree with this statement. In what respects is a university similar or dissimilar to a print shop? Consider, for example, the sequence of operations and the sequence of courses as well as the scheduling of jobs and the scheduling of classes.

   b. In a typical job shop, each job takes a different amount of time. Describe the scheduling problems that would result if every class were a different number of weeks in length.

   c. Is the registration procedure at your university more like one of the other forms of production? Which one?

   d. What would be necessary in order to educate students using a repetitive type of production? Describe the process.

7. Use the model presented in figure 1-1 to compare and contrast these two firms: a manufacturer of doghouses and a dog-grooming service.

   a. What are the major differences in the types and relative amounts of inputs needed?

   b. How do the conversion processes differ? Is the customer involved in the conversion process?

   c. Are there differences in the flows of funds and/or information from the environment to the firms? Explain.

8. Why is mass production found only in the twentieth century?

9. Most large banks have a facility called the operations center. What is the purpose of this facility and what work is performed there?

10. What is the purpose of programs offering certification, for instance, as a CPIM or C.P.M.? What is the value to the person who is certified? How does this compare to licensing accountants, doctors, or lawyers?

11. When manufacturing a product, the firm begins with raw materials, feeds them through a conversion process, and ends up with a finished product ready to sell. Explain why these steps are reversed in the decision-making process to introduce a new product.

12. Visit a McDonalds or other fast food restaurant and watch the process of preparing the basic food items as well as the order filling

and interaction with the customer. Now describe in detail how you would design a totally automated fast-food franchise. Specifically:

a. How would the raw material have to be packaged and stored?

b. How would you replace the cooks in the food preparation areas?

c. How would you design the customer contact interface (does an automatic teller give you any ideas)?

d. What control systems would you suggest to control quality and to assure that the customer is satisfied?

13. In 1960, we divided work into very small jobs and made them as standardized, routine, and repetitive as possible. What is the rationale for doing that? For example, does it save the company money in wage rates, training costs, efficiency of production, or in other ways? On the other hand, what problems do you think this caused with respect to:

a. Motivation of the worker.

b. Pride in craftsmanship.

c. Quality of the product.

d. Flexibility of the firm and ability to meet changing demand.

What remedies do you suggest to combat these problems?

14. Explain how each of the following might have a positive or negative effect on national productivity measured as total outputs in the private sector per worker hour.

a. Changes in the amount of spending on research and development.

b. Aging of the workforce.

c. Increased pollution controls.

d. Changes in government regulations.

e. Increase in employee ownership and profit sharing.

15. Suppose you are planning to open a new business: a combination pizza parlor and self service laundry. Discuss each factor in table 1-3 with respect to your new business venture.

16. What difference does it make if the level of productivity in Japan surpasses the U.S.? Would it make a difference in your job opportunities? Your salary expectations? The products you buy? How much you pay for them? Any other effects to you personally?

17. Two computer software development firms are located in the same industrial park. One claims to be product focused while the other is much more process focused. Which one is likely to produce large quantities of standardized products such as spreadsheet or word processing programs? Which one would develop custom programs for special applications? What else can you say about the facilities, organization, and method of operations of these two firms?

18. Explain what is meant by "time-based competition." Under what circumstances is time more important than costs to the producer of the product or to the customer?

CHAPTER

2

Product Design
and Development

The purpose of any organization is to produce products that customers are willing to buy. But this task is not as easy as it seems. Not only are customer needs and preferences constantly changing, but competition and advancing technologies also continually make products obsolete. Most firms monitor shifting attitudes and demographics through market research and keep abreast of technological changes that might affect their industry. This information is fed into the firm's research and development activities to create new products or modifications of existing products to keep the firm competitive.

For example, not too many years ago the slide rule was a common product in a mature and stable market. Today, it is difficult to find a slide rule; they have been displaced by electronic hand-held calculators. Companies making slide rules either were forced out of business or they had to design and develop new products that matched some other consumer need. At the same time, new products caused new firms to flourish in a Darwinian-like battle between innovative companies and those still producing obsolete products. Similar circumstances have faced manufacturers of watches, cigarette lighters, computers, home appliances, and other products.

Remember, products include services as well as manufactured goods, and the same pressures for product innovation apply. Consumer attitudes toward physical fitness have changed, and consumers have more leisure time and more money to spend. Recent research has provided new knowledge linking diet and exercise to health and longevity. The result has been an explosion of new firms and new industries geared to take advantage of the opportunities. Innovative products abound in health clubs, diet foods, athletic equipment, and videotapes to help consumers develop their own fitness programs.

Few products are completely new; most "new" products are developments or refinements of existing products. And, contrary to what some might believe, new products seldom come from the mind of the eccentric inventor working in a garage. Most often they emerge from corporate or government research laboratories after months or years of tedious work. Sometimes we can trace the history of a product and chronicle its development through a series of minor and major breakthroughs in technology or creativity.

For example, the first "washing machine" was a rock beside a stream. Later came the washboard, and, finally, the first crude machines consisting of a tub, an agitator, and a wringer. The major difference between the latter machine and the washer of today is the addition of automatic devices and electronics that enable the machine to perform preset functions. The modern washing machine has achieved the goal we have set for our "factory of the future"; it is fast, efficient, almost totally automatic, yet flexible and adaptable. In the future, we may see another major breakthrough in the method of washing clothes, such as the use of microwaves, sonar, lasers, or some technology not yet discovered.

Similarly, in services, major breakthroughs are interspersed with many minor refinements. The movie industry traces its origin to the Greek theater more than two thousand years ago. It then progressed through traveling shows, vaudeville acts, silent films, talkies, color movies, and videotape. In between were thousands of refinements that improved the quality of the sound and picture, as well as many developments in the artistry of motion-picture production.

Product Life Cycle

In the marketplace, most new products go through a product life cycle of five stages (figure 2-1):

1. **Introduction:** The product is brand new, high priced, and does not always work well. Furthermore, market awareness and acceptance of the product are minimal, with sales volume at a low level and growing very slowly. The only customers for the product at this point are the wealthy and the adventuresome.

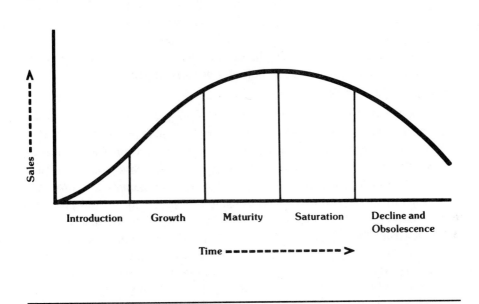

Figure 2-1. Stages of the Product Life Cycle

2. **Growth:** The product is now accepted in the marketplace and is making rapid sales gains as a result of the combined effects of promotion, distribution, improved dependability, standardization, increased use, and lower selling prices. Customers buy the product with little prompting, but substantial profits gained by the innovating firm lure competition into the marketplace. The product begins to sell in much larger quantities as it becomes more commonly used.

3. **Maturity:** Now a number of competitors have entered the market. The rate of sales growth begins to slow because of the declining numbers of people who still are unaware of the product. By now, the product has proved itself dependable in performance, and, because of increased competition, the product now is reasonably priced.

4. **Saturation:** At this stage, nearly everyone who wants the product has bought it. Sales thus level off at a rate determined by replacement demand plus sales resulting from population growth. Product promotion is very important in this stage, since the products of competitors differ very little, if at all. In our society, the markets for most automobiles, household appliances, and television sets have reached this stage.

5. **Decline and Obsolescence:** In the final stage, products are edged out of the market by better products or by substitutes that are enter-

ing the growth and maturity stages of their life cycles. This does not happen to all products; for example, scissors have been around for a long time, and newer products, such as electric scissors, have not replaced them. On the other hand, the slide rule had been at the saturation stage for a long time before it was driven from the marketplace by the electric calculator.

One excellent illustration of the typical product life cycle is the Polaroid camera. Radically different from other cameras at the time it was introduced, the Polaroid initially was a very expensive toy for the rich. Compared to the Polaroid of today, these early models were crude, inconvenient to use, and often unreliable, yet the camera was successful enough to survive the introduction stage and experience rapid growth in the market. Technical refinements of the camera have made it more convenient to use, and patent protection has kept most direct competition at bay. Today, the Polaroid camera is a mature product, perhaps entering the saturation stage with competition coming from 35mm cameras and video cameras. If no further refinements are made, this product, too, will eventually fall into decline and obsolescence.

Product Strategy

Successful companies formulate strategies to guide their decisions and actions. Within an overall business strategy, a firm should have compatible strategies for marketing, finance, operations, and indeed, every part of the organization. From the set of strategies, it can then develop more specific goals and objectives, policies, and operating procedures.

Important in the set of strategies is the product strategy which guides the firm in the development of new products, modification of existing products, and the elimination of old products that no longer fit with the company's mission. A product strategy contains several dimensions.

First, the firm must decide what part of the market to compete in by establishing the **level of product**. The level connotes a certain market segment and usually a price range. Depending on the product involved, the level may imply certain features, capacity, or performance characteristics. For example, a manufacturer of dinnerware may chose to compete at the low end of the market, with the least expensive china for everyday use and not try to compete with the fine-china firms of the world. To use a service example, a barbershop may choose the market for basic barbering services at reasonable prices or cater to consumers wanting expensive styling and conditioning treatments. Rare is the firm that can compete at all levels.

The second dimension of the product strategy is **product line**. Some firms achieve a competitive advantage by offering a limited line of products and providing better products, faster delivery, or some other feature to make up for the lack of depth. Fast-food restaurants, convenience markets, and many small manufacturers are examples. On the other hand, some firms strive to offer a complete array of products to their customers. Contrary to the strategy of the convenience market, some traditional grocery stores have added departments for sporting goods, lawn-care products, appliances, pharmaceuticals, eyeglasses, and even a branch bank to attract customers who want one-stop shopping. Interestingly, both strategies are successful.

The third dimension of product strategy is **product availability**. Some manufactured items are available almost anywhere, while others can be purchased only through company-owned or franchise outlets such as Radio Shack. Some manufacturers limit the geographic region in which their products are sold. Until recently, Coors beer was available only west of the Mississippi. For services, availability takes on different meanings. Number of outlets, hours of operation, and delivery or house-call policy determine when and where the service is available.

A complete product strategy will consider, at a minimum, the level, line, and availability of products to be offered by the firm. In addition, however, the strategy should incorporate other factors relevant to the firm such as resources available, supplier relationships, marketing and distribution channels, market segments served, and company image and reputation. Products that do not fit in the product line with respect to these factors are candidates for abandonment; new products that do fit are candidates for development.

Product Strategy at Bic Pen

The Bic Pen Corporation is an interesting example of a product strategy. The company was formed to produce the original Bic pen, which combined the design of the common lead pencil with the technology of the ballpoint pen. The first Bic pen was the same color, the same size, and the same configuration as the pencil, but it had a ballpoint cartridge in a plastic casing. As the product became successful, the company introduced different points and ink colors while staying with its original philosophy of producing a high-quality, inexpensive product with a high market volume that permitted economies of mass production.

Later, Bic produced a felt-tip pen, but the pen was not introduced into the marketplace quickly enough. Gillette had researched and developed the new Flair pen, patterned after the early fountain pens, and the Flair was a great success. Bic's version, the Banana, was fashioned after the successful "stick" version of its pens, but the design and timing in the market led to its downfall.

Bic learned from this experience and entered the market with an entirely new product, the Bic lighter. Like the pen, the lighter was a reliable, inexpensive, disposable, high-volume, mass-produced item using plastic and metal as its primary materials. Bic could produce the lighter using the same technology, the same knowledge, and often the same marketing channels. The Bic lighter was a huge success; Gillette's version, the Cricket, could not catch up.

Bic's next major product introduction was a disaster. For reasons that were related more to corporate finance than to following a consistent product strategy, Bic began to market pantyhose produced by a French subsidiary under the name "Fannyhose." The differences in technology of the process, market, marketing channels, and competition were too much for Bic to overcome.

But Bic was too strong a company to let one product lead to its downfall. It swallowed its losses and returned to the product strategy that had spelled success by introducing the Bic disposable shaver, another highly successful product. Today, Bic continues its research and development into new or modified products that fit with the strategy and philosophy of the company.

Research and Development

Research and development (R&D) refers to those investigative activities leading to the discovery of new knowledge (research) and the translation of this new knowledge into marketable products (development). R&D has taken us from 78-rpm phonograph records (that shattered when dropped) to 45-rpm records, LP albums, casette tapes, and compact discs. Digital tape is still in the R&D lab but is about to emerge.

Not every firm engages in R&D activities. Some buy research results through patent rights or some other form, and others simply copy products that have already reached the market. In some industries, however, it is essential to spend considerable amounts of money on R&D to maintain a competitive position. In those businesses, R&D efforts can be applied in a number of ways.

New Products

New products usually are brought into existence for one of three basic reasons:

1. **To fill a gap in an existing product line.** For example, a home-appliance producer may decide to manufacture a home air conditioner to make its line of home appliances more complete.

2. **To supplement an already complete product line.** For example, a housepaint manufacturer may decide to produce paintbrushes to supplement an already complete line of home paints.

3. **To capitalize on a potential market opportunity not related to existing product lines.** For example, a full-line manufacturer of plastic toys may see a potentially strong market for plastic sports equipment. This reason for introducing new products carries the most risk, since the company may be getting involved with markets and production processes about which it knows very little. Additional skills in product design, development, production, and marketing may be required to make the product successful.

One method of entering new product areas is to undertake a full-blown R&D effort of gathering new knowledge and translating this knowledge into the desired products. Although this type of effort has resulted in the manufacture of products such as the polio vaccine, television, and the jet engine, its high cost and associated risks normally limit such activity to the larger firms. On the other hand, the payoff to the firm making such a breakthrough through its own R&D efforts can be impressive.

Another way a firm can enter a new product area is to buy the R&D efforts of other firms. This often is done by marketing finished products under the buying company's own label. For example, a manufacturer and marketer of drafting supplies, such as rulers, triangles, and templates, may round out its product line by purchasing mechanical drawing instruments (which it does not produce) from a manufacturer in Germany and marketing them under its own label. The private product lines or brands of most large retailers are good examples of this practice. Although this practice tends to minimize R&D costs and risks, it also reduces the possibility of the substantial profits that often result from breakthroughs due to internal R&D activities.

Still another way a firm can enter a new product area is to merge with a firm that already has product lines in that area. The acquired firm has the skills necessary to produce and market the new product or product line. Mergers, however, do not always produce the anticipated results. Often a merger will cause new organizational problems that adversely affect the new company's operations.

Modification of Existing Products

One reason for modifying an existing product is to improve its customer appeal. This can be accomplished by (1) reshaping the product to conform to current styling trends; (2) adding new features that will set the product uniquely apart, as was the intent when the remote-control channel selector was added to the color television product package; or (3) giving the product a new package that will produce a new look or image.

Another reason for modifying an existing product is to reduce its production costs. One of the best ways to reduce production costs is to redesign the product so that the cost of its materials is reduced. For example, a product often can be modified, without changing its functional performance, so that its production will require less material, less expensive material (such as the substitution of plastic for metal), or both. Furthermore, material costs and assembly costs often can be greatly reduced if the product is modified to include the use of standard parts and components.

New Uses for Existing Products

Exploration of new uses for an existing product is often another objective of a firm's R&D efforts. R&D efforts are aimed at discovering ways that an existing product, or a slightly modified version of it, can be adapted to new markets. For example, a manufacturer of an industrial-grade liquid floor cleaner might take this same cleaner, dilute it, and market it as a liquid floor cleaner for households. This type of R&D activity allows a firm to satisfy a greater number of customers within the realm of its existing products.

New Packaging

Changing the packaging of an existing product involves changes in the size, shape, layout, or other external characteristics without affecting the product's purpose. Packaging changes often have the effect of creating a "new" product by giving regular customers, or customers in new markets, the existing product in a new form or in a quantity that is more satisfactory. For example, Anheuser-Busch produces only ten distinctively different beers (such as Bud, Bud Light, and Michelob) but it supplies over 1500 different combinations of containers, sizes, and packages to its distributors.

By offering attractive packages, a firm often can compete more effectively. A better box, wrapper, label, can, or bottle may even enable a relatively small and unknown firm to market successfully against established competitors.

Creating a Model

The immediate outcome of a successful R&D effort is the creation of a model or prototype of the product. For a manufactured item, this may be a physical model, while in services it may be a detailed set of specifications with a demonstration or "dress rehearsal" of the service to be performed. One reason for creating a prototype is to assure that the ideas upon which the product is based are feasible. A second reason is to help management visualize how the product will look and perform. Although these initial models may be changed before final production, they provide the basis for decisions regarding final product specifications, facilities design, and materials required.

Product Design

Taking a model and modifying its design into a product that can be produced and marketed profitably requires information input from a number of areas within the firm as well as from the marketplace. Factors such as alternative material costs, use of standard parts and components, results of product tests, and inputs from market research, all must be considered. Once this needed information is gathered and properly analyzed, the specifications of the final product can be determined.

Material

Often the product designer can choose from several different materials. For example, automobile hoods can be made out of aluminum, steel, or fiberglass. In choosing from available material alternatives, the designer must consider (1) the performance requirements of the product, (2) the relative costs of the alternative materials, (3) the relative processing costs associated with the alternative materials, (4) the effect of each material on the appearance of the final product, and (5) the relative availability of each material.

When two or more of the alternatives can produce the required performance, the lowest-priced alternative does not automatically win out. It may be that the highest-priced material costs less to process. Thus, the highest-priced alternative may be the most desirable alternative when *total* production costs are considered. For example, aircraft producers save a substantial sum of money by using higher-priced bronze rather than steel extrusions in aircraft elevator and rudder counter-weights. Even though bronze is higher priced than steel, the savings in machining time more than offsets the increase in material costs.

A material alternative also may be desirable from the standpoint of performance, cost, and appearance but may be obtainable from only one supplier. In this case, a material decision is also a supplier decision, and the firm should carefully evaluate the reliability of the supplier's ability to meet desired future quantity requirements and delivery schedules. At a minimum, this decision calls for a thorough investigation of the supplier's available plant capacity, financial strength, and labor situation.

Value Analysis/Value Engineering

Value analysis/value engineering (VA/VE) involves an organized, systematic study of every element of cost in a part, material, or product to ensure that it fulfills its function at the lowest total cost. VA/VE is the study of function and value. **Function** refers to the job that the material, part, or product performs. For example, the function of a ballpoint pen may be to write. **Value** is defined as the lowest end cost at which the function may be accomplished at the time and place required and with the quality required. For example, if the only function of a ballpoint pen were to write, the least expensive pen probably would do the job. If, on the other hand, the pen must fulfill an additional function, such as indicating status, then perhaps a more expensive, gold-filled pen would be required.

Although it may sound technical, VA/VE actually is a straightforward, basic approach designed to reduce material and production costs while ensuring that the product still fulfills its intended function in a satisfactory manner. A VA/VE study cannot be done effectively unless the function of the product is first determined–that is , "to write" or "to connote status." Once the function of the product has been determined, the remainder of the study involves asking and objectively answering a number of basic questions about the particular item. Most companies develop a checklist to systematize this activity. In some cases, these checklists consist of hundreds of questions, such as

1. Would a less costly design work as well?

2. Can a standard item be used?

3. Can the product's weight be reduced?

4. Can a less expensive material do the job?

5. Can the costs of packaging be reduced?

6. Is the capacity of the item greater than required?

By answering such questions thoughtfully, analysts generally will arrive at alternatives. If the answer to a particular question is not entirely satisfactory, this becomes the starting point for a more detailed investigation. The use of a well-developed checklist of questions focuses attention on those factors that may further reduce production costs.

The cost savings attributed to VA/VE efforts have been impressive. For example, one firm that had been using a specially designed screw costing 15¢ each found a way to make the screw for 1.5¢, resulting in an annual savings of $20,000. In another instance, a gasket costing $4.15 each when made in-house was found to cost 15¢ when purchased from an outside supplier.

Standardization

Standardization is the process of establishing agreement upon uniform identifications for certain characteristics of quality, design, performance, quality, and service. A uniform identification that generally is agreed upon is called a *standard*. For example, if a person in the United States buys an electric appliance such as a toaster, the buyer knows that this toaster will operate on the same voltage available from the electrical outlets at home. Why? Because in the United States the voltage in homes has been standardized at 110 volts. Likewise, when you buy a light bulb, you know that the bulb will screw into your sockets at home because light-bulb sockets in the United States are standard. Just think of the problems that would exist if each typewriter manufacturer's typewriter keyboard were arranged in a different configuration!

Standards do not exist for consumer products alone. They also exist for a wide variety of items used in manufacturing, such as nuts, bolts, screws, and electric motors. Without these standards, there could be no assembly line, since there would be no interchangeable parts. The lack of standards also would complicate repair services greatly. Many of the items we use on a daily basis would cost more to buy and maintain.

There are several reasons for incorporating, whenever possible, standard parts and components into the design of a product. The use of standard items in a company's products permits the company, as a whole, to purchase fewer items in larger quantities at lower prices. If fewer items are purchased, then fewer items need to be processed and stocked. This has the immediate effect of lowering purchasing, receiving, inspection, and accounts-payable costs. In addition, stocking fewer items makes controlling inventories and production easier and less costly, and it greatly simplifies assembly operations. Furthermore, since suppliers generally stock standard items in their inventories, deliveries can be made more quickly, allowing the firm to maintain lower inventory levels, which, in turn, result in another substantial saving. Thus, lower prices, lower processing costs, lower inventory costs, and lower scheduling costs are all reasons why a firm uses standard parts and components in the design of its products. As a result, a product can be brought to market at a lower total cost.

Modular Design

Modular design refers to designing products with separate sections or modules. When an item fails, the whole module (of which the item is a part) is removed and replaced with a new module. The module that has failed either can be repaired at a central facility (which is usually less costly than on-site repair), or it can be discarded. For example, if a transistor in a television set fails, the whole printed-circuit board (of which the transistor is a part) is removed and replaced.

The basic reason why industries, such as electronics, have turned to modular design has been the high cost of repair labor, which has made breakdowns associated with conventional forms of design extremely expensive. Under the modular design concept, the on-site time it takes to repair a complicated piece of electronic equipment is greatly reduced. If the replaced module is worth repairing, the repair work then can be accomplished at a central facility utilizing less expensive labor.

Modular design also is gaining rapid acceptance in the home-building industry. In this case, the impetus behind modular design is the high cost of construction labor. Under the modular design concept, standard house components (such as the bathroom) can be mass produced at a central facility with less expensive assembly labor. The components then are transported to the building site and put together, requiring only a fraction of the time and expensive labor associated with conventional construction methods.

Computer-aided Design (CAD)

Computer-aided design (CAD) is a complex and imaginative new tool that is revolutionizing product design. CAD first was used in the aerospace industry and soon was adopted by the automobile industry to help deal with the engineering and design nightmare of downsizing the entire fleet of America's gasguzzling cars. Today, because of the declining prices of computer equipment and the increased capabilities of computer software, CAD techniques commonly are used in many other industries as well.

Basically, CAD consists of a computer that draws pictures, on a television screen or cathode-ray tube (CRT), of what the engineer has designed. The sophisticated CAD software is able to draw lines between points, creating a three-dimensional drawing that can be rotated to show all sides of the design. As a result, CAD greatly speeds up the normally slow and laborious work of drafting.

CAD is an especially effective way to design and analyze products because the computer communicates with the designer directly through pictures. By looking at these pictures, the designer is able to absorb and interpret the informational content of the design much faster than if he or she were looking at an array of numbers or words and then trying to translate them into mental pictures. Furthermore, if the necessary programming has been done, the designer can analyze and test the things designed by subjecting them to electronically simulated temperature changes, mechanical stresses, or other potential problems the product is likely to encounter in its real-world application. For example, color graphics can be used to show heat or stress points of a design in red and cool points in blue, thus enabling the engineer to understand more easily the design's temperature fields.

Such on-screen testing and analysis can save huge amounts of time and money associated with the more traditional way of designing a product–that is, building a prototype, testing it, modifying the design, and retesting the prototype. Products designed using a CAD system are more likely to work properly when built, since many of the problems associated with a new or modified product can be removed before the product leaves the design stage.

Market Research Inputs

Thus far in our discussion, all the inputs to the product design process have come from within the firm. But because the success of a product ultimately is determined by consumers, they also should be allowed to express opinions about the products design. This important information is gathered through market research.

In the initial stage of a product's development, market information concerning the product's salability normally is gathered through the use of a questionnaire. The questionnaire is a list of carefully phrased questions to be used to guide a series of personal interviews with potential customers or to elicit information in a mailing to specially selected potential customers.

Information collected should indicate the size (quantity) of a potential market over time for alternative product characteristics (designs, packages, quality, and reliability levels, as well as any other selected operating features) and alternate prices. The survey also should provide valuable information concerning the activities of major competitors, styling trends, and predictable seasonal variations in sales, if they exist.

Information gathered this way can be extremely useful in guiding a product through its final design and development stages. Without such information, it would be difficult to differentiate between products that only seem to be a good idea from those that have sound market potential. For example, consider the individual who decided he had the greatest idea in the world for packaging and marketing unprocessed wheat bran. He packaged his product in a rustic brown paper bag with an eye-catching sea-gull logo printed on the front. A recipe incorporating bran was printed on the back of the bag, and a copy of a copyrighted bran recipe was included inside. Our entrepreneur also decided to price his product far below his competitors in order to gain immediate market acceptance. The whole idea seemed so good that the fellow proceeded, without conducting even the most basic market research, to buy 20,000 printed bags, enough bran to fill them, and enough master cartons to ship them. The initial investment was $10,000.

When sales did not pick up as rapidly as expected–in fact, they never even got off the ground–the bran man decided to conduct a survey to find the problem. The results indicated that the bag idea, although quaint and seemingly clever, was unattractive to retailers because the bags couldn't be stacked on the shelf the way conventional cereal boxes could. Furthermore, since unprocessed bran was a slow-moving item regardless of its price, most retailers were reluctant to give the product any shelf space to start with. To make matters even worse, the master cartons were the wrong size; when the allocated shelf space was completely filled, there still were some bags of bran left in the carton, which then had to be put in inventory in the storeroom. Conclusion: The idea was a loser to start with. Cost of the market survey: less than $100. Had this individual conducted the survey *before* taking action, he would have saved himself $9,900 and a lot of grief.

Resources

The resources of a firm, including its facilities and equipment, the skills of its personnel, and its financial strength, have an important impact on the final design of each product that will be manufactured. The closer the production requirements of a product match the capabilities of a firm's existing equipment and personnel resources, the more efficient will be the manufacturing process. On the other hand, the less the production requirements of a product match the firm's resources, the less efficient the product will be to manufacture. For example, if a firm currently produces products on an assembly line, it probably would not be in the company's best interest to initiate a new product requiring much custom work at individual work stations. Such a move probably would be inefficient because the workers would have to learn new skills, new equipment would have to be purchased, material handing patterns would have to be altered, and inventories would have to be adjusted.

The design of a product should not be approved nor the decision made to produce it until the firm objectively examines its financial condition to ensure that it has the necessary dollar resources to see the product through to the point where it begins to return a profit. For a major new product (especially one requiring substantial investments in new equipment and facilities), this often takes a long time, since buildings may have to be built, equipment purchased and installed, and raw materials and parts purchased. In addition, the actual production of a brand-new product initially proceeds slowly because it usually takes time to work the "bugs" out of a new production system. Each of these activities takes time and is costly. But no money is coming in from the new product's sales to help offset these costs. To make matters worse, when the product finally does hit the market, initial sales normally are slow until market acceptance for the product is gained. Thus, if a firm doesn't have the financial resources (cash or credit) to offset these initial costs, the company may go out of business before the product ever has a chance to realize its long-term potential.

Testing

Before a product is placed into production, prototypes of the product should be tested sufficiently to ensure that the final product will perform its intended function. This is the stage of product design at which steel-belted tires run over boards full of nails, and wristwatches are thrown into cement mixers or worn by football players during practice. The main concerns here are quality and reliability as they relate to the product's intended function.

Another important factor in product testing is consumer safety. Product recalls are expensive, both in terms of the cost of the recall and the damaging effect on a company's image. A good example is the product-recall problem Firestone Tire and Rubber Company faced with certain models of its steel-belted radial tires. One major goal of product testing should be to preclude such product-use problems and recalls.

Pilot Production Run

After all the information concerning materials, VA/VE, standardization, market research, company resources, and product testing have been incorporated into the product design, a complete set of tentative specifications is drafted, and the product is put through a pilot production run. For a manufactured product, the pilot run involves the manufacture of a small quantity of a new product under stimulated normal-production conditions. For services, the pilot may involve a trial run of the process using other employees or even real customers as "guinea pigs."

In either case, the purpose is to test the product and the process to remove any defects or inefficiencies that are revealed. Once this stage is completed, the product design becomes definite, and product specifications can be finalized.

Designing Services

Throughout this discussion, the term *product* has referred to both manufactured items and services. It may be helpful, however, to use a service example to illustrate specifically how the concepts apply.

Years ago, innovative entrepreneurs borrowed ideas from the automobile assembly line to create the automatic car wash. At first a novelty, the car wash is now in the saturation stage of the product life cycle, where it is likely to stay until some radical new technology displaces it. The earliest car washes used rough brushes that scrubbed the car, but continued research and development has developed a variety of better cleaning equipment as well as more effective detergents, spray waxes, vinyl dressings, and other products.

Most car washes today offer a menu of options for the customer. Like the product line in a manufacturing business, the car wash offers a line of services including wash, spray wax, floor-mat cleaning, dressings for tires and vinyl roofs, and perhaps other special features as the car passes down the line. Often, several of these options are packaged as "sets" with special reduced prices. Larger car washes may have separate facilities for waxing, interior cleaning, and detailing.

Like manufacturing, services use materials, and the components of the service (such as the elements of the car wash) are subject to value analysis/value engineering, standardization, and modular design. Although CAD systems exist expressly for the design of physical products, services may also employ computer simulations or other sophisticated tools in their design. Certainly market research plays a major role in the development and refinement of services that meet the needs of customers, and the service firm must consider its resources in the selection of products to offer. Many car washes sell accessories for automobiles, but few go so far as to offer maintenance or repair for cars.

Finally, the service must be tested and perhaps subjected to a pilot run before it is open to the public. Each of the components of the car wash, such as the spray wax, should be tested on different paints and exterior surfaces and under different temperature and weather conditions. In the pilot run, each combination of services (wash, wax, etc.) should be tested on several cars to assure that the modules that work well separately do not work together to form an incomplete combination that turns the finish on your new Corvette into a sticky mess.

Product Description

After a product design is established, much supporting work must be done before finished products can be produced. Material must be ordered, employees trained, and all production activities scheduled. Control systems for quantity, quality, time, and cost must be in place. None of these activities could begin to occur with any degree of coordination without the entire product being completely, clearly, and accurately described with a set of product specifications, a bill of materials, and a route sheet.

Product Specifications

Product specifications refer to the detailed description of the product. For a manufactured item, the description usually includes a list of the product's measurable characteristics (dimensions, weight, volume, and tolerances), the different parts and components that go into the product, and a detailed set of directions for assembling the unit. For a complicated product such as an aircraft, teams of experts develop thousands of pages of descriptions and blueprints showing every part, dimension, material, and method of assembly. But even simple products may require detailed descriptions. The U.S. government specification for a mousetrap, for example, contains more than 120,000 words and many pages of supporting documents.

Service specifications normally include a list of resources needed such as material, tools and equipment, and labor, as well as a detailed set of directions for delivering the service and a list of measurable characteristics that determine satisfactory performance. In many services, the product specifications are even more important than they are for a manufactured item. For example, if a customer is buying a lawn mower, he or she can examine the product, check its specifications visually, test the item, and then make a decision to purchase. But if the customer is buying a lawn-service, he or she must trust the written product specification to made the purchase decision. In this case, as with many services, the product is created, produced, and delivered simultaneously. There is no way to examine the service before it is performed.

Bill of Materials

In addition to clear, complete, and accurate product specifications, a bill of materials (B/M), usually developed by the designer from the product specifications, lists all the components, including the quantities of each, required to produce one unit of the finished product. For example, the bill of materials for a bicycle would specify the two pedals, two handle grips, and one seat (among other things). An example of the bill of materials for the manufacture of a yo-yo is illustrated in figure 2-2 and for a car wash in figure 2-3. (A more detailed and complex bill of materials is shown in chapter 4).

An important function of the bill of materials is to permit a production schedule to be "exploded" into a list of required raw materials. **Exploding** means that the quantity of finished product in the production schedule is multiplied by the quantities of components in the bill of materials. For example, if 2,000 yo-yos are scheduled for production next month, we will need 4,000 wooden discs, 2,000 connecting pins, 2,000

Product Description
Yo-Yo

Part or Material Number	Part Description	Quantity per Assembly
2010	Wooden Disc	2
2011	Connecting Pin	1
2012	3 Feet of String	1
2013	Glue	.04 oz.
2014	Paint	.1 oz.
2015	Cardboard Box	1

Figure 2-2. Bill of Materials for a Yo-Yo

Product Description
Car Wash

Material Number	Material Description	Quantity Per Unit (Washing One Car)
3010	Detergent	3 oz.
3011	White-wall Cleaner	1 oz.
3012	Water	12 gals.
3013	Hot Wax	4 oz.

Figure 2-3. Bill of Materials for a Car Wash

strings, 80 ounces of glue, 200 ounces of paint, and 2,000 cardboard boxes.

After computing the total number of each component needed for production, the purchasing department can then check the firm's inventory to see if any of the parts currently are in stock. Purchasing then will buy those materials needed to complete the production schedule.

For example, if 4,000 wooden discs are needed and 1,500 units are in stock, purchasing must acquire an additional 2,500 discs to fulfill the requirement.

For services, it is important that some unit of service be agreed upon and that the bill of materials be expressed in these terms. For carpet cleaning, 1 square yard is a frequently used unit, while in roofing the common unit of measure is 100 square feet. In many service industries, the unit is a transaction (such as in a bank) or a customer served (as in a restaurant). In the car wash example, the unit is one car; so a forecast of 500 cars for the coming week could be multiplied by the bill of materials to determine the needed amount of detergent, wax, and other materials.

Other Supporting Documents

Certain situations might require the employment of other supporting documents to communicate the product specifications to purchasing, scheduling, quality control, production control, and other units within the organization as well as to the sales force and to the customer. Blueprints, models, pictures, route sheets, and assembly diagrams are applicable to manufactured products. Services may require written descriptions,

Product Description
Yo-Yo

Operation Number	Dept. Number	Machine Number	Operation Description	Setup Time (Min.)	Per Piece Time (Min.)
1	13	383	Paint wooden discs	1.3	.015
2	8	211	Connect discs with con-necting pin	.75	.02
3	6	101	Attach string	.5	.01
4	7		Inspect		
5	21	622	Package	1.0	.015

Figure 2-4. Route Sheet for a Yo-Yo

diagrams, samples, demonstrations, or even videotapes of the service being performed.

An example of a route sheet for the manufacture of yo-yos is figure 2-4. It lists the sequence of production operations necessary to make the finished product, including inspection and assembly operations. The route sheet contains a separate entry for each operation performed on a different machine or in a different work center. As an aid in production planning and scheduling, the route sheet almost always includes the standard times allowed for setting up each operation and for producing each piece after the setup has been approved. Additional examples of a route sheet and other production documents are given in chapter 3.

Break-Even Analysis

One way to evaluate the potential of a new product or changes in an existing product is to use break-even analysis. Actually, break-even analysis is a general tool that finds the intersection between two or more factors and defines ranges in which one option is better than another. The factors may be two cost structures, two revenue functions, revenue plotted against cost, or any other factors that can be plotted as linear or non-linear functions.

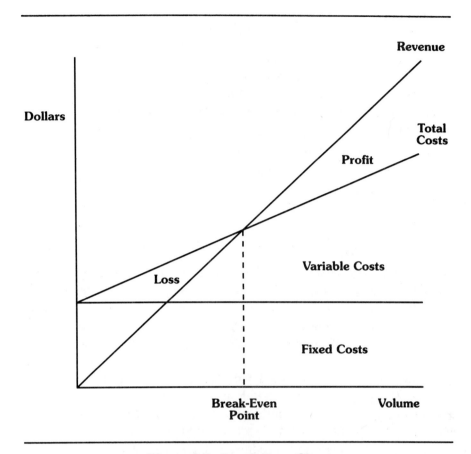

Figure 2-5. Break-Even Chart

Basic break-even analysis plots fixed costs, variable costs, and revenues as a function of volume as illustrated in figure 2-5. **Fixed costs** are those costs that do not change as the production of the product increases. Examples include rent, utilities, office salaries, and other expenses which accountants call "overhead." **Variable costs,** as the name implies, correspond directly with the number of units produced. The primary components of variable costs are direct material and direct labor, but other costs, such as packaging materials and supplies consumed in the manufacture of the unit also may be included. **Revenues,** for purposes of break-even analysis, are derived as a constant price for each unit sold.

Below the break-even point, the total costs (sum of fixed plus variable costs) exceeds total revenue and the firm is experiencing a loss for this item in this range of volume. Above the break-even point, the firm is making a profit and, under these simple assumptions, the higher the volume the greater the profit.

To calculate the break-even point directly, let

$$p = \text{Price per unit sold}$$
$$v = \text{Variable cost per unit produced}$$
$$F = \text{Fixed cost for the period}$$
$$Q = \text{Number of units produced and sold in the period}$$

We set the total revenue equal to the total costs and solve for the quantity at the break-even point:

$$pQ = F + vQ$$

$$Q = \frac{F}{p - v}$$

As an example, suppose the variable cost of the product was $20 per unit and the fixed cost was $50,000 per month. The proposed selling price is $30. The margin per unit ($p^v - {}^v v$) is $10 and the break-even point is then 5,000 units per month ($50,000/$10). Above 5,000 units per month, the product will yield a profit; below that point it will experience a loss.

Sensitivity analysis allows the decision makers to vary parameters of the model until they are satisfied with the outcome. For example, if the current sales projection for this item is 4,000 units per month the managers will have to decide whether to increase the selling price, try to reduce costs, operate initially at a loss to gain market penetration, or cancel the introduction of the product. (You should be able to verify that sales of 4,000 would generate a loss of $1,000 per month).

Break-even analysis can be made more complicated, but more meaningful, by adding some other features. For example, when the process reaches normal capacity, the firm may be able to work overtime at an increased wage rate up to some limit set by a union contract. On the break-even graph, the variable cost line would increase at a greater slope over this range. If a second shift were added, additional fixed costs would probably be incurred causing the total cost line to jump up at that point and then continue to rise at the variable cost rate. Finally, the assumption of a constant price for the complete range of volume may not be valid. Larger volumes may require a lower selling price, thus the revenue line may not be linear.

Additional applications of break-even analysis will be found in other parts of this book. Later in this chapter, research and development efforts are evaluated using a model for the time needed for product profits to break even with development costs. In chapter 3, alternative locations are evaluated in terms of where their relative costs break even. In general, break-even analysis is a useful tool with many applications.

Evaluating Research and Development

Of all the areas of the business firm, research and development has always been considered the most difficult to evaluate because of the uncertain links from research activities to research results and because of the time involved. A researcher or design engineer may work on a project for months or years, only to find that the resulting product is not salable. Even if the product seems promising, the value of the engineer's work may not be known for several years.

For these reasons, many firms engage in R&D based on faith and fear; they have faith that their efforts will produce usable products, and they are afraid *not* to have an R&D department for competitive reasons. The size of the R&D budget differs considerably among industries, but often the decision is made to devote a given percentage of sales to R&D, under the logic that as the firm gets larger its R&D effort should grow in proportion.

Traditional measures of R&D effectiveness have focused on two factors: control of projects underway and final results. Most R&D projects start as proposals that are approved for funding. As the project unfolds, it is monitored for time and cost relative to the budget and schedule contained in the proposal. If possible, the project will contain milestone events that mark the accomplishment of each phase of the project. At such times, the project often undergoes an intense evaluation, and a decision is then made to continue, change, or abandon the project.

Upon completion, the projects should produce measurable results in the form of new products, process improvements, or patents for new discoveries. These results can be evaluated along with other outcomes, such as papers presented at scientific meetings or reports published in scholarly or trade journals.

Break-Even Time

Recently, Hewlett Packard, a major manufacturer of computers and electronic equipment, developed a concise way of evaluating its R&D efforts from initial idea to the time the idea becomes a successful product in the marketplace. This model, called Break-Even Time, is not a remedy for all R&D evaluation problems, but it combines in a single measure the time and costs of development with the profit from the sale of the product.

An example will illustrate the R&D process at Hewlett Packard and help explain the Break-Even Time (BET) diagram in figure 2-6. A new product, such as the Hewlett Packard plotter, begins as an idea in phase

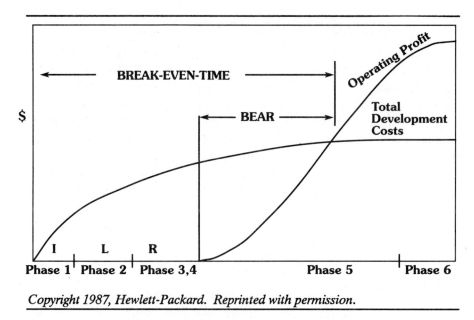

Copyright 1987, Hewlett-Packard. Reprinted with permission.

Figure 2-6. Break-Even Time Model

1, when the idea is explored and a decision is made to develop the idea as a laboratory project (phase 2) into a workable product. In phase 3, the prototype is further developed so that it can be manufactured efficiently, and it is then released to the manufacturing division for production.

At this point, the graph indicates that the majority of development costs have been expended, but the product has not yet been manufactured or sold. As it enters this next stage (phase 4), the product will incur manufacturing costs such as setup, material, labor, and overhead, to produce the initial stock of the item. As these units are sold (at a profit) the total profit attributable to this product begins to accumulate. Eventually, if the product is successful in the market, it will earn enough profit to cover all of its development costs. At this point, the new product has truly reached break-even for the company.

The primary objective in this analysis is to minimize the break-even time, defined as the time from the beginning of exploration of the idea until the product that stemmed from that idea has earned enough profit to cover all of its development costs. A second objective is to minimize break-even after release (BEAR), the time from the beginning of manufacturing until profits cover development costs.

At first, the emphasis in this standard of measurement seems to be on time—on doing things rapidly; and, indeed, part of it is. In the fast-changing electronics markets, a new product that is late in the market will lose a lot of profit to the competition. John Young, the president of

Hewlett Packard has said that a project that is six months late is far worse than a project with a 50 percent overrun in development costs.

But very rapid development of new products will not be beneficial in the long run if the development work is not done well. Problems in the manufacturing stage could slow down the time the product takes to reach the market, and hidden defects in the design could eat away the profits in warranty costs. If, on the other hand, development is very effective at removing all bugs before release to manufacturing, the startup time can be reduced and some manufacturing problems eliminated, thus allowing the product to reach the market and begin earning more profit sooner. On the graph, the operating profit line climbs at a steeper slope and reaches break-even sooner.

The break-even-time model helps us focus on the critical factors in research and development:

1. Maximize the effectiveness of development activities in creating salable products

2. Minimize the time required to develop an idea

3. Keep development costs under control

4. Coordinate the relationship between development and manufacturing

5. Develop products that are cost effective to manufacture

6. Develop products that will return a good profit.

Research and development may always be the riskiest part of any business firm, but doing these activities a little better than the competition will enhance one's chances for business survival and even success.

Organizing For Product Development

The functional organization chart, in which operations, marketing, finance, research and development and other functions are completely separate departments has many advantages, but in today's fast-paced competitive environment the disadvantages are beginning to take their toll. The typical pattern in the past was for R&D to design and develop a new product and then "throw it over the wall" to manufacturing engineering who tried to determine if and how it could be manufactured. If there were problems, it would be "thrown back over the wall" to be redesigned; if it could be manufactured, it was then "thrown over the wall" to marketing to see if they could sell it. This process and attitude has caused some to refer to the departments as "silos" to indicate that little coordination took place at the operations levels of these functions.

Today, many firms have broken out of the "silos" by forming **cross-functional teams** for product development. As soon as the idea is deemed worthy of development as a likely product offering, a project team is formed with representatives from marketing, production, purchasing, and sometimes even outside vendors to jointly develop a product that is manufacturable and salable. When the design engineer says a certain material should be used, purchasing may say that the material is too difficult to obtain, production may have concerns about the ability of present equipment to cut that material, and marketing could have information from its research that indicates a different material is preferred by customers. These differences are resolved within the team, with minimal delays, so that when the product design is finalized, problems in manufacturing and marketing are minimal.

Firms in industries characterized by time-based competition, such as computer hardware or consumer electronics, have found project teams essential to their survival. As the success of this approach increases, we are likely to see even more rapid innovation in product development and introduction.

Key Concepts

Definitions of most key concepts are found in the Glossary

Product Life Cycle	**Computer-Aided Design (CAD)**
Product Strategy	**Service Design**
Product Level	**Product Specifications**
Product Line	**Bill of Materials**
Research and Development	**Route Street**
Value Analysis	**Break-Even Analysis**
Modular Design	**Break-Even Time**
Standardization	**Cross-Functional Teams**
Pilot Production Run	

References

Albrecht, Karl, and Zemke, Ron. *Service America!* Homewood, Ill: Dow Jones-Irwin, 1985.

Dumaine, Brian. "How Managers Can Succeed Through Speed." *Fortune.* 119 (February 13, 1989): 54-59.

Groover, J. D., and Zimmers, E. W., Jr. *CAD/CAM: Computer Aided Design and Manufacturing.* Englewood Cliffs, NJ: Prentice-Hall, 1984.

Haas, Elizabeth A. "Breakthrough Manufacturing." *Harvard Business Review.* 65 (March-April 1987): 75-81.

Hayes, R. H., and Wheelwright, S. *Restoring Our Competitive Edge: Competing Through Manufacturing.* New York: John Wiley & Sons, 1984.

House, Charles H. and Price, Raymond L. "The Return Map: Tracking Product Teams." *Harvard Business Review.* 69 (January-February 1991): 92-100.

Stalk, George and Hout, Thomas M. *Competing Against Time.* New York: The Free Press, 1990.

Takeuchi, Hirotaka, and Nonaka, Ikujiro, "The New Product Development Game." *Harvard Business Review.* 64 (January-February, 1986): 137-146.

Whitney, Daniel E. "Manufacturing by Design." *Harvard Business Review.* 66 (July-August 1988): 83-91.

Discussion Questions

1. A list of manufactured products is given below. Describe the progression of each product through the product life cycle, ending at the point where you think the product is today. Include in your discussion how long the progression took, the entry or exit of competitors at various stages, product price changes from stage to stage, and other factors relevant to the product life cycle.

   a. Automobile

   b. Television

    c.   Compact disc

    d.   Duplicating machine

    e.   Personal computer

2. In the same manner as question 1, above, discuss the life cycle of the following services:

    a.   College education

    b.   Golf course

    c.   Automatic bank teller

    d.   Convenience market

    e.   Home-security system

3. Under deregulation, banks have been able to offer many new products that combine services previously offered only by other financial institutions and to develop some new products that have never been offered previously by any financial institutions. Describe several new products developed by banks in the last five years. Suggest at least one new product that banks might develop in the future.

4. Outline the elements of Bic Pen Corporation's product strategy. Name several current or new products that would fit the strategy.

5. One application of R&D is modification of existing products. Select a product (manufactured item or service and suggest how it might be modified to better fit your needs as a customer.

6. Standardization exists for many, but not all, products in the United States. Give several examples of a lack of standardization that (a) was created because of independent development by different companies, or (b) was created purposely for competitive reasons.

7. Although some products are standardized in the United States, they are not necessarily standardized across international boundaries. Give examples of this lack of standardization. What problems does this create, and how are the problems resolved?

8. Select a product such as a disposable cigarette lighter and discuss how the product should be tested and under what conditions it should be tested before it is released for sale throughout the United States.

9. Suppose you are planning to develop a new "same-day" document-delivery service in your hometown.

    a.   Write a detailed description of this product.

b. Explain how you would do market research on the product.

c. Should you do a pilot run of the product and, if so, how would you do it?

10. For the Break-Even Time model, made two lists of factors: one for those that would reduce break even time and another for those that would extend it.

Problems

1. The owner of the car wash forecasts that 500 cars will be washed this week. Currently in stock he has

Detergent   400 oz.
White Wall cleaner   0
Hot wax   1,000 oz.

How much of each item should the car wash owner order to be able to meet the needs for this week's production?

2. Use the information from figure 2-4 to determine the total amount of labor for setup and production of one batch of 2,000 yo-yos. Would the same amount of labor be required if the yo-yos were produced in four batches of 500 each?

3. A book publisher has fixed costs of $300,000 and variable costs per book of $8.00. The book sells for $23.00 per copy.

a. How many books must be sold to break even?

b. If the fixed cost increased, would the new break-even point be higher or lower?

c. If the variable cost per unit decreased, would the new break-even point be higher or lower?

d. If the fixed costs were increased by $40,000 and, at the same time, the variable costs were reduced by $2.00 per unit, would the firm be better off or worse off? (Be sure to give a complete answer!)

4. In the problem above, suppose the first 10,000 books are sold at $23.00 but then they must be discounted to $18.00 to sell the rest. Under these conditions, what volume is necessary to break even?

5. A manufacturing process has a fixed cost of $150,000 per month. Each unit of product being produced contains $25.00 worth of mate-

rial and takes $45.00 of labor. How many units are needed to break even if each completed unit has a value of $90.00?

6. Assume a fixed cost of $900,000, a variable cost of $4.50, and a selling price of $5.50.

   a.   What is the break-even point?

   b.   How many units must be sold to make a profit of $300,000?

   c.   How many units must be sold to average $.25 profit per unit? $.50 profit per unit? $1.50 profit per unit?

7. Mr. Aldo Redondo drives his own car on company business. His employer reimburses him for such travel at the rate of 36 cents per mile. Aldo estimates that his fixed costs per year such as taxes, insurance, and depreciation are $2052.00. The direct or variable costs such as gas, oil, and maintenance average about 14.4 cents per mile.

   a.   How many miles must he drive to break even?

   b.   If he buys a new car that has a fixed cost of $2292.00 per year and a variable cost of 12 cents per mile, will he be better off or worse off?

8. An import company buys foreign-made sewing machines for $125.00 per unit and sells them door to door with salesmen who receive a 40% commission. If fixed costs of the operation are $210,000, what is the minimum price that must be charged if the firm is to avoid a loss on a shipment of 5,000 machines?

9. Lauri Clifford is in the business of organizing and conducting executive training seminars. Her relevant costs are as follows:

   Each executive is charged $150.00 per day.

   Each executive pays for his or her own hotel room.

   The meeting room for the seminar costs $60.00 per day.

   Lunch and breaks cost $24.00 per person per day.

   Instructors are paid $150.00 per hour for a six-hour day.

   Each executive receives a $30.00 book at the seminar.

   Promotional materials prior to the seminar cost $900.00.

   a.   If the seminar is two days long, how many executives must enroll for Lauri to break even? How many for a three-day program?

   b.   Lauri has promoted a two-day seminar and, at present, she has sixteen people enrolled. If she can cancel the hotel arrangements and return the books without penalty, should she cancel or continue with the program? Explain relative to the break-even point (or points).

c. Biltwell Toy Company wants a special program for thirty of their managers. Since there is no promotion cost, they expect a 10% reduction in the rate charged. How long must the seminar be for Lauri to make a profit?

10. A firm is selling two products, chairs and bar stools, each at $50.00 per unit. Chairs have a variable cost of $25.00 and bar stools $20.00. Fixed costs for the firm are $20,000.

    a. If the sales mix is 1:1 (one chair sold for every bar stool sold) what is the break-even point in dollars of sales? In units of chairs and bar stools?

    b. If the sales mix changes to 1:4 (one chair for every four bar stools) what is the break-even point in dollars of sales? In units of chairs and bar stools?

11. Your company is about to receive an order for a small manufactured part, but you do not yet know the size of the order. There are three ways it can be manufactured:

    Method 1: By hand, using normal tools, a worker can produce two units per hour.

    Method 2: For $300.00 we could buy specialized tools that would allow a worker to produce four units per hour, but the tools would be worthless after the job was finished.

    Method 3: For $900.00 we could rent a semi-automatic machine (for as long as we need it) which would enable the worker to produce eight units per hour.

    The same worker is utilized in each alternative. She is married, has two teenage daughters, works 37.5 hours per week and earns $12.00 per hour. For what size order would we produce the product by hand? With the specialized tools? With the machine?

12. On a graph, draw a total cost line that represents normal variable and fixed costs up to point A. In the next range of volume, from A to B, workers earn overtime pay at time and a half (remember that labor is only part of variable costs). At point B, the maximum allowable overtime, add a second shift that includes some additional fixed costs and a shift premium of 10%.

Next, overlay several revenue lines that intersect the total cost line at different points (including a revenue line that intersects at more than one point) and interpret the results.

3

Location, Layout, Work Study, and Productivity

Suppose you wanted to start your own small business. In addition to developing a marketing plan and arranging financing, you would have to develop an overall business strategy and decide what products you want to produce, as we discussed in chapters 1 and 2.

This chapter continues the discussion of the design functions necessary to set up an effective and efficient production system. Later, chapter 4 will cover the forecasting, planning, and scheduling of production within the facility, and chapter 5 with deal with the complexities of acquiring the raw materials, parts, and supplies needed. Chapters 6 and 7 will focus on activities for managing the materials in inventory and controlling the quality of the process.

Necessary design functions covered in this chapter include finding a proper location for the facilities, deciding on the best layout of the work flow within the facility, studying the work to determine the best methods, measuring the work to establish time standards, and evaluating individual and firm productivity.

Although these functions must be performed at the startup stage of a new business to avoid chaos, it is equally important for existing businesses to reevaluate their operations periodically to maintain an effective system in the face of changing product lines, growth of the firm, and the many changes in the environment over time. As a business firm evolves, it usually finds that locations, layouts, process designs, and measurement systems that worked well in the past have become obsolete with the addition of new products, new equipment, and different demands by customers. For some firms, such as high-technology manufacturers and multilocation retailers, these decisions must be made very frequently, sometimes monthly or even weekly. For other firms in basic industries such as steel or mining, years may pass before the firm feels the need to reevaluate.

Facilities Location

An improper location for a manufacturing firm usually results in increased production and distribution costs, placing an otherwise efficiently managed company at a competitive disadvantage. The location of service facilities is critical because proximity to the customer and a convenient location may be the major factor in determining the success of the enterprise. The location decision takes on added significance because that choice, once made and implemented, cannot be changed without considerable cost.

Key Factors for Location Choices

The facilities location decision generally involves selecting the region, selecting a particular community within the region, and finally selecting a specific site within the community. At each stage of this process, factors requiring serious consideration include:

1. **Proximity to product markets.** For manufacturing firms, distance to the customer influences transport time, shipping costs, and the ability to service the customer's needs. for many service firms, the location must be where the customers are, in high traffic areas with easy access.

2. **Relationship to other facilities.** A multilocation firm may select a location for an additional facility to provide the best coverage of the market territory it serves. In other instances, it may be an advantage to group several facilities of the firm in the same area.

3. **Access to materials and suppliers.** If raw materials are bulky and costly to transport (such as iron ore), a location near the source is cost effective. If suppliers of tools, equipment, components, and materials are concentrated in one area, it may make sense to locate near those firms.

4. **Transportation and communication access.** Prompt, regular, dependable, low-cost shipment and communications facilities are essential to many organizations. The firm may require easy access to major airports, rail lines, truck routes, waterways, or even to financial communication centers.

5. **Labor market concentration.** The objective is to develop and maintain an effective work force with a minimum of recruiting and training costs. Favorable regional wage rates are a positive factor in situations where labor cost represents a major part of total operating cost. Firms requiring high levels of technical personnel must choose locations attractive to these mobile employees.

6. **Relationship to competition.** In some industries, locating as far from competitors as possible is the best strategy, while in other industries, similar firms tend to cluster in an area to their mutual advantage.

7. **Climate.** Climate may be a major factor in some production processes such as testing facilities or technologies that must operate with strict controls on temperature, dust, and other environmental features. A mild climate, such as in the Sunbelt states, also may be more attractive to the desired labor supply.

8. **Quality of Life.** Community facilities and living conditions such as schools, churches, medical facilities, recreational and cultural opportunities, available and affordable housing, municipal services, and environmental quality are important in recruiting and maintaining an adequate work force.

9. **Laws, regulations, services, and taxes.** Local laws and regulations may favor some industries and discourage others. Pollution controls and special fees are examples. From a cost perspective, the firm must judge the relative value of services provided (such as fire and police protection, utilities availability, and waste removal) relative to the fees, rates, and taxes for the area.

10. **Facilities cost.** Whether remodeling an existing facility or constructing a new one, the firm must consider the costs of land and construction as well as the availability of suitable sites. The choice of urban, suburban, or rural locations will greatly influence these costs even within the same area.

11. **Inducements.** Many communities make financial or tax inducements to attract a type of industry or a specific firm. Sometimes these inducements can be the deciding factor.

12. **Special requirements.** The technologies of some industries impose special demands on the location decision. For example, brewing firms must have access to an ample supply of fresh water, and a toxic waste disposal firm must deal with the political ramifications of its desired location decision.

Location Decision Making

Some firms, such as convenience stores, fast-food restaurants, motel chains, and gasoline distributors, locate new facilities frequently. In these companies, departments of experts in the field of location-analysis methods and real estate are continually working on location projects. Depending on the firm, they may make decisions at the department level or make recommendations to higher levels of management for a final decision.

In other firms, where the decision to locate or relocate is made infrequently, the typical procedure is to establish a committee, gather data, perhaps hire specialized consultants, meet with representatives from possible sites, and eventually present a recommendation to top management for a decision. When General Motors decided to locate its new facility in Tennessee, the press followed the process over years of study because of the impact this decision would have on some small community.

Analysis Methods

A variety of approaches, methods, and quantitive tools are available to make the location decision. Several of the more important methods are reviewed here.

Weighted Factor Method. One way to make the location decision is to assign weights to the regional, community, and site factors considered important. Each alternative site is evaluated on each factor, evaluations are multiplied by the weights, and the weighted evaluations are totaled for each site to provide insights into the location decision.

Weights may be assigned objectively, such as weighting the factor for utilities costs based on its percentage of total costs of the firm, or they may be subjectively determined based on the judgment of the decision makers involved. Similarly, the ratings of each proposed location for a given criterion may be objective or subjective depending on the nature of the criterion, the available data and the preferences of the decision makers.

Table 3-1 provides an example of this method. Notice that, for this firm, the industrial park emerged as the preferred location even though each of the other sites was better on one of the criteria.

Break-Even Analysis. Another approach is to make a location break-even analysis. First, relevant fixed and variable costs are determined for each proposed location. Next, the total cost curves for each alternative are plotted on a single graph (figure 3-1). Then, based on forecasted level of activity, the alternative location with the lowest total cost is selected.

In this example, Houston has very low fixed costs (such as land prices) but very high variable costs (such as wage rates). It would be the lowest cost alternative for projected volumes up to V1. In the range between V1 and V2, Denver, with a higher fixed cost but lower variable cost, would be best. Above V2, Chicago is the low cost location. New York would never be chosen since its costs are higher for any projected volume. If the decision is to be made strictly on cost and the projected production rate is V3, Chicago is the preferred site.

Simulation. Sometimes the location selected determines the type of facility that can be built, which, in turn, affects the operating costs and perhaps the revenues for the facility. One way to handle the complicated interactions of site costs, facility costs, and impact on the firm is to simulate the operation of this alternative over time to see the likely results.

A large motel chain built a simulation model to do just that. Some of its locations are in rural areas where two major interstate highways intersect. A facility here would require larger dining facilities (since there were few alternatives for the traveler) but no banquet facilities for local club meetings. The demand is almost exclusively from travelers staying only one night, and this has implications for the configuration of the rooms, staffing of employees, registration procedures, and many other factors.   By contrast, small-town locations and downtown metropolitan locations would differ considerably on these factors.

For each proposed location , the type of facility was plugged into the simulation, along with specific data on the cost of the land, traffic rates on the highways, number of nearby competing facilities, and other relevant data. The computer then simulated the operation of the facility for several years, and projected revenues, costs, profits, and other data with distributions on the degree of risk involved. At this point, the decision makers can adjust input data (such as more or fewer rooms in the facility) and make successive runs of the simulation until they are satisfied with the combination of factors for that project and make a decision.

Table 3-1

Weighted Factor Analysis of Locations

FACTORS (weights)

SITES	Land Cost (.40)	Possible Expansion (.10)	Transportation Availability (.30)	Amenities (.20)	Total Weighted Factor
Industrial Park					
Evaluation	8	5	8	8	
Weighted	3.2	0.5	2.4	1.6	7.7
Rural					
Evaluation	10	10	4	1	
Weighted	4.0	1.0	1.2	0.2	6.4
Central City					
Evaluation	2	0	10	6	
Weighted	0.8	0.0	3.0	1.2	5.0
Suburban					
Evaluation	6	5	6	10	
Weighted	2.4	0.5	1.8	2.0	6.7

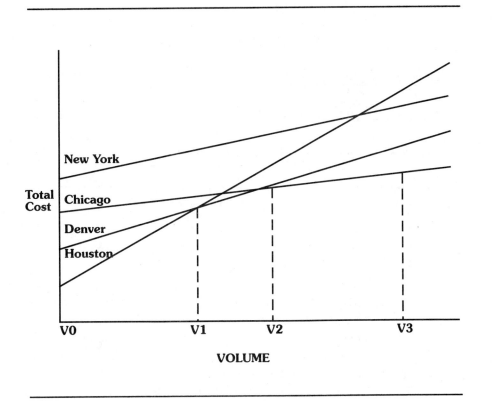

**Figure 3-1. Total Costs for Alternative
Locations Compared to Volume**

Linear Programming. A special form of linear programming known as the transportation method is especially useful for the firm that has multiple plants serving multiple warehouses. When deciding to locate a new plant or a new warehouse, this quantitative tool will evaluate each proposed site in terms of its impact on the cost of the entire system, particularly the transportation and distribution costs. The analysis provides the optimal distribution of products from plants to warehouses, including the proposed facility.

As an example, one firm has manufacturing plants in Chicago, Los Angeles, and Phoenix. These plants supply distribution centers in regional locations which, in turn, supply retail outlets throughout the country. An additional distribution center is needed and two sites, A and B, have been proposed. The matrix in figure 3-2 shows the three plants with their production capacities and the demand from the four distribution centers, including the new one. The numbers in the upper left corner of each cell represent the transportation costs of shipping from a plant to a distribution center.

DISTRIBUTION CENTERS

PLANTS	I	II	III	New	CAPACITIES
Chicago	8	10	15		1000
Los Angeles	12	7	4		1500
Phoenix	14	10	8		1200
DEMAND	900	1300	800	700	

**Figure 3-2. Matrix For Transportation Method of
Linear Programming**

Each proposed location is plugged into the last column of the matrix with its appropriate transportation costs, and the allocation problem is solved to yield the optimal distribution of products from the plants to the regional centers. (Solution techniques are explained in most operations-research texts and are available in many computer programs.)

Figures 3-3 and 3-4 are the solution matrices for the two proposed sites. Site A would receive 100 units of product from Chicago and 600 units from Los Angeles to fill its demand of 700 units. The low-cost solution for site B would involve shipping all 700 units from the Phoenix plant and making necessary adjustments in other shipping schedules to assure that supply from the plants meets demand from the distribution centers. With site B, total shipping costs for the system would be $3,000 less. This is then factored in with the other costs for the two proposed sites, and a final decision is made.

Facilities Layout

Facilities layout is the overall arrangement of machines, personnel, materials handling, service facilities, and aisles required to facilitate efficient operation of the production system.

Several specific objectives of good facilities layout include the following:

1. Minimizing materials handling and plant transportation requirements. This reduces the costs and time to move materials through the production process and reduces work-in-process inventories.

DISTRIBUTION CENTERS

PLANTS	I	II	III	A	CAPACITIES
Chicago	8 900	10	15	4 100	1000
Los Angeles	12	7 100	4 800	6 600	1500
Phoenix	14	10 1200	8	10	1200
DEMAND	900	1300	800	700	3700

TOTAL COST = $27,100

Figure 3-3. Solution Matrix For Proposed Site A

DISTRIBUTION CENTERS

PLANTS	I	II	III	B	CAPACITIES
Chicago	8 900	10 100	15	6	1000
Los Angeles	12	7 700	4 800	10	1500
Phoenix	14	10 500	8	4 700	1200
DEMAND	900	1300	800	700	3700

TOTAL COST = $24,100

Figure 3-4. Solution Matrix For Proposed Site B

2. Maximize the return on the fixed investment in facilities by minimizing the amount of floor space required. Floor congestion and production bottlenecks should be eliminated.

3. Utilizing labor efficiently and effectively by minimizing the distance and time to obtain materials, tools, and supplies; by facilitating main-

tenance and housecleaning; and by facilitating production supervision and use of support personnel.

4. Reducing the hazards affecting employees and products. Provision of adequate exhaust ducts, guard rails, and operating clearances makes the job safer.

5. Providing for a smooth, logical flow of customers through the process where applicable.

6. Providing flexibility for expansion caused by growth, new products, and new processes.

The net effect should be to increase efficiency, reduce costs, and improve employee and customer satisfaction.

Regardless of how effective the original layout is, changes are inevitable. Changes in demand, the introduction of new products, product-design changes, obsolescence of processes or equipment, changes in safety and personnel needs, and changes made to reduce costs may prompt a new layout.

Manufacturing Layout

Four basic layout patterns are used in manufacturing operations:

1. Process layout

2. Product or line layout

3. Fixed-position layout

4. Group or cellular layout

A **process layout**, which is used in the job-shop or intermittent-production system, groups similar equipment together. For example, all drilling equipment would be in one area, all grinding equipment would be in another work center, and all milling equipment in still another. Figure 3-5 presents a graphic representation of a process layout. The variable-path nature of materials handing in process layouts eliminates much of the savings possible from the use of chutes, conveyors, or transfer machines.

The process layout is used where volume is low, several products are made, and processing flexibility is desired. General-purpose, low-cost machines generally are used. If one machine breaks down, the work usually can be shifted to other, similar machines. Because equipment in a process layout does not depend on a given sequence, machines that produce excessive noise, vibration, fumes, or heat can be located in isolated areas.

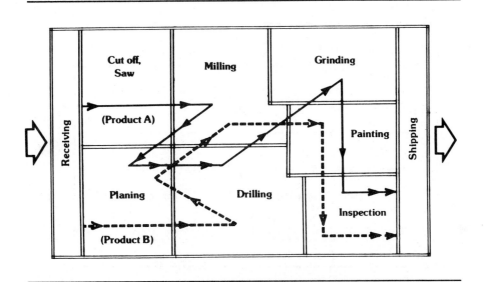

Figure 3-5. Process Layout Showing Movement of Two Different Products

There are several disadvantages to the process layout: more complex planning and control because of routing, scheduling and cost-accounting requirements; costlier materials handling; larger work-in-process inventories; increased storage and floor area requirements; increased costs for more skilled labor; more frequent inspection requirements; and more extensive supervision requirements.

A **product or line layout** arranges the equipment according to the progressive steps by which the product is made. Product layout is used in the repetitive production system, in which the number of end products is small, the parts are highly standardized and interchangeable, and the volume is large. Figure 3-6 presents a graphic representation of a product or line layout.

Product or line layout permits the use of costly, specialized, high-volume equipment; materials handling is simplified by means of transfer machines or conveyors; both production control and job training are easier; less inspection is required; there is less work-in-process; smaller aisles are required; and the floor area is more productive.

Disadvantages of the product or line layout include the higher initial equipment investment; greater vulnerability to work stoppage; the highly repetitive nature of the work; and the inflexibility that makes it more costly when changes are made because of product redesign.

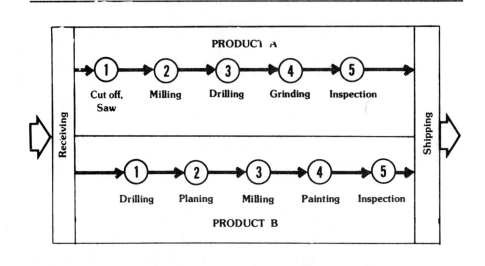

Figure 3-6. Product or Line Layout Showing Movement of Two Different Products

With a **fixed-position layout,** the product remains in one position because of its bulk or weight, and the workers, materials, and tools move to it. This layout normally is used in making items such as locomotives, ships, or large printing presses in project production.

A **group or cellular layout** is indicated when a product is manufactured by means of group technology; that is, equipment and operations that have a common sequence for a family of parts or products are grouped together. This permits economic production of very small lots, thereby minimizing work-in-process inventories, space requirements, and production leadtimes. In layout by process, machines are grouped by type, and parts travel long distances between steps. By applying group technology with a cellular layout–that is, by combining several steps within an independent machining cell–production lead time can be reduced, and less space is required. Figure 3-7 shows the differences between process layout and cellular layout.

Other types of layout include marketing, storage, yard, and office. A **marketing layout** is arranged primarily to facilitate the sale of products, such as in a supermarket. A **storage layout** is designed to fill an inventory and stock-keeping function, providing effective use of storage facilities and materials-handling equipment. A **yard layout** is used for outside storage, thereby reducing the need for inside facility requirements. An **office layout** facilitates the work of clerical and administrative

Before: Process Layout

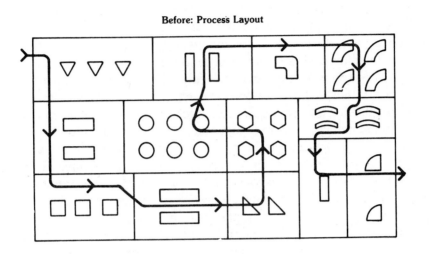

After: Cellular Layout

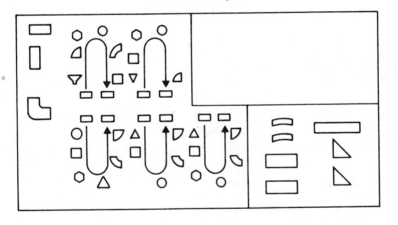

Figure 3-7. Layout by Process Versus Cellular Layout

employees. In addition, many flow process operations, such as in an oil refinery, are laid out according to the technology of the process.

Service Layout

Service organizations, such as banks, insurance companies, hospitals, restaurants, and offices, face many of the same layout problems as manufacturing organizations. The primary difference is that their facilities exist to bring customers together with the organization's services. The layouts provide easy automobile entrance into parking areas from which sidewalks and well-marked entrances guide the customer into the service facility. Receiving or holding areas, cash registers, service counters, and employee work stations frequently are part of a service layout.

Service layouts receive and serve the customer or process physical materials. A hospital, for example, may have a product or line layout for preparing serving trays; a process layout for various medical technologies, such as laboratory tests, radiology, and surgery; and a fixed-position layout within an operating room or intensive-care facility.

Restaurants also could have mixed layouts. For example, a buffet line represents a product layout, and a seated dining area represents a fixed-position layout. The kitchen itself, with its freezers, grills, ovens, dessert areas, and salad areas, represents a process layout.

In office automation and clerical applications, the primary considerations are the location and movement of people, paperwork, and equipment.

Layout Cost Comparisons

As volume increases, the cost advantage moves successively from fixed-position layout, to process layout, to product layout. For this reason, many companies strive for high-volume operations to permit use of product layout in a repetitive production system.

In actual practice, most firms use a combination of layouts. For example, machining operations, even in large-volume operations such as those in the automobile industry, frequently are performed with a process layout. Automobile assembly operations, on the other hand, normally use a product or line-layout pattern.

Layout Analysis

The layout analyst frequently starts the manufacturing layout by locating the receiving and shipping departments, which are influenced by the location of rail lines, highways, and existing or potential dock facilities. Then the analyst must determine the size and shape of the other departments.

For process layouts, the primary consideration is minimizing materials handling costs. The analyst may simply work with templates and judgement to determine the most logical layout for the process demands and the space available, or a number of tools may be employed to assist in the analysis. For example, CRAFT (Computerized Relative

Allocation of Facilities) allows the analyst to input material flow and cost data together with a block diagram of the facility into a computer program that will make successive changes in the layout and compute corresponding total costs. It saves a tremendous amount of the analyst's time, but cannot guarantee that the final layout is the optimum, especially for complicated facilities with many work centers.

For product layouts, balance is the key criterion. Each step in the process should provide equal capacity so that material flow will be uninterrupted.   With line-assembly operations, workers should be assigned to each successive set of work stations so there will be a minimum of idle time in the assembly line. This process is called *line balancing.*

Layouts for service industries in which the customer is not present (such as offices) follow the same guidelines, except that the flow of material may be reports, documents, or other forms of information. When the customer is a part of the process, as in retail stores and personal services, generally the flow of the customer is plotted first to maximize efficiency and convenience, and then the equipment, materials, and service operators are placed in positions to support the primary customer flow.

Process charts and flow diagrams help determine the most effective patterns. Often, the actual placement of equipment, materials, work stations, counters, and other components is decided after experimentally placing templates or three-dimensional scale models in position on a floor plan.

Materials Handling

Materials handling frequently is considered the twin of facilities layout because the type of materials-handling equipment utilized influences the plant layout, and vice versa.

Materials-handling equipment is classified as either fixed-path or varied-path equipment.   Fixed-path equipment (conveyors, chutes, cranes, and hoists) is relatively inflexible and handles material in large volume, normally in a continuous flow. Varied-path equipment (forklift trucks and four-wheel trucks) is flexible and normally handles materials in lots. Fixed-path equipment occupies space constantly, while varied-path equipment occupies space only intermittently.

Where variability is not required, there is a tendency to use fixed-path equipment for several reasons: (1) lower initial cost, (2) lower operating cost (no operator is required), (3) less supervision required, and (4) less space required.

A recent trend in some facilities is to use automated materials-handling systems. Automatic storage and retrieval systems (AS/RS) place pallet loads within very large storage racks by means of automated stacking cranes. A computer locates an empty rack cell, directs the stacking crane to place the pallet within the rack, and then records the pallet's location for inventory purposes and automatic retrieval when desired. Robotic carriers automatically convey loads between the rack area and specified delivery areas by using wires installed in the floor to guide the carriers to their destination. These systems do not require operating personnel, and it is even possible to operate in total darkness.

Data Needed for Layout Planning

The layout analyst requires certain types of information. For example, the bill of materials (B/M) specifies the kinds of materials and parts required to make a unit of product (see chapter 2). This, coupled with the forecasted demand for end products and spare parts, helps determine the scale of operations. In addition, the analyst must know the sequence of operations for processing and assembling parts into the end product. A master route sheet helps in making these determinations. With information concerning the products, product mix, market demand, and work standards, the analyst can determine the number and kinds of machines and tooling systems required and can proceed to make an effective layout.

Equipment Types and Their Selection

Equipment affects labor requirements, quality control, production capacity, and job design. Selection of equipment is based primarily on the product design, product volume, quality requirements, and cost considerations.

Firms must determine whether a specific type of work requires general-purpose machines or special-purpose machines. General-purpose machines–lathes or drill presses, for example–are capable of handling a variety of jobs. On the other hand, special-purpose machines, such as an automated transfer line, usually are faster and more efficient, but changing these complex systems to handle different product designs is difficult and costly.

General-purpose machines are less costly then special-purpose machines, have a broad range of job applications, are relatively simple to maintain, and have less obsolescence. On the other hand, they usually have slower operating rates, are less productive, have less consistent quality, and involve large work-in-process inventories. Special-purpose machines are extremely costly and normally are used only for high-volume production.

Numerical-control (N/C) machines are the most costly general-purpose machines, but they are faster and more efficient than other general-purpose machines. Such machines are preprogrammed, by means of computerized commands, to perform a cycle of operations repetitively. Since production is almost automatic, labor costs are reduced because a single operator often can operate several machines at the same time. Quality is improved and is more consistent. Tooling costs and lead time requirements also are reduced considerably. The primary disadvantages of N/C machines are their higher initial cost, the need for specially trained programmers, and higher maintenance costs.

Automated batch manufacturing systems (ABMS) or transfer machines are superior to N/C machines when large volumes are involved. Parts are attached to a conveying system and carried through a system of individual machines that transform the parts into finished units. All product handling is eliminated, except in the first and last operations. In one early installation, 42 machines were connected to perform 530 operations required to machine engine blocks. The ABMS reduced time from nine hours per block to less than 15 minutes.

Computer-aided manufacturing (CAM) is a sophisticated extension of direct numerical control of machine tools, robots, and inspection machines. Ideally, CAM interfaces with computer-aided design (see chapter 2). Data bases developed by CAD are used to manufacture tooling, program tooling for N/C machines, and program inspection machines in the development of CAM applications. In the future, information may pass directly from CAD to CAM via the data base with minimal use of engineering drawings. The CAD/CAM linkage greatly shortens the time between design and production. For example, in designing and making hydraulic tubing for aircraft, one manufacturer reduced the work force from twelve to three persons; time from release of the drawing to finished product was reduced from six weeks to eighteen minutes.

Industrial robots are increasingly used for highly repetitive manual jobs. The robots are computer controlled and usually are programmed initially by being hand guided through the required operation. Their greatest disadvantage is the initial cost; however, their operating costs usually are low, and they are easy to reprogram for other jobs.

Equipment in many service firms is following the same trends as in manufacturing. Restaurants and bars use automatic dispensing equipment, and the use of mini- or microcomputers in office applications make many of the tedious operations automatic.

Maintenance

Maintenance operations include all efforts to keep production facilities and equipment in proper operating condition. The four types of maintenance operations are (1) **breakdown repair,** (2) **millwright** (people who move and install equipment) activities and minor construction, (3) **preventive maintenance,** and (4) **custodial services.** Breakdown and millwright are called irregular maintenance because the demands for such services occur at irregular intervals and impose variable loads on the maintenance department. Preventive and custodial may be called regular or periodic maintenance for they may be performed on a set schedule.

Much attention has been given to the proper relationship of breakdown repair to preventive maintenance. Breakdown repair is a special problem because breakdowns are random, creating peaks and valleys in the work load. Queuing theory and Monte Carlo simulation (two specialized operation research techniques) are methods of analyzing breakdown waiting lines and distributions to determine personnel and scheduling requirements. In any case, the uneven maintenance work load may cause the maintenance department to operate inefficiently. However, in the interest of maximizing performance of the manufacturing departments, the firm may decide to accept some inefficiencies in the operation of the maintenance department.

Preventive maintenance (PM) is performed before the equipment breaks down so that it continues to operate satisfactorily and reduces the likelihood of breakdown. Its primary advantages are that it enables maintenance crews to schedule their time evenly, tends to minimize equipment breakdowns, and may be scheduled to avoid work stoppages. PM schedules may be based on calendar time or equipment usage time. To function successfully, a good PM program depends upon records, which include a maintenance history for each piece of equipment. These permit analysis of breakdown frequency and causes, thereby providing a basis for improving the PM procedure.

Two modifications of a PM program designed to reduce costs are group replacement and standby equipment. **Group replacement** applies to a large group of identical components, such as light bulbs. Analysis based on failure-probability distribution may justify replacing components after a certain time, along with units that already have failed, rather than replacing the units individually as they fail. In **standby equipment** analysis, the minimum total cost between the costs of lost service due to out-of-service machines versus the costs of keeping extra machines on hand to avoid a shutdown is sought.

In the past, maintenance was not a high priority for a service firm. But as service firms become more automated and use more sophisticated equipment, they are subject to the same dependencies on maintenance as manufacturing firms. American Express, for example, depends heavily on the proper functioning of its computer equipment for the rapid and accurate processing of customer information. Even minor breakdowns for very short periods can be extremely costly.

Maintenance of computers and other office equipment may be done by the firm's employees, by the company that sold the equipment to the firm, or by an independent maintenance contractor. Some estimates say that 1 percent of the purchase cost is spent monthly in maintenance. With the amount of electronic equipment now used in industry, and with the great need for maintenance, electronic-equipment and office-systems maintenance has become a service industry in itself.

Energy Management

Energy is one of the major purchased resources most firms use. Since the oil crunch of the early 1970's, the high costs of oil and petroleum derivatives have focused much more attention on energy management. Energy sources such as coal, nuclear power, hydrogenerated electricity, wood, the sun, geothermal heat, shale oil, and wind are possible energy alternatives. Government programs and tax incentives now encourage investments in energy-conserving devices and materials, such as more efficient motors or insulating materials.

Many firms now have formal energy-management programs (EMP). Such programs start with an audit to determine an organization's current energy utilization. The gross energy audit measures total energy consumption and identifies the types of energy used. A detailed energy audit determines how much of each type of energy is being used and where (i.e., which process, operations, or machines).

Energy-management programs seek improvements through several types of conservation methods: (1) process changes, (2) product changes, (3) materials conservation, (4) heat-recovery applications, (5) improved equipment controls, (6) housekeeping practices, and (7) facilities design and insulation. Through these programs, many firms actually have reduced their energy requirements even in the face of organization growth.

Work Study

In the broadest sense, every organization is concerned with providing goods or offering services while utilizing men and women, machines, materials, and facilities as resources. All operating units should be concerned with performing their work more effectively, efficiently, and economically. Work study is an effective way to coordinate and use available resources. Work study means finding the most effective way of doing a job. It involves analyzing present and preferred work systems to develop an optimal transformation of resources into desired products.

The competitive pressures on today's manager greatly increase the need for work study. Specifically, work analysis should result in greater productivity through improved methods that normally permit an increased output with the same or less effort. Additional benefits often include reduction in worker fatigue, improved workplace layout, better product design, more efficient materials handling, and increased safety.

Work study is best applicable to large-scale repetitive manufacturing operations with standardized products and materials. In automobile manufacturing, for example, where millions of essentially identical units will be produced, work is studied in great detail to eliminate any wasted motion, to make the job easier to perform, and to find the right sequence of operations for maximum efficiency. Volume justifies the time and effort taken in work study.

But work study is finding more and more applications in the office and in a variety of service operations. Bank tellers, for example, can provide better, quicker service if their job has been studied to determine the proper equipment, layout of the workstation, arrangement of materials, and procedures for each type of transaction. Although less routine than a job on an auto assembly line, the teller's job can be standardized for most typical transactions and the unusual cases handled as exceptions. Financial institutions, insurance companies, and even health-care facilities are finding that work study is not limited to manufactured products.

Those who perform work studies should be creative, questioning people who love efficiency and abhor waste. It has been claimed that work study is 80 percent attitude and 20 percent knowledge. The person who is continually trying to find faster, more effective ways of doing things or who manages to do several tasks at once is a good candidate for a work-study position. Given the proper skills and management support, that individual can pay the company back in cost savings that equal many times his or her salary.

Work study can be applied in three separate phases:

1. Analysis of the initial design of the product and the process;

2. Periodic reviews of an existing method to see if further improvements can be made;

3. Special studies to resolve problems or to incorporate changes made to the product or process.

An organization's work is accomplished by a series of interdependent operations performed by individuals at work stations. Depending on the process, the tasks may be connected in a line (as in auto assembly) or separate but linked (as in the claims-processing department of an insurance company). The job of the work study analyst is to break down the work into its necessary elements, analyze each element to make it as efficient as possible, and combine the elements into a process that effectively produces the desired product. Key among the tools and techniques available are work-study charts.

Work-Study Charts

Charts using special symbols and formats enable the analyst to describe existing operations and processes and make changes on paper before real work is modified. Besides being useful analysis tools, charts aid in communicating proposed changes to management, employees, and others. The most commonly used charts are (1) process charts, (2) flow diagrams, (3) assembly charts, (4) multiple-activity charts, and (5) operation charts.

The American Society of Mechanical Engineers (ASME) has established a set of five symbols that are now standard in constructing process charts:

1. A large circle ◯ denotes an *operation*.

2. An arrow ⇨ denotes the *transportation* or movement of worker or material more than three feet.

3. A square ☐ denotes an *inspection* for quality or quantity.

4. A large letter d D denotes a *delay*.

5. An inverted triangle ▽ indicates *storage*.

In a **process chart**, chronological steps of the process are listed following the worker, the product, or, in some cases, the customer. Time, distance, or other relevant descriptive information may be included also. It is then possible to summarize the data to determine how much time is spent in operations, inspections, transporting, storage, necessary delays (such as waiting for glue to dry) or unnecessary delays (such as waiting in line for processing).

Figure 3-8 is an adaptation of a more detailed process chart taken from a commercial bakery. In this case, the chart follows the activities of

PROCESS CHART

Process: <u>Mixing and</u>
        <u>baking chocolate</u>
        <u>chip cookies</u>

Department: <u>Bakery</u>

Subject charted: <u>Baker</u>

Method: <u>Current</u>

Charted by: <u>LLC</u>

Summary			
Activity	Steps	Time	Distance
Operation ○	8	60.6	
Transport ⇨	6		162
Delay D	3	37.5	
Inspect ❐	4	3.9	
Store ▽	0		
Totals	21	102.0	162

Step No.	Time (min)	Distance (feet)	○	⇨	D	❐	▽	Description
1	13.0		X					Assemble ingredients
2		25		X				Take to counter
3	9.0		X					Assemble mixing tools
4		31		X				Take to counter
5	4.0		X					Combine flour, baking soda, and salt; set aside
6	10.5		X					Combine other ingredients, beat until smooth
7	7.8		X					Add flour mixture and chocolate chips
8	0.3					X		Inspect mixture for consistency
9		62		X				Obtain cookie sheet, take to counter
10	11.2		X					Drop cookies onto sheet

Figure 3-8. Process Chart

Step No.	Time (min)	Distance (feet)	O	⇨	D	☐	▽	Description
11		11	X					Go to oven
12	0.1			X				Set oven temperature
13	12.0				X			Allow oven to preheat
14	0.1					X		Check oven for correct temperature
15		22	X					Obtain cookies, take to oven
16	10.0				X			Bake cookies
17	0.6					X		See if cookies are done
18		11	X					Take cookies from oven to counter
19	4.5		X					Remove cookies from sheet
20	10.0				X			Allow cookies to cool
21	2.0					X		Taste test final product

Figure 3-8. (Continued)

the baker, but a different chart could be created to follow the product (cookie mix) especially if several workers were involved in the process. Such a chart would then plot the operations performed, transportation of the mix, and time that the mix was delayed or in storage. How the chart is constructed depends on the purpose of the analysis.

Analysis of the process can proceed using questions such as the following:

1. **Can unnecessary work be eliminated?** Could a transportation be eliminated, for example, by performing two operations at the same work station?

2. **Can operations or elements be combined?** In one instance, a manufacturer of wood products found that he could move the product to the next work station while the finish on the product was drying; thus he combined the elements of transport and delay.

3. **Can the sequence of operations be changed?** Sometimes simply asking the question leads to new creative solutions such as attaching the wheels to a toy as an early step in the assembly process so the unit is easier to transport to successive work station.

Advanced texts and work-study manuals contain long lists of questions such as these to help guide the thinking and stimulate the creativity of the work-study analyst.

A **flow diagram** (figure 3-9) uses the ASME or other symbols connected by arrows on a floor plan of the facility to depict the flow of the product as it is completed. With this tool, one or several products can be traced to predict problems that could arise with material handling, bottleneck operations, or needed layout changes. Flow diagrams have become frequently used in service businesses to track the flow of customers through a facility. Although customers in a grocery store may be free to choose their own route, patients in a hospital may be charted as

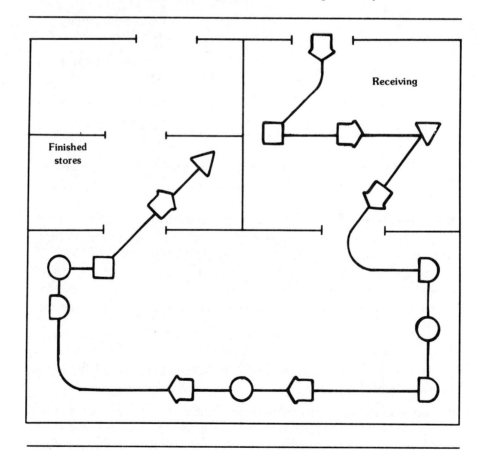

Figure 3-9. Flow Diagram

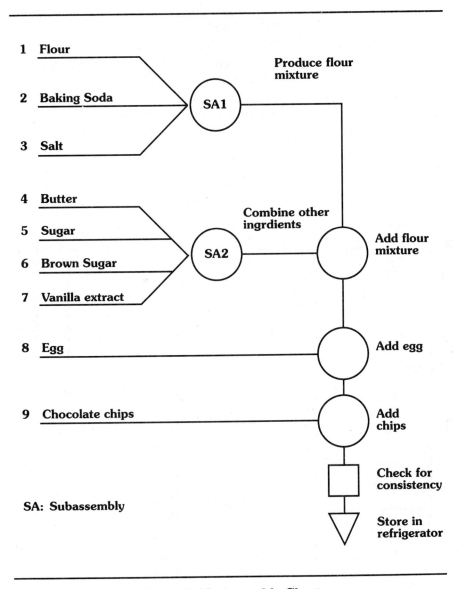

Figure 3-10. Assembly Chart

they progress through laboratories and other facilities to give the analyst insights into developing a more efficient system.

An **assembly chart** focuses on the subassemblies of components and the final assembly of those components into a finished product. Combined with the bill of materials and route sheet (see examples in chapters 2 and 6), the assembly chart gives a good picture of the elements of the product and the sequence of production. The assembly chart also may be called a "gozinto" chart (we will not try to convince you that the chart was developed by an Italian scientist name Vito Gozinto).

Illustrated here (figure 3-10) is an assembly chart for the cookie mix example. Imagine what the assembly chart would look like for a Boeing 767 aircraft or even for a personal computer!

When one worker can operate two or more semiautomatic machines such as a turret lathe or a copy machine, a **multiple-activity chart**

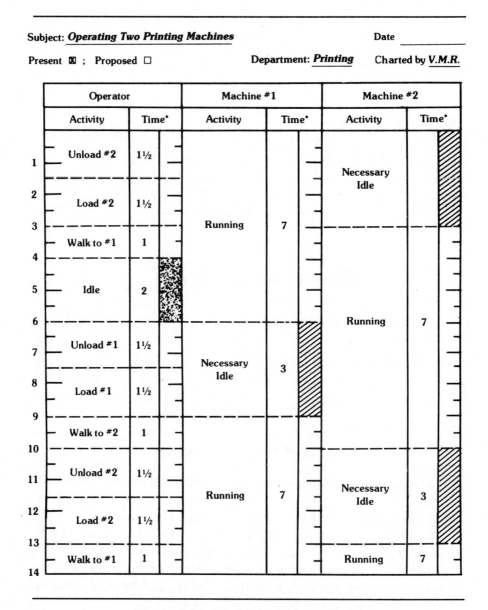

Subject: ***Operating Two Printing Machines***   Date _____

Present ☒ ; Proposed ☐   Department: ***Printing***   Charted by ***V.M.R.***

	Operator		Machine #1		Machine #2	
	Activity	Time*	Activity	Time*	Activity	Time*
1	Unload #2	1½			Necessary Idle	
2	Load #2	1½	Running	7		
3	Walk to #1	1				
4						
5	Idle	2			Running	7
6						
7	Unload #1	1½	Necessary Idle	3		
8	Load #1	1½				
9	Walk to #2	1				
10	Unload #2	1½			Necessary Idle	3
11			Running	7		
12	Load #2	1½				
13	Walk to #1	1			Running	7
14						

Figure 3-11. Multiple-Activity Chart

(figure 3-11) plots activities against a time scale to determine the cycle time and calculate worker and machine utilization. In the example, both printing machines are operating at 100 percent capacity because the only idle time is that which is necessary for loading and unloading. The operator, however, is idle two minutes in every ten-minute cycle, for a utilization rate of 80 percent. This idle time may be acceptable, or it may be put to use to complete additional duties, such as quality-control checks, which could be performed while both machines are running.

The **operation chart** (figure 3-12) also may be called a left-hand/right-hand chart or a "simo" chart (for "simultaneous motion"). The most detailed of the charting techniques, the operations chart depicts every motion of both hands of the operator during the work cycle. Because it is so detailed and difficult to construct, it is used only for manipulative operations with very short cycle times and very high volumes.

Although the chart in Figure 3-12 uses the ASME symbols, other variations are available. Frank and Lillian Gilbreth, pioneers in the field of work study and time-and-motion analysis, used countless feet of film of workers to devise a set of standard motions they called Therbligs. Each of the seventeen fundamental Therbligs–such as reach, grasp, and release–has a precise definition, a standard time, and a symbol with a color code to permit detailed analysis of existing jobs or the design of new jobs, using the Therbligs as building blocks and applying the principles developed in their lifelong study of work. Today, a number of systems of predetermined motion-times are available. Among the most common are Methods Time Measurement (MTM), Basic Motion Time Study (BMT), and Work Factor.

Together, these charts and the principles of work study form the basic "tool box" for the work-study analyst.

Work Measurement

Work measurement often is misunderstood because the time-study analyst may be perceived as trying to achieve a speedup of work to squeeze every ounce of work out of the employee. This image holds true especially when the analyst approaches the worker with a stopwatch in hand! Actually, work measurement does for the labor resource what material control does for the material in the process. Specifically, it attempts to determine the standard time, defined as the time required for a normal worker with normal skill and effort, to perform a task over an extended period, with allowances made for breaks, personal time, fatigue, and working conditions.

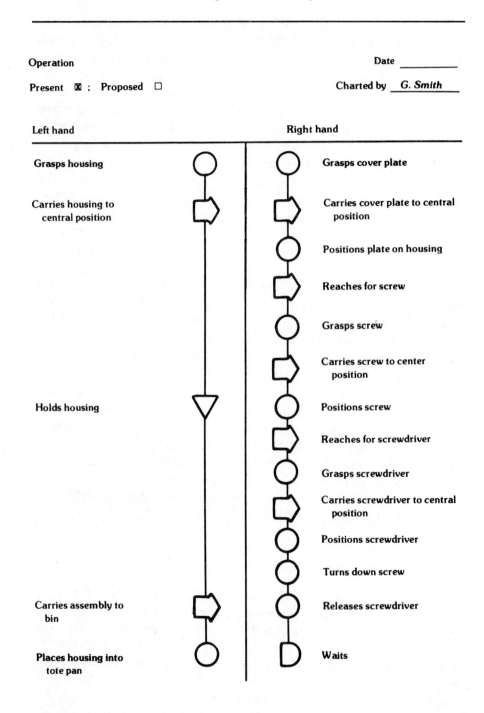

Operation _____   Date _____

Present ☒ ;   Proposed ☐   Charted by _G. Smith_

Left hand			Right hand
Grasps housing	○	○	Grasps cover plate
Carries housing to central position	⬡	⬡	Carries cover plate to central position
		○	Positions plate on housing
		⬡	Reaches for screw
		○	Grasps screw
		⬡	Carries screw to center position
Holds housing	▽	○	Positions screw
		⬡	Reaches for screwdriver
		○	Grasps screwdriver
		⬡	Carries screwdriver to central position
		○	Positions screwdriver
		○	Turns down screw
Carries assembly to bin	⬡	○	Releases screwdriver
Places housing into tote pan	○	D	Waits

Figure 3-12. Operation Chart

Knowing the standard time allows production planners and others in the organization to have the information needed to

1. Schedule the amount of labor needed to complete a job;

2. Determine the amount of additional labor needed because of non-productive time;

3. Calculate the amount of labor per unit of product to determine pricing and other decisions;

4. Evaluate proposed work improvements by comparing before and after standard times.

Several methods are used to establish work standards:

1. Estimates based on historical data;

2. Stopwatch time studies;

3. Predetermined time-and-motion study

4. Work sampling

Estimates Based on Historical Data

Estimating the standard time for a job is the easiest method to use but also the least precise. It involves making an educated guess of the time needed to perform a job before the job is done. Formal analysis would use past data from similar jobs in a statistical model to project a reasonably accurate estimate. Informally, an experienced operator can use judgment to compare the current job to others that have been done in the past.

Often, this is the most reasonable and cost-effective method to use (and the method you use most often to estimate the time to do a job, travel to a meeting, or write a term project). In a job shop, for example, a machinist must drill a hole in each end of a shaft in a batch of twenty units. If other methods of time study were used, the batch would be completed before the standard time was established and the information would then be useless for planning purposes. The machinist just uses experience in drilling a hold in this type of metal and estimates that it will take three minutes per piece or about one hour for the entire job. The estimate will be accurate enough for this purpose, but if we had dozens of machinists drilling millions of holes in millions of shafts, we would use a more detailed method of analysis.

Stopwatch Time Study

A direct time study applies to visible work that is routine and repetitive (as opposed to mental work). Operating a machine or assembling identical units of product are examples of work that can be observed in which the operator performs the same motions over and over again. A skilled time-study analyst can observe the job, time the operator with a stopwatch through repeated cycles, and analyze the data to arrive at a standard time.

Since the standard will later be applied to all operators performing this job, the standard should be set for a normal worker, not an exceptionally fast or skilled one. To meet this objective, the analyst first selects a typical worker for the study and then applies a judgmental rating factor to the study. Just as you could judge whether a person was dealing cards at an exceptionally fast or slow rate, the analyst is trained to judge the rate or efficiency of the operator being observed.

Finally, since the time standard will be applied to work over the course of the day, week, or month, allowances must be made for worker fatigue, personal time, and interference such as breakdowns, shortage of material, or machine reloading.

The example in figure 3-13 will illustrate how the work standard is determined. Mary Alice, a good worker in the copy department, is assigned the task of checking, duplicating, and mailing reports received from a government agency. The analyst timed Mary Alice under normal operating conditions for thirty consecutive reports and averaged the timeat 18.7 minutes per report. Having judged Mary Alice as working at 90 percent of normal, the analyst multiplies the cycle time by the rating to get a normalized cycle time of 16.83 minutes per report.. Allowances in this study are factored in using a formula to assure that 15 percent of the final standard time is allotted to allowances. The result is a time standard of 19.8 minutes per report, which can be applied to any operator performing this job.

Application of the standard is illustrated in figure 3-14. Jane, another worker in the department, worked forty hours and produced 131 reports. Application of the time standard tells if she is working below standard and needs counseling, retraining, or a reprimand; working at standard and deserves a compliment; or working well above standard and deserves a reward. Although the supervisor should look at the data from several operators over a longer period of time to determine the normal variability in the work, it appears from the analysis in the example that Jane is doing very well and may receive a bonus for her superior work.

SUMMARY OF WORK STUDY DATA

Operator: Mary Alice

Working Conditions: Standard

A.	Cycle time (from time study)	18.7 minutes per report
B.	Rating (by analyst)	90%
C.	Normalized time (A x B)	16.83 minutes per report

D. **Allowances**

Fatique	5%
Personal	5%
Delay	5%

Total   15%

E. **Allowance Factor** $\dfrac{1}{1-\%}$ 1.176

F. **Standard Time (C x E)**   19.8 minutes per report

Standard:

19.8 minutes per report
0.33 hours per report
3.03 reports per hour
0.05 reports per minute

Figure 3-13. Calculation of Standard Time

Predetermined Time-and-Motion Study

Predetermined time standards are used as building blocks to determine the standard time for a complete job. Elements of work are studied to establish a standard time, and the time for the job is simply the sum of the times of the elements in it.

At a gross level of analysis, the owner of a housecleaning service may establish time standards for units of work, in this case the time needed to clean a bedroom, bathroom, kitchen, den, or other units of the house. Then, when planning the time needed or the price to charge for a job, the owner needs to know the number and type of rooms the house contains. From that preliminary estimate, adjustments may then be made for special cleaning problems such as wood floors, patio doors, or teenagers' bedrooms.

APPLICATION OF STANDARD TIME

Jane worked a forty-hour week and completed 131 reports.
What is her performance rating?

Method #1: TIME. How long should it have taken a worker to complete 131 reports?

Actual time	=	40 hours
Standard time	=	131 x 0.33 = 42.23 hours
Performance	=	standard/actual= 42.23/40 = 108%

Method #2: UNITS. How many units should a worker complete in 40 hours?

Actual units	=	131 reports
Standard units	=	40 x 3.03 = 121.2 reports
Performance	=	actual/standard= 131/121.2 = 108%

Figure 3-14. Calculation of a Performance Rating

At a detailed level of analysis, Therbligs or similar systems for analyzing hand movements, such as MTM, BMT, or Work Factor, can be used to describe every movement required to perform a given task. Since every Therblig has an associated time standard, the time for the task is the sum of the times of the motions involved. Allowances are then added to establish the time standard for the complete job. Since this method requires a skilled analyst and a great deal of time, it is applicable to jobs with short cycle times and high volumes.

Work Sampling

For work that is routine but not strictly repetitive, work sampling may be used to establish a standard. The analyst observes the worker at random times throughout the day for a period of days or weeks, recording from each observation what type of work the operator is doing. For example, a forklift driver may be traveling loaded or unloaded, may be loading or unloading, may be servicing the truck, may be taking personal time, or may be performing some other activity. Using the principles of probability theory, the analyst can determine the percentage of time in each category and begin to establish the amount of time needed to perform nonrepetitive activities to accomplish a given amount of work such as unloading a truck or picking parts from a warehouse to fill an order.

Because of the nature of the jobs, work sampling often can be applied to clerical work and to jobs in many service firms more effectively than other methods for establishing time standards.

Regardless of the method used, establishment of time standards is necessary if the work of the organization is to be planned, scheduled, and controlled in an effective and efficient operating system.

Managing Repetitive Work

For many years, scientific principles of work study were applied to make tasks routine and structured in the interest of efficiency. The byproduct of those efforts was to create boring, meaningless jobs in many industries. Today we recognize that there must be a balance between technical efficiency and the creation of jobs that are desirable, rewarding, and humanistic. In many cases, the routine jobs have been replaced by robots and other automated equipment. In other circumstances, cross training and pay-for-skill investments have allowed job enrichment and job rotation programs to pay dividends.

Inefficient and unproductive tasks are not rewarding for the worker nor for the company. The objective of work study is to reduce inefficiency and standardize procedures for tasks so that they can then be combined into jobs that are both productive and meaningful.

Individual and Organizational Productivity

In chapter 1 we covered the importance of national productivity in affecting our standard of living and international competitiveness. Here we will explore productivity of individual employees and of organizations. First we will cover the fundamental concepts of productivity as they apply to any industry and to any level of analysis. Then we will look at the basic differences in the productivity concept at the level of the individual worker and of the business firm.

Fundamental Concepts of Productivity

Productivity is a ratio of outputs to inputs. **Outputs** include all products–goods or services–produced by the individual worker or by the business firm. **Inputs** include the four basic factors of production: labor (including direct, indirect, and managerial), materials (direct and indirect such as supplies), capital (land, facilities, equipment, inventories, and other assets), and energy (gas, electricity, heating oil, and fuel).

Partial productivity refers to a ratio of output to one of the input factors such as labor. Units produced per worker hour, for example, is a partial productivity measure. Partial measures are useful in tracking the utilization of one resource, but they can be profoundly affected by changes in the other resource inputs. Examples of typical partial productivity measures are illustrated in figure 3-15. **Total productivity** refers to the ratio of outputs to the combination of all inputs. Although much more useful as a concept, it is difficult to find a common unit to combine the amounts of labor, capital, materials, and energy in the ratio. If dollars are used, the total should be discounted to remove the affects of price changes from the measure; true productivity is a measure of the physical quantities of outputs and inputs.

Productivity analysts are more concerned with the changes or **trends** in productivity than with their absolute levels. Knowing that a worker loaded sixteen tons in four hours yields little information without some comparison or benchmark. If this is more than the other workers or more than this worker has done in the past, then the productivity ratio takes on some meaning.

Any productivity ratio can be increased in five basic ways:

1. **Producing more outputs from the same inputs.** This could be termed "working smarter." Reducing waste in any of the resources or finding productive uses for byproducts are just two of the ways this can be accomplished.

2. **Producing the same outputs from fewer inputs.** Sometimes the output is "fixed" such as a police department serving a given population. Better technology, improved communications, reduced paperwork, and streamlined methods may allow fewer police officers to serve the community with better service and faster response time.

3. **Increasing outputs more than inputs are increasing.** By adding more advanced equipment, better raw material, higher skilled workers, or by realizing economies of scale, the firm is in a stage of "controlled growth;" getting bigger but also getting better.

4. **Reducing inputs more than outputs are reduced.** The other side of the coin can be called "managed decline" and can be achieved by selling unproductive divisions, combining product lines at one facility, and other forms of downsizing.

TYPICAL PRODUCTIVITY RATIOS

LABOR

$$\frac{\text{units produced}}{\text{production employee}} \qquad \frac{\text{customers served}}{\text{cashier}}$$

$$\frac{\text{tons shipped}}{\text{manhours}} \qquad \frac{\text{designs approved}}{\text{engineer}}$$

$$\frac{\text{value added}}{\text{employee}} \qquad \frac{\text{sales}}{\text{payroll}}$$

MATERIALS

$$\frac{\text{tons out}}{\text{tons in}} \qquad \frac{\text{value of shipments}}{\text{value of materials}}$$

$$\frac{\text{customers served}}{\text{paper utilized}} \qquad \frac{\text{production}}{\text{purchase \$}}$$

$$\frac{\text{hamburgers served}}{\text{gallons of ketchup}} \qquad \frac{\text{photos accepted}}{\text{rolls of film used}}$$

CAPITAL

$$\frac{\text{bushels}}{\text{acre}} \qquad \frac{\text{output}}{\text{space utilized}}$$

$$\frac{\text{revenue miles}}{\text{seat miles}} \qquad \frac{\text{units produced/day}}{\text{units of inventory}}$$

$$\frac{\text{units produced/day}}{\text{machine hours}} \qquad \frac{\text{sales}}{\text{square foot}}$$

ENERGY

$$\frac{\text{tons processed}}{\text{BTUs used}} \qquad \frac{\text{degree-days of heat}}{\text{gallons of oil}}$$

$$\frac{\text{production}}{\text{utility \$}} \qquad \frac{\text{value added}}{\text{energy cost}}$$

$$\frac{\text{Ingots made}}{\text{KWH}} \qquad \frac{\text{miles}}{\text{gallon}}$$

Figure 3-15. Partial Productivity Measures

5. **Increasing outputs while reducing inputs.** This may be viewed as the best of all worlds, but it does frequently happen in rapidly advancing industries. The history of the hand-held calculator is a prime example.

Finally, it should be noted that increased productivity does not mean, as commonly believed, reduced quality. In fact, the opposite is usually true; increased productivity and improved quality go together. Reworking or scrapping of rejected products and redoing services that were not properly performed wastes resources. If the products were produced right the first time, the resources used to rework them could be put to more productive uses.

Individual Productivity

Conceptually, individual productivity refers to the ratio of the output of one individual's job to the resources used. As a practical matter, individual productivity is almost always measured as a labor partial and occasionally as a material partial if the worker has control over the amount of scrap and waste produced. In manufacturing, outputs may be physical products such as parts produced, bricks laid, or chairs painted. In services, common output measures are transactions, paperwork processed, or customers served. On the input side, labor may be measured as number of hours worked, number of employees, total compensation or a variety of other ways. No universal measures of individual productivity exist; specific measures are developed to fit each application.

Methods for improving individual productivity covers the entire fields of technology, psychology, human relations, industrial engineering, and probably several others. Everything we have learned about making individuals and processes more effective, more efficient, more timely, and more quality conscious applies to making them more productive.

Firm Productivity

At the firm level, productivity generally means the utilization of all inputs–labor, materials, capital, and energy–to produce all of the outputs of the firm, goods and services. To measure productivity, the firm has two basic choices: develop a family of partial measures or use a total productivity measurement system.

A **family of measures** is a set of partials for all four resources that use the same or similar output measures and together cover all of the outputs and inputs of the firm. For example, TRW developed its corporate measures by using discounted sales as the output measure. They formed five ratios by dividing sales by (1) number of employees, (2) total compensation, (3) total materials costs, (4) real net plant, property, and equipment, and (5) units of energy consumed. Two other measures, value added per employee and value added per total compensation allowed them to better track and evaluate the labor component. Together, these seven ratios gave a comprehensive picture of resource utilization in each of the operating units and could be summed to yield an indicator of total corporate performance.

Total productivity measurement is based on the relationship of productivity to profitability and price recovery. To illustrate this relationship, start with the basic accounting equation:

$$\text{Total revenue} = \text{units produced (and sold)} \times \text{output prices}$$

On the input side, resources are purchased in units (such as hours of labor, tons of material, dollars of capital, and kilowatt hours of electricity) and a price per unit is paid (wage rates, price per ton, interest on capital, and price per kilowatt hour). Another accounting equation says that the total costs of the firm is the sum of all of the resources purchased:

$$\text{Total costs} = \text{input units used} \times \text{input unit prices}$$

Profitability may be defined as the ratio of total revenue to total costs. It defines the percent of revenue that covers costs and therefore the percent of profit out of revenue. If we use the two equations above to form a profitability ratio we find that:

$$\frac{\text{Total revenue}}{\text{Total costs}} = \frac{\text{output units} \times \text{output prices}}{\text{input units} \times \text{input prices}}$$

and a mathematical manipulation of the equation yields:

$$\frac{\text{Total revenue}}{\text{Total costs}} = \frac{\text{output units}}{\text{input units}} \times \frac{\text{output prices}}{\text{input prices}}$$

The first ratio is profitability, as defined earlier. The second ratio, output units to input units, is the definition of productivity for the firm. The third ratio is called price recovery; it measures the degree to which changes in input prices (such as wage rate increases) are passed on to the customer in the form of higher prices or are absorbed by the firm. This equation, productivity = productivity X price recovery, allows the firm to

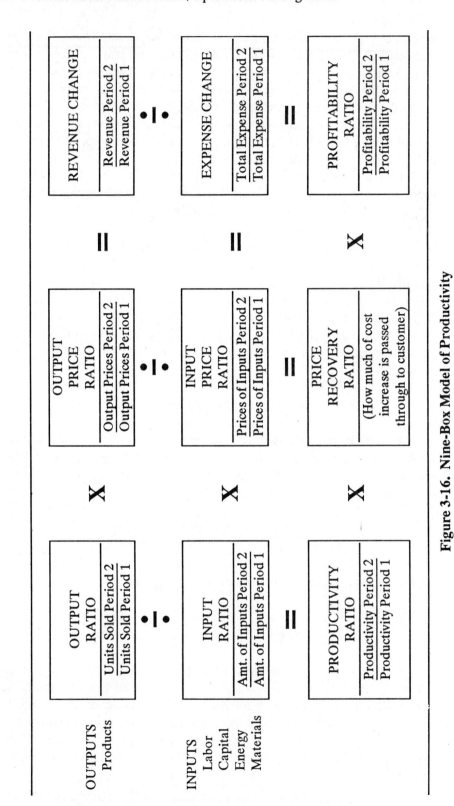

Figure 3-16. Nine-Box Model of Productivity

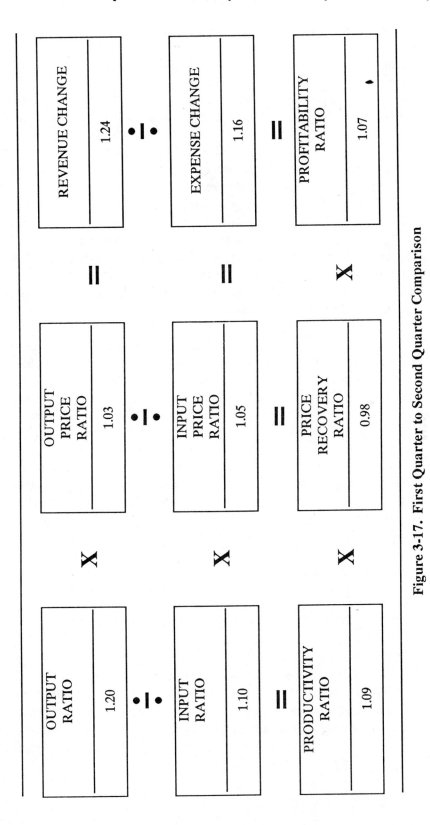

Figure 3-17. First Quarter to Second Quarter Comparison

clearly see that productivity increases allow the firm to be more profitable and allow it to hold the line on its product prices even though it is
paying more for labor, capital, materials, and energy. Some oil companies and other firms should get this message.

Several complex methods are available, some on computer programs,
to perform the calculations of this model with the firm's data. A basic
method, illustrated in figures 3-16 and 3-17 will help explain how the
process works. The "Nine-Box Model" is patterned after the nine elements of the equation above; however, each box represents the change in
that element over a time period as explained in figure 3-16. The first box,
output units, is the units of output in the second period compared to the
units of output in the first period. Figure 3-17 contains data comparing
the first quarter with the second quarter of the current year. The number
1.20 means that twenty percent more units were produced and sold.
Similarly, the average price of the outputs in the second quarter were
three percent higher (1.03) than they were in the first quarter. Multiplying these two figures means that the firm plans to increase total revenues
by 24 percent.

The firm believes it can achieve the twenty percent increase in output
with only a sixteen percent rise in total expenses since some economies of
scale are possible, but it knows it is facing a five percent inflation rate in
the prices of its inputs. Working backwards (right to left) in row two of
the matrix, one can derive that this represents a ten percent increase in
the amount of inputs without having to identify the physical unit of
measure.

The bottom row of the matrix can be interpreted the same as the
model of equations for profitability. The first column indicates that if the
firm is to produce twenty percent more product with ten percent more
resources, it must achieve a nine percent increase in productivity by some
means. The price recovery ratio at the base of column two says that the
firm is absorbing some of the inflation in input prices–good news to its
customers. Finally, column three states that a 24 percent increase in
revenues combined with a sixteen percent rise in total expenses will yield
a seven percent improvement in profitability.

If the Nine-Box Model is used with past data, it indicates how well
the firm performed as a whole and whether its profitability was derived
more from better resource utilization or from simply overcompensating
for inflation with large price increases for its products. More often,
however, the model is used as a planning tool. With sensitivity analysis,
the firm can determine if its projections fit together (for example, can it
sell twenty percent more at the higher price) and if the plans are realistic
(for example, how can it achieve a nine percent productivity improve-

ment in all resources). Fine tuning the matrix will provide a plan that the firm can implement.

Managing productivity of individuals and organizations has become one of the top priorities of business firms facing international competition. In the future, only those who are most effective in the utilization of their resources will survive.

Key Concepts

Definitions of most key concepts are found in the Glossary

Location Factors	**Multiple Activity Chart**
Weighted Factor Analysis	**Operation Chart**
Transportation Method of Linear Programming	**Maintenance**
Simulation	**Standard Time**
Break-Even Analysis	**Stopwatch Time Study**
Process Layout	**Predetermined Motion-Times**
Product Layout	**Work Sampling**
Cellular Layout	**Partial Productivity**
Fixed-Position Layout	**Total Productivity**
ASME Symbols	**Price Recovery**
Process Chart	**Profitability**
Flow Diagram	**Nine-Box Model**
Assembly Chart	

References

Barnes, Ralph M. *Motion and Time Study: Design and Measurement of Work.* 7th ed. New York: John Wiley & Sons, 1980.

Buffa, Elwood S., Armour, Gordon C., and Vollman, Thomas. "Allocating Facilities with CRAFT." *Harvard Business Review* 42 (March-April, 1964): 136-158.

Francis, Richard L., and White, John A. *Facility Layout and Location: An Analytic Approach.* Englewood Cliffs, New Jersey: Prentice-Hall, 1987.

Greene, T. J., and Sadowski, Randall P. "A Review of Cellular Manufacturing Assumptions, Advantages, and Design Techniques." *Journal of Operations Management 4* (February 1984): 85-97.

Hyer, N. L., and Wemmerlov, Urban. "Group Technology and Productivity." *Harvard Business Review* 62 (July-August 1984): 140-149.

Schmenner, Roger W. *Making Business Location Decisions.* Englewood Cliffs, New Jersey: Prentice-Hall, 1982.

Tompkins, James A. and White, John A. *Facilities Planning.* New York: John Wiley & Sons, 1984.

Voss, C. A. *Managing New Manufacturing Technologies. Operations Management Association Monograph No. 1.* East Lansing, Michigan: Michigan State University, 1986.

Discussion Questions

1. Many cities and towns have an "automobile row," where car dealers are located side by side for several blocks. What are the advantages and disadvantages of a car dealer locating beside a competitor? What types of firms try to locate *away* from their competitors?

2. Name a type of firm for which each of the following factors would be the most critical location criterion:

   A. Closeness to raw materials

   B. Land cost

   C. Available skilled labor supply

   D. Climate

3. A manufacturer of kitchen cabinets chose a location just outside city limits on county land. List the advantages and disadvantages of this location compared to a nearby location just inside city limits.

4. A toy manufacturer makes wooden pull toys, stuffed animals, and a series of board games in small lot sizes. Discuss the advantages of a cellular or group layout as compared to a process layout for this company.

5. If you were assigned to do a layout for a grocery store and you knew that most customers traveled through the store from left to right, where would you place frozen foods, canned goods, produce, meat, dairy foods, and other items? Why?

6. If a time standard is set too tight (that is, if there are not enough allowances of if the rating is too severe), what problems would this cause? What problems would occur if the standard is too loose?

7. In applying a time standard, do you divide actual work by the standard, or do you divide the standard by the actual work? Explain.

8. Work sampling can be used to help establish a time standard for nonrepetitive work, but it can also be used as a tool for identifying inefficient work. Explain how this might be done.

Problems

1. In the example of the transportation method of linear programming, suppose we had to ship 100 units from the Chicago plant to a new location, site B. Make the necessary adjustments in the other cells to ensure that the rows and columns have the proper totals, and then calculate the new total cost for this alternative.

2. If the cycle time for an operation is eight minutes, the rating is 110 percent, and allowances total 20 percent, what is the standard time?

3. Choose a task that is familiar to you, such as changing a tire, preparing a meal, or performing an activity at work, and construct a process chart describing the present method including all operations, transportations, inspections, and delays. Analyze the job and make suggestions for improvement. Construct a chart for the improved method.

4. In the multiple-activity chart example, add a third machine for the worker to operate, and chart the worker and three machines through two complete cycles. Calculate the machine and operator utilization. What are the advantages and disadvantages of three machines compared to two machines?

5. The current method used to bake cookies as depicted in the process chart in figure 3-8 can be improved. Examine the method to see where you can eliminate an activity, combine two activities, or change the sequence of activities. Construct a new process chart and compare your summary with that of figure 3-8.

6. An operator was time studied for six continuous hours during which time he completed 57 units. The analyst thought the subject was not a very good worker and rated him during the study at 85%. Normal allowances for this job total 12%.

   A. Calculate the cycle time, the normalized time, and the standard time.

   B. Interpret the difference between the cycle time and the normalized time. What do these two figures mean? How are they different from the standard time?

7. A job was timed for twenty cycles with the following results:

Cycle	Minutes	Cycle	Minutes
1	38	11	42
2	46	12	31
3	48	13	93
4	50	14	41
5	36	15	39
6	38	16	46
7	53	17	42
8	48	18	50
9	39	19	44
10	45	20	55

   Operating conditions were normal except for cycle 13 when the operator was interrupted by the supervisor with a question about a fellow worker. Normal allowances for this job are 7% for fatigue and 10% for personal time. The analyst considered the worker to be keeping a normal pace throughout the study. Calculate the standard and express it as minutes per unit, hours per unit, units per minute, and units per hour.

8. Later in the month, the worker from the problem above worked five 8-hour shifts plus four hours of overtime and produced 48 units. What was his performance rating for this week?

9. Three employees worked together on several jobs over a three-day period (eight-hour shifts). We cannot tell the performance of each individual, but we can determine the performance of the three as a team using the information below. (Hint: compare total hours worked to total standard hours of work completed.)

JOB	UNITS	STANDARD
1	140	7 units/hr
2	1500	120 units/hr
3	750	25 units/hr
4	180	16 units/hr

10. A firm has appointed a committee to make a location decision for their new warehouse. The committee decided that the three critical factors are land cost, utilities cost, and proximity to transportation. They attached weights of 0.60, 0.30, and 0.10 respectively to the three factors. Three sites are being considered. Land costs are $50,000 for site A, $30,000 for site B, and $20,000 for site C. Utility costs are the same at sites A and B, but twice as much at site C. Since proximity to transportation is a matter of judgment, the committee rated site A as 0.45, site B as 0.35 and site C as 0.20 (where a lower number represents closer proximity).

   A. Use the weighted factor method to determine the preferred location.

   B. Would your decision change if the three factors were weighted equally?

11. Alpha-Omega is a pizza delivery service that is always located in small towns with large college campuses. It is considering opening a new location in Bloomington, Indiana. If it locates close to the campus of Indiana University, rent on the facility will be high, but the delivery cost will be low. The farther it is from the campus, generally the lower is the rent but the higher is the delivery cost per pizza to the campus. They have gathered the following data on several possible sites:

SITE	RENT	DELIVERY COST PER PIZZA
W	$2600/month	$ .50
X	1600/month	1.25
Y	800/month	3.25

   A. Use break-even analysis to determine the range of volume per month for which each site is the low cost alternative. Draw a graph to support your findings.

   B. If the projected volume is 1500 pizzas per month, which location would yield the lowest cost?

12. Use the following data and calculate all of the elements of the Nine-Box Model.

    • Output this year will be 6% more units than last year.

    • Output prices will be lowered by 10%.

    • Total expenses will remain the same.

    • Resources will average 5% increase in prices.

    A. Interpret the meaning of productivity, price recovery, and profitability according to your calculations. What does this mean to the sales manager and to the production manager? What will this mean to the firm's competitors?

    B. Is this a good plan? What must be done to make this plan work? Would you like to work for this company? Would you like to invest in this company? Why or why not?

13. A firm is suffering the problems of recession and expects the number of units shipped to decline by 15%. It feels it cannot raise its prices at present; but, because of the recession, it expects only a 2% increase in the prices of the resources it must purchase. Use the Nine-Box Model to determine what the firm must do to maintain its profitability at a constant rate in these tough times. Do you think it can do it? How?

14. Draw a graph with the Y-axis scale from –30% to +30% and the X–axis representing eight quarters of performance. Starting at 0,0 plot a productivity line that represents a steady increase of 3% improvement per quarter. Then draw a price recovery line that shows a steady decrease of 2% per quarter. Using the formula, Profitability = Productivity X Price Recovery, calculate the profitability increase each quarter (starting at 0) and plot it on the same graph.

    A. Interpret the results of your graph with a general rule.

    B. If the firm had a 3% increase in price recovery and a 2% decrease in productivity each period, how would the graph be different?

    C. Which firm (A or B above) would you like to work for? Which would you invest in?

    D. If both price recovery and productivity were increasing, what would the graph look like? If both were decreasing, where would the profitability line be on the graph?

4

Forecasting, Planning, and Scheduling Production

So far, we have explored how a product is designed and what steps are necessary to get both the product and the physical facility ready for actual production. In this chapter we discuss how the demand for a product is estimated and then, based upon this estimate, how the actual production is planned and the required resources scheduled.

These three activities are closely tied together in a hierarchical arrangement, with forecasting at the top, followed by planning, and then scheduling. The forecasting and planning of production is an on-going process of updating and revising as the market and conditions change. This chapter concludes with project management tools that address the planning of major one-time endeavors.

Forecasting Demand

The basis for all business activity is a forecast of demand, which indicates that the venture will be profitable. Perfect forecasts, however, are rare. Realizing this, the forecaster must make an effort to develop forecasts that represent the best estimates of future demand. The six basic steps to be reviewed are (1) separating dependent from independent demand, (2) determining the forecasting horizon, (3) selecting a model, (4) assessing the proposed model, (5) applying the model that passes initial assessment, and (6) monitoring the performance of the model to determine the justification of continued use of the selected model.

Dependent and Independent Demand

The forecaster actually must forecast *two* types of demand–dependent and independent.

Dependent, or internal, demand is derived from the demand for some other product or item. Raw materials, components, and subassemblies are examples of items subject to internal demand; that is, they are dependent upon the demand for the final product. The paper used in printing this text is dependent upon the demand for this and other texts to be printed. This paper raw material faces only an internal demand as specified by a detailed component list of materials required to manufacture various books (the bill of materials, see chapter 2).

Since the bill of materials for a product indicates, in detail, the requirements for items facing internal demands, the forecaster also must be concerned with external demands. External demands, which are unrelated to the demands for other items produced by the firm, also are known as **independent** demands. Items that have independent or external demands usually are final products or items used for maintenance and repair purposes. Using the previous example, the forecaster must determine the demands for the various books to be published by the firm. The demand for products that have an external or independent demand must be forecast.

Forecast Horizon

Once the items to be forecast have been selected, a decision must be made about the time period of the forecast. This is done by establishing the forecast horizon, which depends upon many variables. As the horizon is pushed out, confidence in the accuracy of the forecast drops, and the forecasting methodologies become more costly to develop and utilize. Selection of the forecast horizon must consider the product's life cycle, the manufacturing cycle, the firm's ability to gather the necessary production resources, and the cost of developing a forecasting model. The product-life-cycle concept maintains that a product goes through predictable stages: introduction, growth, saturation or maturity, and then decline. Different forecasting models are appropriate depending on the current stage of a product. An industry may experience a manufacturing cycle that requires new models or major new-product introductions at reasonably consistent intervals. Such cycles that exceed annual seasonal patterns will tend to extend the forecast horizon. The forecast horizon must provide adequate visibility into the future for informed decision making as it pertains to plant expansion or contraction and, on a day-to-day basis, sufficient visibility in terms of the purchase of materials and the design of an efficient production plan.

Selecting the Model

Before discussing the actual types of forecasting models, let us consider the criteria for selecting a model. These criteria are listed in exhibit 4-1.

Once decisions concerning each of the criteria have been made, the actual model that best fits this set of decisions may be chosen.

Methods of forecasting. Three general categories of forecasting methods exist–judgmental, intrinsic, and extrinsic. Each differs in terms of the kinds of data utilized and the settings in which each is most effective.

Judgmental methods, or qualitative rather than quantitative methods, rely on expert opinions regarding the future. Two examples of judgmental forecasting techniques are the Delphi technique and market-survey techniques.

The Delphi technique utilizes several experts in the area to be forecast. Instead of bringing these experts together and perhaps having their reputations influence one another, the employing firm does not reveal the identities of the experts to each other. The forecasts of these experts are summarized and fed back to each contributor, and their individual revisions are solicited in light of the anonymous views of the group. After several revisions, it is hoped that a consensus can be reached based on the shared expertise. This technique applies where quantitative data are unavailable and judgments of knowledgeable persons can be obtained economically.

Market surveys attempt to measure customer intentions by collecting a sample of opinions. The sample may consist of forecasts by sales personnel, stated intentions of key customers, or a representative consumer panel. Key customers may be especially effective for some industrial suppliers who might have sales concentrated among a small number of accounts. Consumer panels often provide an economical measure of a new consumer-product market. Consumer-opinion surveys, while expensive, are particularly relevant where the firm has no historical experience–for example, when it is introducing a new product.

Intrinsic models, or time-series models, extrapolate historical data patterns into the future. The type of intrinsic model used depends on the historical pattern of the forecast variable (e.g., sales units). Time-series

---

Exhibit 4-1

Forecast Model Selection Criteria

1. Who will use the forecast, and what are their information needs?

2. What are the relevance and availability of historical data?

3. What degree of accuracy is desired?

4. What time period (horizon) is to be forecast?

5. How much time is available for making the analysis and forecast?

6. What is the cost/benefit (value) of the forecast to the company?

---

data can be plotted on graph paper and analyzed for the four basic components of variation. These components are (1) seasonal, (2) trend, (3) cycle, and (4) the residual, unexplainable component, or random "noise." Graphic illustration of these influences is shown in figure 4-1.

In the fourth, and simplest case, there are no apparent cycles, seasons, or trends. The goal is to smooth out the random noise so that production levels and staffing are not changed in response to transient conditions. Simple models, such as moving averages, weighted-average models, and exponential smoothing techniques, apply in this case.

A **simple moving average** merely sums the data for the most recent months and divides by the number of months. Take a three-month moving average, for example, where the sales were: January, 1,200 units; February, 1,300 units; and March, 1,100 units. The three-month average is 1,200 units, and this would be the forecast for April. Now April has come and gone. April's sales were 1,150 units. To compute the new three-month average, the oldest month is dropped (January's 1,200 units), and the newest demand is added (April's 1,150 units) to get (1,300 + 1,100 + 1,150) ÷ 3 = 1,183.3 or 1,183 units.

A **simple weighted average** works in much the same way. The three-month moving average really applied a weight of one-third to each of the months. In our previous example, we would get the same answer if we added 1/3 x 1,300 plus 1/3 x 1,100 plus 1/3 x 1,150. The advantage of a weighted-average approach is that it allows different emphasis on different pieces of data. For example, we might want to place more importance on last month than on the month before. In the case of retail

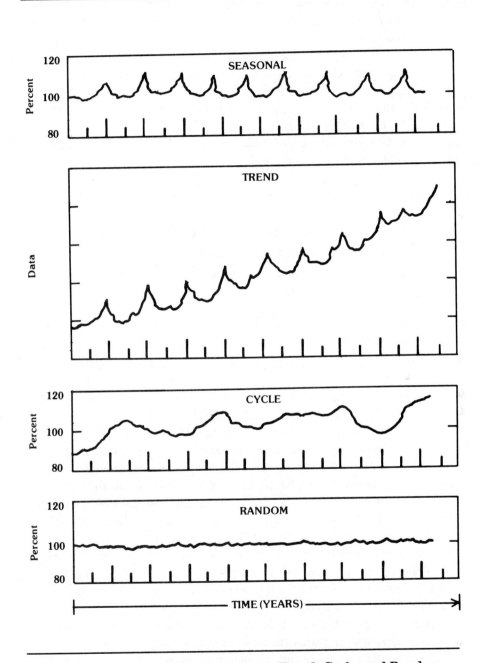

**Figure 4-1. Illustrations of Seasonal, Trend, Cycle, and Random
Time-Series Fluctuation Cycles**

sales, we might want to place more emphasis on Thursday through Saturday sales and less on Monday through Wednesday sales. The weighted-average approach allows this flexibility.

A final variation is **simple exponential smoothing.** In this case, we apply a weight, alpha, to the most recent demand. Although alpha can be any value between 0 and 1, typical values are between .1 and .3. The balance of the weight (1-alpha) is placed on the previously exponentially smoothed average. An equivalent approach is to apply the weight, alpha, to the forecast error of the previous period. These two approaches are represented by the following formulas.

$$SF_{t+1} = \alpha(A_t) + (1 - \alpha)(SF_t) \text{ or } SF_{t+1} = SF_t + \alpha(A_t - SF_t)$$

Where: SF_t is the smoothed forecast for period t

SF_{t+1} is the smoothed forecast one period in the future

A_t is the actual demand in period t

α is the weighting constant alpha

The three methods–moving average, weighted average, and exponential smoothing–are illustrated in table 4-1. Check to see if you can compute the averages illustrated in table 4-1. Note that the exponential-smoothing model consists of two multiplications and one addition. The moving-average method consists of one addition per month and a division. The weighted-average method consists of one multiplication and one addition per month. The relative efficiency of exponential smoothing is one of its advantages; it also requires the storage of less data.

When a trend is clearly present, the simple moving-average models and exponential smoothing lag behind actual demand and therefore do not perform very well. Trends can be handled by making a trend adjustment to the simple exponential-smoothing model. An alternate method is to use **linear regression** to determine the slope (trend) of the historical data. This method finds the straight line that minimizes the squared errors, as measured by the vertical distance between the historical points and the trend line. Extending this trend line into the future provides a forecast of the expected average sales or other forecast variables. Random variations about these forecast points are to be expected. Also, standard statistical measures are available to evaluate whether or not the trend is statistically significant. If the trend is not significant, then the simple moving average or similar models would be more appropriate. Finally, to be valid, regression models require a significant number of data points and should not be extrapolated into the distant future.

Table 4-1

Methods of Smoothing Random Variations

Month	Demand	3 Month (Moving Average)	3 Month (Weighted Average[a])	Exponential Smoothing[b]
January	1,200	—	—	1,200 (assumed base)
February	1,300	—	—	.1(1,300) + .9(1,200)=1,210
March	1,100	1,200	1,183.33	.1(1,100) + .9(1,210)=1,199
April	1,150	1,183.33	1,158.33	.1(1,150) + .9(1,199)=1,194

[a]*Weight 1 = $1/6$; weight 2 = $2/6$; weight 3 = $3/6$*
[b]*Alpha = .1: The values are the smoothed average for the associated month. The average, therefore, for April (1194)–would be the forecast for May.*

Another matter of concern to the operations manager is the seasonal component. Time-series models handle this by deseasonalizing the data. One approach is the **multiplicative model,** where a trend line is computed. The trend could be zero, in which case the line represents the average level. Next, each data point is divided by the point on the trend line for the corresponding observed data at that point in time. This tells us what percentage the demand is of the trend line. For example, if the data point is 120 percent of the trend line, then the actual demand can be found by 1.20 x point on the trend line. If we compute these percentages for several years, we can average the percentage for January, February, and so on or for quarter 1, quarter 2, and so on; then these seasonal percentages can be used to forecast the future. First, find the trend point for the future period, and then multiply that value by the seasonal percentage to get the desired forecast. This approach is illustrated in table 4-2 and figure 4-2.

The influence of a cyclical factor on time-series models will not be discussed here, but one example would be the demand for yo-yos, where the product falls in and out of favor regularly over long time periods.

Extrinsic models attempt to forecast desired variables, such as sales, based on variables outside the system. These models are referred to as causal models because they hypothesize a cause-and-effect relationship between the independent and the dependent (forecasted) variables. The statistical techniques of correlation analysis and regression analysis are the primary means for specifying these relationships. An example of a

Table 4-2

The Multiplicative Model

Actual A(t) $=$ Trend Component T(t) $\times$ Seasonal Ratio S(t) $+$ Random Component

Forecast F(t) $=$ Trend Component T(t) $\times$ Seasonal Ratio S(t)

Yr	Qtr	Past Demand A(t)	Computed Trend T(t)	Seasonal Trend/Dem A(t)/T(t)	Average Seasonal S(t)	Model Forecast F(t) = T(t) x S(t)	Random Component A(t)-F(t)
1	1	18	15	1.2	1.25	18.75	-0.75
	2	20	20	1.0	1.00	20.00	0.00
	3	20	25	.8	.85	21.25	-1.25
	4	33	30	1.1	1.05	31.50	1.50
2	1	45.5	35	1.3	1.25	43.75	1.75
	2	40	40	1.0	1.00	40.00	0.00
	3	40.5	45	.9	.85	38.25	2.25
	4	50	50	1.0	1.05	52.50	-2.50

Table 4-2 (Continued)

As a measure of random component (forecast error), we compute the Mean Absolute Deviation (MAD)

$$= \frac{\Sigma \; |A(t) - F(t)|}{n}$$

$$= (.75 + 0 + 1.25 + 1.5 + 1.75 + 0 + 2.25 + 2.5) \,/8$$

$$= 1.25$$

Forecast for Next Year

Yr	Qtr	Computed Trend T(t)	Average Seasonal S(t)	Model Forecast F(t)
3	1	55	1.25	68.75
	2	60	1.00	60.00
	3	65	.85	55.25
	4	70	1.05	73.50

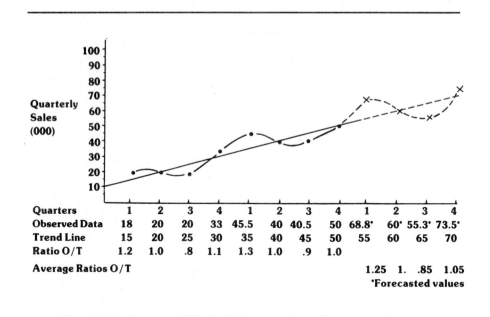

Quarters	1	2	3	4	1	2	3	4	1	2	3	4
Observed Data	18	20	20	33	45.5	40	40.5	50	68.8*	60*	55.3*	73.5*
Trend Line	15	20	25	30	35	40	45	50	55	60	65	70
Ratio O/T	1.2	1.0	.8	1.1	1.3	1.0	.9	1.0				
Average Ratios O/T									1.25	1.	.85	1.05

*Forecasted values

Figure 4-2. Multiplicative Model for Trend and Seasonals

causal model in forecasting would be a model relating housing permits to lumber sales. By statistical analysis of historical data, it may be found that lumber sales are highly correlated to housing permits and lag behind the permits by two months. Such a model is of great value to the lumber producer, since the number of housing permits issued is easily obtained, and the fact that it provides a two-months' warning of changes in demand is very useful.

Assessing the Model

Now the forecaster must reexamine the model to see whether it adequately describes the forecasting situation under the real constraints of time and cost. The model usually is assessed by using historical data to make forecasts for periods in which the level of activity is known. Then, by comparing the model's forecasts with the known outcome, the forecaster can determine the model's predictive ability. If the resulting forecasts are either positively or negatively biased to an unacceptable degree or the magnitude of the errors is excessive, the forecaster must return to the selection step in an effort to reformulate the existing model or choose a different one.

The magnitude of the forecast errors is often measured by the mean absolute deviation (MAD). The MAD is computed by taking the actual demand minus the forecast for a set of historical data. The absolute values (ignore minus signs) of these errors are summed and divided by the number of values to arrive at the average, the MAD. We use the absolute values to reflect our equal concern for under and over forecasting errors (see table 4-2). The procedure is easier than computing the standard deviation of the errors and serves the same purpose. Within other constraints, the model that provides a smaller MAD is preferred to one with a larger MAD.

Bias in a forecasting model may be evaluated by computing the running sum of the forecast errors (RSFE). Consider a model that consistently provides forecasts on the low side. The error (actual minus forecast) would be consistently a positive value, and, hence, the RSFE would become a bigger positive value each period. The same would be true if the model consistently provided forecasts on the high side, except the RSFE would become a bigger negative number. An unbiased forecasting model would tend to overforecast about as often as it would underforecast; therefore, the errors would tend to cancel each other out, resulting in a small RSFE. The MAD and the RSFE are useful measures of a forecasting model's performance.

Applying the Model

Here the acceptable model is put to work in a real forecasting situation. When the model is first put into action, previous forecasting methodologies typically are continued as backup. By continuing to use the old method, the forecaster has the forecast from the previous technique to use in evaluating the new model.

Evaluating the Model

Because forecasting methodologies are adaptable to computer applications, it is tempting to give the computer total forecasting responsibility. Although safeguards may be built into the computer model to recognize when the forecast exceeds some set of reasonable limits, the human touch is required to make a good evaluation of any model.

Forecast evaluation is a continuing process that requires the forecaster to monitor the validity of each new forecast. Only through judgment can one recognize external variables that cause fundamental changes in the forecast variable.

Planning for Production

The overall mission of the organization, as discussed in chapter 1, provides the foundation for the planning process. Figure 4-3 shows operations strategy as an equal partner with marketing and financial strategies. These three legs of the competitive strategy must reinforce each other and integrate with strategies in other relevant functions. For example, a marketing strategy emphasizing products that are highly engineered to unique customer specifications is effective if the special competence of manufacturing is flexible production of make-to-order products. A manufacturing strategy based on standard products would not support this marketing strategy. Conversely, targeting a highly competitive, mass, consumer market would call for a different production strategy, possibly with highly automated processes and standardized products. The integration of the organization's operations strengths with the firm's marketing and financial strengths is necessary for a successful business plan.

The Business Plan

The planning process generally follows the organizational hierarchy from the top down; however, this need not exclude information and initiatives flowing up from lower levels in the organization. A knowledge of internal competitive strengths at all levels is the foundation of an effective mission and business plan.

As plans evolve from the broad concept of mission to the specifics of detailed production schedules, the time frame changes from long range (more than a year or two) to medium range (three months to a year) and finally to short range (up to three months). The shift from a broad perspective to a more narrow focus requires that the units used to measure business activity become more specific. In the long term, business activity is measured in aggregate units such as total revenue, total employment, or total facility size. In the near future, plans are broken down into revenue by products, employment in terms of hours by job categories, and facilities by some appropriate measure of capacity of production work load.

At the top level we are looking at marketing plans and projected levels of business by market segment. In manufacturing or service firms these levels may be measured in sales dollars; in a not-for-profit organization budgeted dollars may be used. Since this level takes a relatively long term view, changes in capacity are considered.

A business plan in dollars must be converted into units of productive resources: labor hours, facility space, aggregate inventory, and capital equipment. This process might take the quarterly sales revenue targets

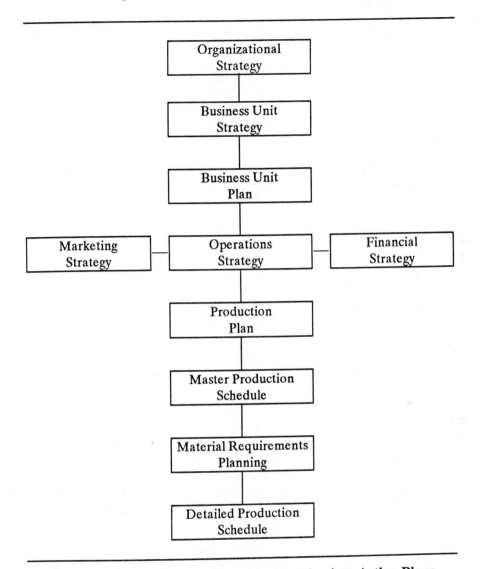

Figure 4-3. Transforming Strategic Planning into Action Plans

for the next five years and estimate the required resources using historical ratios (such as .006 hours of direct labor per sales dollar). If we have a large number of diverse products, we will need to specify the sales targets by product line. Product line sales can then be translated into resource requirements which, in turn, allows us to project capacity requirements over an extended period of time.

Capacity, measured in space, equipment, or employees, can be increased or decreased in the long range. The projection of key resource requirements identifies where and when capacity shortages and surpluses exist. These capacity gaps guide plans for hiring and training programs, facility expansion or contraction, and additions of new equipment and process technology.

The immediate part of the business plan–the next four quarters–will need to be refined into a more detailed production plan.

The Production Plan

Planning in the mid-range is more constrained than in the long-range. For example, facility size and locations may be fixed and changes in work force and technology may be limited to minor adjustments. These restrictions to current capacity are particularly challenging in the face of highly seasonal demand and sales targets. Strategies for dealing with seasonal demand range from level production at one extreme to flexible production plans at the other.

A **level production strategy** establishes a steady production plan which produces and stores enough extra units during the slack season to meet demand during the peak season. If the product can not be stored economically as in unique, make-to-order items, an alternative leveling strategy is the back-order approach. The firm might "store the demand" in the sense of accepting the purchase order but promising a delivery date farther into the future. In times of peak demand, promised delivery dates are extended; in slack periods they are shortened. Whether this plan works depends on the strategies of competitors and the needs of the firm's customers.

The motivation behind a level production plan is better utilization of our facilities and equipment and the elimination of the need to hire, layoff, and rehire workers with the shifts in demand. Some firms find a level production plan most economical; others find it impossible and must use a more flexible approach.

A **flexible production strategy** is sometimes called a "chase" strategy because capacity changes are made to try to follow (or chase) demand as closely as possible. If the firm can change the volume and variety of products quickly, it will reduce the inventory and back-order costs associated with a level strategy. However, flexible production capability may require extra equipment, space, and human resources to meet peak demand levels and bear the costs of idle or under-utilized people and facilities during slack times. Alternatively, the firm may alter employee capacity through the use of overtime, temporary or part-time workers, hiring, and layoffs as needed. In some labor markets and some industries (such as harvesting and food processing) this practice is common and accepted. Similarly, short term capacity supplements for facilities can be obtained by sub-contracting or by renting additional equipment and space.

The motivation behind a flexible strategy is the reduction of inventory and yet a fast response time to changes in demand. Given a well designed facility and cross-trained workers, a flexible approach need not endure excessive costs of changing output levels.

Service firms, for the most part, cannot inventory finished products; they can, however, attempt to level their rate of production by influencing demand. Many service firms offer specials or discounts at slack times in an effort to move some customers from the peaks to the valleys. Also, they may attempt to schedule all non-customer contact activities such as set-ups, clean-ups, and maintenance in slack times. Mainly, however, service firms are forced to use a chase or flexible strategy.

There are several approaches to evaluating the merits of these production planning alternatives. Balancing the trade-offs between inventory/back-orders versus costs of changing capacity can be done by trial-and-error methods, mathematical programming, or heuristic decision rules. Graphical and spreadsheet tools can facilitate the process of evaluating a proposed plan by allowing quick detection of policy violations such as exceeding a permissible inventory level or requiring unauthorized back-orders. Spreadsheet tools significantly reduce the time to compute the cost of a proposed plan, thus permitting the planner to consider many possible alternatives before committing to a production plan.

The production plan is still in aggregate terms, that is, units by product families and labor in terms of representative standard hours. Translating the production plan into the manufacture of specific products on specific dates is the task of scheduling.

Scheduling Production

Once the production plan has been developed according to the planned resources available and the market demand, the disaggregating process begins. The goal is to establish a realistic master production schedule from which detailed shop loadings and job-order sequences are derived. The disaggregation process is illustrated in figure 4-4.

The Master Schedule

The master schedule states the desired quantities to be produced by end product or product group. It also indicates when the "end items" are to be available. The guiding principle for setting a master schedule is to make it realistic. A common error in practice is to schedule excessive

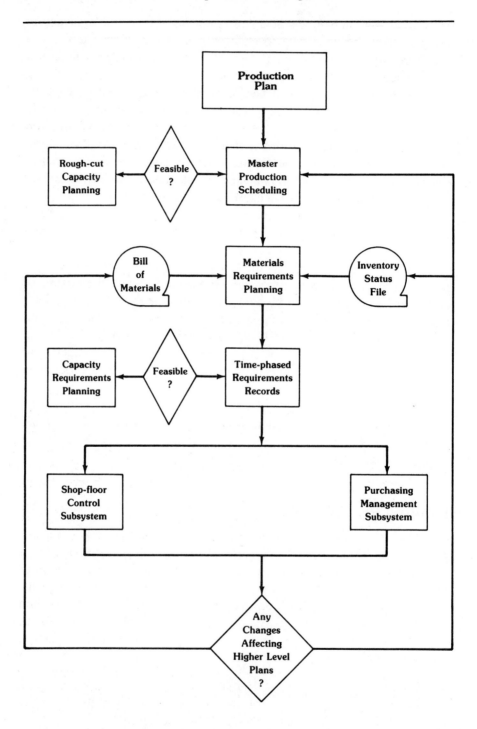

Figure 4-4. The Detailed Schedule

production quantities, even though it is not remotely possible to achieve the schedule.

Difficulties can occur when the product mix differs from the typical mix assumed in the aggregate plan. The organization may not be able to adhere to the aggregate plan without using expensive strategies such as excessive hiring and firing or massive inventory buildup during slack periods. The assignment of specific products to be made in specific periods brings with it the need to check the demands on the productive resources of the organization. This roughcut capacity planning focuses on key resources that might bottleneck the flow of work through the organization. The master production schedule should be modified until a feasible schedule is obtained, that is, one that does not exceed planned capacity in the facility. The master production schedule is the basis for planning the detailed requirements for assemblies, parts, and raw materials that make the final product. This planning process is very complex when many different products, parts, and materials are involved. Such environments often use the materials requirements planning approach to perform the detailed computations.

Materials Requirements Planning (MRP)

Materials requirements planning was originally viewed as an inventory system because the approach specified order quantities and the timing of the orders. MRP has since taken on a larger role that includes short-and medium-range corporatewide planning as well as the setting and maintenance of work priorities in the factory. MRP uses three data bases to perform its functions: the master production schedule, the bill of materials file, and the inventory status file.

To illustrate the way MRP translates the master production schedule into detailed, time-phased material plans, we will develop a bill of materials (B/M) for a mass-produced picture frame. This product will be considered one of many variations. Possible variations derive from choices of three sizes, five colors, seven frame materials, and ten mats. These choices lead to 1,050 unique end products made from less than seventy-five parts and twenty-five raw materials. A bill of materials for one of these products is shown in figure 4-5 in two formats: a structure tree B/M format, and an indented B/M format.

Inventory status must be maintained on each unique inventory item. Such information as the quantity on hand and on order must be accurately recorded along with precise storage locations of the material. Each inventory item will have a lot-sizing rule to guide how much to order when a shortage is anticipated. Furthermore, the data base will contain the planned lead times required to purchase or make each of the inven-

Level	Part No.	Description	Quantity per Parent
0	10141101	10 x 14 Assembled Frame	no parent
1	101411xx	10 x 14 White Frame	1 each
2	000001xx	White Antique Stain	2 ounces
2	101401xx	10 x 14 Frame-xxxxx-Pine	1 each
3	100001xx	10 inch Mitered Pine Sides	2 each
3	001401xx	14 inch Mitered Pine Top/Bottoms	2 each
3	08010001	Staples	8 each
1	10140001	10 x 14 Glass	1 each
2	20280001	20 x 28 Plate Glass	1/4 sheet
1	10140001	10 x 14 White Mat	1 each
2	20280001	20 x 28 White Mat Board	1/4 sheet
1	1040003	10 x 14 Paper Backing	1 each
2	20280003	20 x 28 Paper Backing Sheets	1/4 sheet
1	10140009	10 x 14 Wire Hanging Packet	1 each

Bill of Materials Showing Indented Format

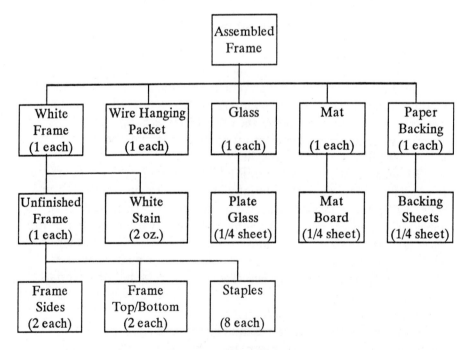

Structured Tree Format

Figure 4-5. Frame Bill of Materials

tory items. We now have the data that MRP uses to develop detailed material plans for several weeks, months, or years into the future. How far we plan into the future is called the planning horizon. The planning horizon is determined by the product that takes the longest time to build. In our simplified example, we will plan only five periods into the future.

The MRP planning process begins with the master production schedule for the end items. These end items are the highest level of the bill of materials, level 0 by convention. The master production schedule identifies the gross requirements for these items and, if appropriate, any independent (direct customer) demand for lower-level components (e.g., replacement parts). The procedure is to try to satisfy the gross requirements from inventory before building more of a product or its parts. Items that are on hand can be used for this purpose and so can on-order material that is expected to arrive in time to meet a specific gross requirement. Once all the on-hand and on-order material has been used to reduce the gross requirements, the remaining requirements are called net requirements. This is the **netting** process.

The projection of a negative balance indicates a net requirement and the need to plan a receipt of the product or material. Since each item is associated with a planned lead time, we must start a planned order earlier than its due date. The start time is the date of the planned order release for that inventory item. This process is often called **time phasing** or offsetting.

The bill of materials for this item is used to identify all the parts and materials that must be on hand at the time the planned order is released. This linking of requirements from one item or parent to a lower-level component is called **exploding** requirements from the planned order releases of the parent to the gross requirements of the components. Note that the bill of materials provides the recipe. If the planned order release for Part No. 101401, unpainted 10 x 14 frame, were 200 units in period 1, then the gross requirements for Part No. 100001, 10-inch sides, would be 400 in period 1 because we need two of these components for each Part No. 101401. Figure 4-6 illustrates these steps, starting with a master production schedule for 100 units of the 10 x 14 picture frame, Part No. 10141101, due in week 3, 50 units due in week 4, and a final batch of 75 units due in week 5. The on-hand inventory for each item is indicated in a box before the first time period. The on-hand line represents projected inventory at the end of the associated period. When the projected balance becomes negative, the negative number is the trigger that caused MRP to plan a receipt which then modified the projected on-hand balance. Order quantities and planned lead times are indicated below each time-phased inventory record in figure 4-6. The lot-for-lot order quantity means that one should order only enough to meet the net requirements for one period at a time.

PART NO. 10141101
10 x 14 Assembled Frame

		Period 1	2	3	4	5
GROSS REQUIREMENTS	from MPS			100	50	75
ON ORDER						
PROJECTED ON-HAND BALANCE	80	80	80	−20* 80	30	−45 55
NET REQUIREMENTS				20		45
PLANNED ORDER RECEIPTS				100		100
PLANNED ORDER RELEASES			100		100	

PLANNED LEAD TIME = 1 Week   ORDER QUANTITY = 100 units

NOTE: A negative projected on-hand balance triggers a planned order receipt which in turn causes the balance to be adjusted.

PART NO. 101411xx
10 x 14 White Frame

		Period 1	2	3	4	5
GROSS REQUIREMENTS	from Part #10141101		100		100	
ON ORDER						
PROJECTED ON-HAND BALANCE	0	0	−100 0	0	−100 0	0
NET REQUIREMENTS			100		100	
PLANNED ORDER RECEIPTS			100		100	
PLANNED ORDER RELEASES		100		100		

PLANNED LEAD TIME = 1 Week   ORDER QUANTITY = Lot-for-Lot

Figure 4-6. MRP Time-Phased Inventory Records

PART NO. 101401xx

10 x 14 Frame, Unfinished, Pine		Period				
		1	2	3	4	5
GROSS REQUIREMENTS	from Part #101411xx	100		100		
ON ORDER		100				
PROJECTED ON-HAND BALANCE	0	0	0	−100 0	0	0
NET REQUIREMENTS				100		
PLANNED ORDER RECEIPTS				100		
PLANNED ORDER RELEASES		100				

PLANNED LEAD TIME = 2 Weeks   ORDER QUANTITY = Lot-for-Lot

PART NO. 0000001

White Antique Stain		Period				
		1	2	3	4	5
GROSS REQUIREMENTS	from Part #101411xx	200		200		
ON ORDER		800				
PROJECTED ON-HAND BALANCE	100	700	700	500	500	500
NET REQUIREMENTS						
PLANNED ORDER RECEIPTS						
PLANNED ORDER RELEASES						

PLANNED LEAD TIME = 2 Weeks   ORDER QUANTITY = 800 ounces

Figure 4-6. (continued)

The power of MRP comes from the improved timing of the correct quantities of materials to support production and the timely updating of job priorities, (i.e., planned order releases and on-order due dates). Any changes in plans because of customer wishes, manufacturing problems or opportunities, or supplier problems can be effectively evaluated using the MRP time-phased records and exception messages provided by MRP systems. Finally, the detailed material plans permit careful analysis of work loads in various work centers in comparison to their capacity. This load analysis is the function of capacity requirements planning.

Capacity Requirements Planning (CRP)

CRP is concerned with the loading of specific jobs onto various work centers for specific periods of time. By combining MRP data on the timing of units needed with standard data on manufacturing processes, one can identify the machine hours and labor hours required by a work center to meet the master schedule. There are two general approaches to loading: (1) infinite loading and (2) finite loading.

Infinite loading assumes that each work center has sufficient capacity to produce whatever it is assigned, using standard manufacturing processes. This approach has the main advantage of being simple. When a plant has more-than-ample capacity, it may be valid to assume that no resource will be strained to capacity. Here infinite loading is both simple and effective. But, regardless of its short-term validity, infinite loading is useful for long-term capacity planning. Because infinite loading assumes use of the primary method of manufacturing and no limit in capacity, it gives a good picture of what capacity the plant should have in the future.

Finite loading does not assume that enough capacity will be available in all work centers and does not restrict itself to the primary method of manufacture. The elimination of these two assumptions makes the analysis much more complicated and time consuming. In essence, when a bottleneck is encountered, the load is shifted to secondary methods in work centers with available capacity, or the load is shifted to different time slots. Allowing loads to be shifted in these ways opens up for consideration thousands of possible schedules. The large number of alternatives makes this problem impressive even when large-scale computers are available. Techniques such as linear programming, simulation, and heuristic rules have been applied to solve this problem. The advantage of finite loading is that it indicates what can be produced in the short term—that is, what is realistic given current conditions.

Sequencing Jobs

The loading of work centers for a block of time does not specify the order in which the individual jobs are to be processed. Often this sequencing is left to the foreman, or a central planning group may specify the sequence based on sophisticated computerized analysis. In either event, some of the common goals are (1) maximum flow through the shop, (2) minimum number of late orders, (3) minimum average lateness, (4) minimum variance from due dates, and (5) minimum cost.

One way to sequence jobs is to use a priority rule. There are many such rules, each with its own unique performance characteristics. One popular priority rule is the shortest-operation-time job first (SOT). This rule is effective with respect to minimizing the average flow time through the shop. Its major weakness is that long jobs continually may be "bumped" to last and thereby delayed excessively. Since long jobs may be the most important jobs, it might make sense to use another priority rule, one called longest-operation-time first (LOT). The performance characteristics of this rule are the opposite of SOT. The choice of a priority rule depends upon what is important to the organization; obviously, no rule will achieve all the possible desirable goals.

Other common priority rules are summarized in exhibit 4-2. First come, first served (FCFS) is an easily defended rule as far as customers are concerned. The various slack rules consider how much time there is between a reference time, for example, time of arrival at a work center, and the due date. Some rules divide this by a measure of the amount of

---

Exhibit 4-2

Job-Shop Priority Scheduling Rules

FCFS   First come, first served–priority based upon time of arrival at the work center or place in line.

SOT   Shortest operation time–process the quickest jobs first. This rule maximizes mean flow rate but tends to delay excessively the important large jobs.

FISFS   First in system, first served–this differs from FCFS, where the priority can change at each work center. For example, air travelers flying standby have priority based on when they started the journey, not necessarily when they arrived at an intermediate stop.

LCFS   Last come, first served–this is a convenience rule, that is, do the job on the top of the stack first.

Critical This is the ratio of time remaining to work time remaining. This
Ratio   is a popular dynamic rule in which a job with a ratio >1 is ahead of schedule, ratio of 1 is on schedule and a ratio <1 needs to be expedited.

---

work that still remains to be done, such as the remaining processing time or the number of operations remaining. Such ratios give a measure of urgency for each job.

Development of Detailed Schedules

When all the aforementioned decisions and revisions have been made, detailed schedules finally will be prepared. Detailed schedules take the job and flow sequences established at the last stage and overlay them on a time scale, which is divided into periods appropriate for the manufacturing setting, extending over the entire planning period. Job shops may require daily scales, while an assembly line might use weekly or longer time frames. **Gantt charts** are particularly useful in blocking out plans and providing quick and easy visual presentation. Figure 4-7 illustrates a set of work orders scheduled using the common Gantt chart symbols. By updating progress on the chart, one can see at a glance the jobs that are behind schedule, on time, and ahead of schedule, as well as the jobs coming up in the near future. Such a chart facilitates the coordination of setups, maintenance, and scheduling of labor crews.

After scheduling conflicts have been resolved, specific start and finish dates are assigned to jobs. These start and finish dates may be set by working back from the due date on a job (backward scheduling) or by starting a job as early as possible (forward scheduling.) Backward scheduling reduces inventory and maintains flexibility on schedule changes as long as possible, at the risk of having more late jobs than with a forward-scheduling approach. In either case, when the start date is reached on a dispatch list, work orders are released to the manufacturing facility, and processing commences.

Progress Control/Shop-Floor Control

Progress control, the final stage in the scheduling process, involves constant monitoring of the jobs as they pass through the facility in an attempt to detect and to resolve problems that may arise. One method of detecting problems or bottlenecks in the flow of jobs is through input/output (I/O) control charts. I/O control monitors planned work input and output against actual input and output by work center. If backlogs arise, the I/O table focuses attention on the work center causing the problem. The importance of bottlenecks has been stressed by the concepts and philosophies such as "optimized production technology" (OPT) and the "theory of constraints" advanced by Eliyahu Goldratt.

Job Order

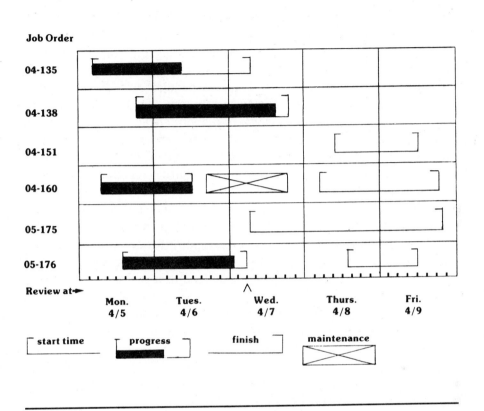

Figure 4-7. Gantt Chart

Bottlenecks determine the flow of products through the factory and thus constrain the supply of products to the customer. If the flow is constrained, then profit is reduced. Therefore, everything should be done to fully utilize the bottleneck facility. Here fewer and shorter setup times are very beneficial. Avoiding delays caused by lack of material or labor or by breakdowns is very important to overall capacity. Do not be distracted from this goal by pressures to appear efficient in non-bottlenecks. Extra setups or other changes in non-bottleneck operations should be considered if they reduce delays at the key bottleneck work centers.

Another approach to shop-floor control is the pull system of the Just-in-Time (JIT) philosophy. Under conditions of a level load on the factory, we can consider using a simple card system, called kanban (or its equivalent) to authorize production. In essence, we produce only when a customer comes to us and makes a withdrawal from our stock. If the withdrawal is from finished goods, then final assembly may make a standard (small, ideally equal to one) replacement lot. The authorization to assemble will lead to withdrawals of parts, which in turn authorizes production of replacement parts. This process repeats back through the system until it reaches the suppliers of raw materials. The kanban approach applies to a repetitive manufacturing environment when a reasonably stable flow and simple sequencing rules can be maintained.

In any system, a job can fall behind schedule. Expediting can get a late job back on schedule by reducing the time spent waiting for jobs ahead of it. This works when some of the jobs ahead of the late one can be delayed. Lot splitting and lap scheduling can speed a job through a facility. By splitting a lot into two or more smaller lots, the first split lot moves on through the system as soon as it finishes an operation. By lap scheduling we transfer part of a lot to the next operation before completing the entire batch. Both lot splitting and lap scheduling reduce normal delays in the system for rush jobs. Alternate routings, using other machines or processes, can be used to temporarily deal with a bottleneck and keep jobs on schedule. If the schedule cannot be maintained, then feedback to the scheduling process may lead to a revised master schedule.

Managing the shop floor requires constant revision of plans. This necessitates accurate and current feedback data on the status of in-process jobs.

Planning and Controlling Projects

The management of major, complex projects typically requires the coordination of several organizational functions for successful completion within time, budget, and resource constraints. A project might be the design, development and introduction of a new model car in time for the 1994 model year, or it could be the development and execution of a new multimedia advertising campaign. A third example would be the design and implementation of the MRP system described earlier in this chapter.

Network techniques, such as PERT, provide an effective way to define the scope, complexities, and key tasks of a project and to schedule and control its activities. PERT and CPM are discussed next.

PERT/CPM

The program evaluation and review technique (PERT) and the critical path method (CPM) are widely recognized and successfully applied techniques that require special attention. These similar methodologies belong to a special set of operation-research techniques known as network models. They are particularly applicable to the management of unique projects that have a broad scope.

PERT and CPM are so similar that it is unnecessary to attempt to distinguish one from the other. PERT originally was developed by the U.S. Navy Special Projects Office and Lockheed Aircraft Corporation in cooperation with the consulting from of Booz, Allen, and Hamilton. It was introduced in 1958 in an effort to reduce the original time forecast for the development of the Polaris ballistic missile and is credited with reducing the time span by several years. CPM was developed in 1957 to help with the scheduling of maintenance in chemical plants. Next to PERT, CPM is the second most widely used system for planning and controlling large projects. Both techniques have been applied to such projects as startups and shutdowns of production facilities; installations of major new equipment, such as computer systems and assembly lines; construction of subdivisions, shopping centers, skyscrapers, dams, and power stations; and virtually all government development contracts.

As a planning tool, PERT allows the manager to plan a project well in advance and estimate its expected completion time and date. This early planning identifies possible bottlenecks and indicates which activities may require modification. For controlling the project, PERT permits the manager to compare the actual and planned progress of each activity. This procedure identifies those activities that are behind schedule and that ultimately may delay the overall project completion date.

PERT analysis proceeds chronologically through the following steps:

1. Identification of **activities** required by the project.

2. Identification of **precedence relationships** among the activities (i.e., which activities must be completed before others can begin).

3. Determination of the **expected time requirements** for each activity.

4. Development of the **network diagram** of activities or **nodes** (squares) and **arrows** showing precedence relationships.

5. Determination of the **earliest start** and **earliest finish** times for each activity.

6. Determination of the **latest start** and **latest finish** times for each activity which will not delay the project beyond the earliest expected completion time.

7. Identification of the activities that form the **critical path.**

Steps 1 through 3 require extensive data gathering from people knowledgeable about the various activities of the project. Their expert opinions form the basis for the PERT analysis, thus they represent a critical input to the planning. It is important to solicit the full and honest cooperation of these people, who, in many cases, will be the same people responsible for the successful implementation of the project.

Network diagramming. The network must flow from left to right so that all prerequisites of an activity are to its left with arrows flowing from the predecessor into the activity. For example, in a simplified equipment installation (table 4-3), activity F must be preceded by Activities C, D, and E. In figure 4-8, therefore, these activities are to the left of Activity F and each has an arrow linking it to Activity F.

In table 4-3, three times are provided by the experts: optimistic, most likely, and pessimistic. Since the actual distribution of times may be skewed instead of symmetrical, it may be difficult for the experts to estimate directly the mean (expected) time. In PERT, the expected time is computed as a weighted average of the three time estimates. Traditionally, the optimistic and pessimistic estimates are given a weight of one, and the most likely is given a weight of four. The computed expected time is the estimate used in evaluating the PERT network.

The precedence requirements in table 4-3 resulted in the network in figure 4-8. Check the network to assure yourself that you understand how the precedence relationships are incorporated into the diagram.

Determining earliest and latest event times. The earliest expected event times are computed first in what is termed the "forward pass." We use a reference time of 0 to mark the beginning of the project. Therefore, 0 becomes the earliest start time (ES) for any task that has no preceding tasks, Activities A and B in our example.

The early finish time (EF) is the early start time plus the expected activity time, EF(A) = ES(A) + Time(A) or 0 + 26 = 26. Similarly, the EF(B) = ES(B) + Time(B) = 0+5 or 5.

The early start for subsequent activities is determined by the early finish times of an activity's prerequisites. Activity D has one predecessor, Activity A. Since the earliest Activity A is expected to finish (EF) is day 26, this is the earliest that Activity D can start, therefore, ES(D) = 26. Activity F has three predecessors, C, D, and E. The last one of these to finish determines when Activity F can begin. Therefore, Activity F has an expected early start of 28, the maximum of [EF(C) = 9, EF(D) = 28, EF(E) = 6]. With the computation of the early finish for Activity G, the forward pass is complete and the expected completion time for the project is found to be 49 days.

The "backward pass" computes the late finish time (LF) and the late start times (LS) for each activity. Our reference point will be the EF time for the entire project because we wish to find the LS and LF times that will <u>not</u> delay the project beyond this time. Therefore, we set the late

Table 4-3

PERT Data on Activities: Precedence and Time Estimates

ACTIVITY Code	Description	TIME Optimistic	TIME Most Likely	TIME Pessimistic	TIME Expected*	Preceding Tasks
A	Acquire Equipment	20 days	25 days	36 days	26 days	None
B	Clear Floor Space	2	5	8	5	None
C	Mark Floor Location	1	3	11	4	B
D	Inspect Equipment	1	1	7	2	A
E	Store Installation Materials	1	1	1	1	B
F	Install Equipment	5	10	27	12	C,D,E
G	Test & Debug Equip.	3	7	23	9	F

$$*Expected\ Time = \frac{t(optimistic) + 4 \times t(most\ likely) + t(pessimistic)}{6}$$

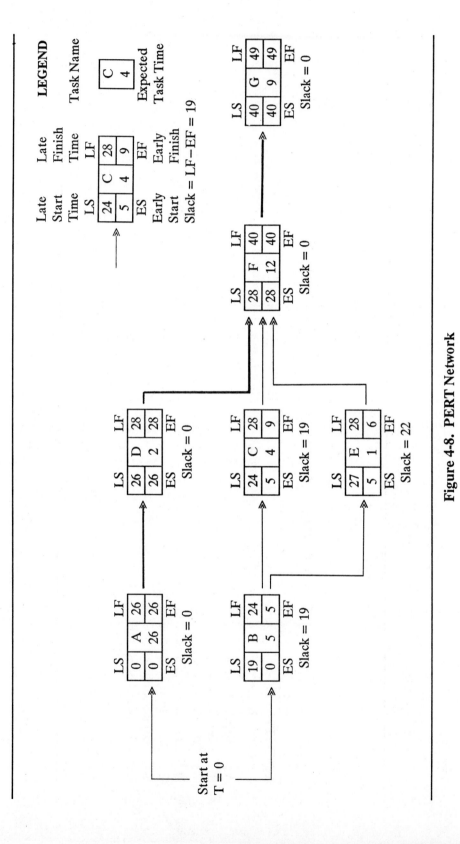

Figure 4-8. PERT Network

finish time for Activity G equal to the early finish time for Activity G, LF(G) = EF(G) = 49.

The late start (LS) is computed by subtracting the activity time from the LF time. The late start for Activity G is 40, LS(G) = 49 − 9. Working backwards, the late finish of a predecessor is set by the late start of the followers, LF(F) = LS(G) or 40. When there are two or more followers, e.g. Activity B, then the smallest LS among the followers determines the LF(B). The late finish for Activity B is the minimum of [LS(C) = 24, LS(E) = 27], that is, 24. Consider what would happen if Activity B finished on day 25, 26 or 27. Would the project still be completed on day 49? The answer is no, the project would be delayed. But since Activity B can begin as early as time 0 and only takes 5 days to complete, the likelihood of that happening is slight. The "backward pass" is complete when all the late start and late finish times have been computed.

The critical path. The critical path consists of the activities associated with the longest-time path from the start of the project to its end. The critical activities must be completed on time or the project will be delayed; in other words, critical activities have zero "slack".

Since we have computed the early finish and late finish times for each activity, we can find the slack, LF − EF, for each activity. (We could use LS − ES to get the same result.) Slack measures how much a task can be delayed without delaying the project. Therefore, a task with zero slack is critical to the timely completion of the project, delaying such an activity delays the project. By arranging the late times on the top of each node and the early times below we are ready to perform the subtraction LF − EF giving the slacks for each activity. Slack for Activity C is LF(C) − EF(C) or 28 − 9 = 19 days of slack. Thus, Activity C could be delayed as much as 19 days without delaying the project's expected completion on day 49.

The critical path in figure 4-7 consists of activities A, D, F, and G. These activities require the most management attention since a delay in any of them would mean a delay in the entire project. On the other hand, the critical path tells us which activities to expedite to finish the project sooner. If management requires the new equipment in operation forty days from now, we will focus our speedup efforts on activities A, D, F, and G. Since we have a great deal of slack in the other activities (19 to 22 days) we need not be very concerned that our expediting will lead to another path becoming critical. In other projects, however, we must be concerned about near critical paths–that is, those with little slack.

Using the PERT Network

The PERT network is not an inflexible, unalterable schedule. It is a dynamic tool that allows new networks to be formulated as changes occur in the schedule because of a lack of resources or in order to utilize available resources more effectively. The planner who understands this flexibility may find that rearranging activities or moving resources to the most critical areas can significantly reduce the total time required.

Key Concepts

Definitions of most key concepts are found in the Glossary.

Intrinsic/Extrinsic Forecasting
  Methods

Components of Variation

Exponential Smoothing

Mean Absolute Deviation (MAD)

Production Planning

Master Schedule

Material Requirements
  Planning

Level/Flexible Production
  Strategies

Indented Bill of
  Materials

Capacity Requirements
  Planning

Job Shop Scheduling
  Rules

Gantt Chart

Progress Control

PERT/CPM

Independent/Dependent
  Demand

Multiplicative Model

Finite/Infinite Loading

References

Chase, Richard B., and Aquilano, Nicholas J. *Production and Operations Management.* 5th ed. Homewood, IL: Richard D. Irwin, 1989.

Goldratt, Eliyahu, and Cox, J. *The Goal.* Revised ed. Croton-on-Hudson, NY: North River Press, 1986.

Goldratt, Eliyahu M. *The Haystack Syndrome.* Croton-on-Hudson, NY: North River Press, 1990.

Hill, Terry. *Manufacturing Strategy.* Homewood, IL: Richard D. Irwin, 1989.

Makridakis, Spyros, and Wheelwright, Steven C. *Forecasting Methods and Applications.* 2d ed. Santa Barbara, CA: John Wiley & Sons, 1983.

Melnyk, Steven A., and Carter, Phillip L. *Production Activity Control.* Homewood, IL: Dow Jones-Irwin, 1987.

Meredith, Jack R., and Mantel, Samuel J., Jr. *Project Management.* 2d ed. New York: John Wiley & Sons, 1989.

Moder, Joseph J., Phillips, Cecil R., and Davis, Edward W. *Project Management With CPM, PERT and Precedence Diagramming.* 3rd ed. New York: Van Nostrand Reinhold Company, 1983.

Vollmann, Thomas E., Berry, William L., and Whybark, D. Clay. *Manufacturing Planning and Control Systems.* 2d ed. Homewood, IL: Richard D. Irwin, 1988.

Wiest, Jerome D. and Levy, Ferdinand K. **A** *Management Guide to PERT/CPM.* 2d ed. Englewood Cliffs, NJ: Prentice-Hall, 1977.

Discussion Questions

1. What are the six basic steps in the forecasting process?

2. How does external market demand differ from internal dependent demand? Why are the differences important?

3. Identify three general types of forecasting models and discuss how they differ.

4. Identify four components that may be found in a set of time series data. Why are these influences important to a forecaster?

5. How can you measure whether or not your forecasting model is doing a good job?

6. Discuss why manufacturing or operations strategies should be developed at the same time and in cooperation with the strategic planning of the other functional components of the organization.

7. Contrast the strengths and weaknesses of level production plans versus flexible rate production plans.

8. Discuss the consequences the following errors would have on the MRP example of a picture frame in this chapter.

    a. Your inventory records say you have 100 units of Part No. 10141101 in the chapter example, but in truth there are only 80 units.

    b. The bill of materials calls for 2 ounces of white antique stain for each frame, but in reality you need 3 ounces.

9. What types of problems justify the use of PERT? Why is PERT particularly helpful in these situations?

10. How do split lots and lap scheduling speed some jobs through the shop?

Problems

1. Given the historical data below, use simple exponential smoothing to forecast sales for July. Use an alpha of .1 and assume that the smoothed forecast for January was 1,100 units.

t	Month	Actual Demand (A_t)	Smoothed Forecast (SF_t)
1	January	1,150	1,100 (initial smoothed forecast)
2	February	1,075	_____
3	March	1,230	_____
4	April	1,020	_____
5	May	1,185	_____
6	June	1,045	_____
7	July		_____

2. Given the data on the four jobs–A, B, C, and D–sequence them into work center 1 based on FCFS, SOT, and critical-ratio priority rules. Which rule gives the smallest average lateness per four jobs? Per late jobs only? Today is Tuesday. The current day is available to schedule as are the days on which a job is received. Work is scheduled Monday through Friday.

Job	Total Work per Job	Work Remaining on Each Job	Date Received	Due Date
A	3 Days	2 Days	Yesterday	Friday
B	2 Days	2 Days	Today	Wednesday
C	5 Days	4 Days	Last Thursday	Next Tuesday
D	1 Day	1 Day	Today	Next Monday

3. Develop the MRP time-phased inventory records for items A, B, C, and D based on the B/M, MPS, and inventory file information provided.

Indented Bill of Materials

Level	Part No.	Quantity per Parent
0	A	no parent
1	B	2 each
2	D	3 each
1	C	1 each
2	D	2 each

Master Production Schedule

Item	Wk. 1	Wk. 2	Wk. 3	Wk. 4
A	0	55	225	200
Others	No independent demand for items B, C, and D			

Inventory Status File

Item	Lot Size	On Hand	On Order	Lead Time
A	200	95 units	200 units due in Wk. 3	1 Wk.
B	L4L*	10	0	2
C	L4L	20	0	1
D	L4L	1200	0	1

L4L = lot for lot

4. Revise the multiplicative model illustrated in Table 4-2 based on the actual demand for Year 3 provided below. Compute the seasonal ratios based on all three years of data. Assume the trend continues rising five units each quarter. Compare the MAD for Year 3 using the new seasonals versus the forecasts using the old seasonals.

Actual Demand for Year 3

Quarter 1	Quarter 2	Quarter 3	Quarter 4
71.50	54.00	55.25	80.50

5. Find the expected time of completion and the critical path for the project defined by the data in the table below.

Task Name	Optimistic Time	Most Likely Time	Pessimistic Time	Task is Preceded by
A	2 days	4 days	12 days	none
B	1	3	5	A
C	4	6	14	A
D	3	5	7	A
E	7	7	7	B, C
F	9	10	11	C, D
G	7	8	15	E, F
H	2	3	4	G

6. Compute the following for the PERT diagram below (assuming that the activity times provided are the expected times):

a. The early start times for each event (ES)

b. The late start times for each event (LS)

c. The critical path

d. The slack times for each event.

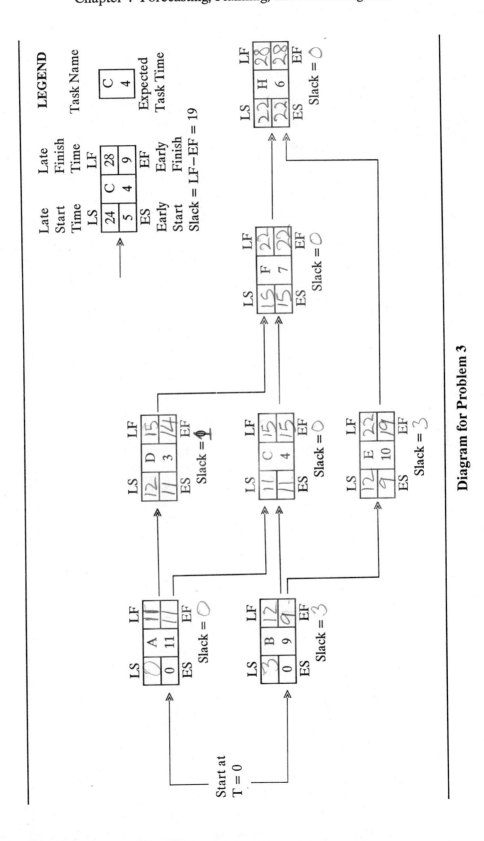

Diagram for Problem 3

5

Purchasing/Materials Management

All organizations (banks, computer manufacturers, hospitals, steel producers, airlines, government agencies, or universities) must have a continuous flow of materials, supplies, and services to support operations. The supply of these items typically is handled through the organization's purchasing department, which has the managerial responsibility of providing, from outside suppliers, a smooth flow of materials, supplies, and services to support operations.

Prior to 1940, most firms regarded the purchasing function as primarily a clerical activity. However, during World War II (1939-1945) a firm's success was not dependent on what it could sell, since demand was almost unlimited. Instead, the ability to obtain, from suppliers, the raw materials, supplies, and services needed to keep the production process operating was the key determinant of an organization's success. Because attention was given to the organization, policies, and procedures of the purchasing function, it emerged as a recognized managerial activity. During the 1950s and 1960s, purchasing continued to gain stature as the techniques for performing the function became more refined and as the supply of people trained and competent to make sound purchasing decisions increased. Many companies elevated the chief purchasing officer to top management status. Today, according to a 1988 study by the Center for Advanced Purchasing Studies, the chief purchasing office in 297 major corporations carries the title of Director of Purchasing (38%), Vice President of Purchasing (23%), Manager of Purchasing (18%), or Vice President of Materials Management (9%). The salary of the head of purchasing often is in the $100,000 range, and substantially higher when bonuses are included.

In the early 1970s, firms faced two vexing problems: an international shortage of almost all the basic raw materials needed to support operations and the fastest rate of price increases since the end of World War II. The Middle East oil embargo during the summer of 1973 intensified both the shortages and the price escalation. These developments put the spotlight directly on companies' purchasing departments, because their performance in obtaining needed items from suppliers, at realistic prices, spelled the difference between success and failure. This emphasized again to top management the crucial role played by purchasing. Although the shortages lessened from 1974 to 1975 because of the worldwide recession, and the inflationary trend moderated in 1982, due to stringent government monetary and fiscal actions and a worldwide glut of crude oil, companies now recognize the importance of a capable, efficient purchasing function. Additionally, the purchasing department plays a key role in combating inflationary pressures by resisting unwarranted price increases.

Indicative of the key role of the purchasing function in the overall performance of the U.S. economy is the attention given to the monthly "Report on Business" (ROB) generated by the National Association of Purchasing Management (NAPM). It collects data on prices, lead times on shipments from suppliers, new orders received, production, and employment from over 250 manufacturing companies at the end of each month. Since the respondents deal daily with the forces of supply and demand in the marketplace, they can spot and report on economic trends well before comparable government data become available. The results from this leading economic survey are widely reported on radio and TV and in the leading newspapers on the first business day of each month, indicating what happened to the economy in the month just ended.

As a result of this recognition of the impact of purchasing decisions on the long-term success of a firm (assuring a reliable supply of needed materials at a reasonable cost), many firms now are emphasizing strategic material planning. This activity attempts to forecast the long-term (five to twenty years) demand, supply, and price of those key raw materials needed to operate the firm based upon a variety of assumptions about the worldwide economic and political environment. If future problems can be spotted now, the firm can take action by, for example, substitution, backward vertical integration, or product line reduction to alleviate the difficulty before a crisis occurs.

Objectives of Purchasing/Materials Management

The main function of the purchasing department is to obtain the *right materials* (meeting or exceeding quality requirements), in the *right quantity*, for delivery at the *right time* and *right place*, from the *right source* (a reliable supplier who will meet commitments in a timely fashion), with the *right service* (both before and after the sale), and at the *right price*. The purchasing decision maker might be likened to a juggler attempting to keep several balls in the air at the same time: The purchaser must achieve several goals–the seven "rights" just listed–simultaneously. It is not efficient to buy at the lowest price, if the goods delivered are unsatisfactory from a quality or performance standpoint or if they arrive two weeks behind schedule, causing a production slowdown or shutdown. The right price may be one that is much *higher* than normal if the item is needed immediately, preventing the buyer from adhering to the normal lead time. The purchasing decision maker attempts to balance out the often conflicting objectives and makes trade-offs to obtain the optimum mix of these seven rights.

A more specific statement of the overall goals of purchasing would include the following eight items. Purchasing should

1. **Provide an uninterrupted flow of materials, supplies, and services required to operate the organization.** Stock-outs (interruptions in supply) of raw materials and production parts would shut down an operation and be extremely costly in terms of lost production, escalation of operating costs due to fixed costs, and inability to satisfy delivery promises to customers. For example, an automobile producer cannot complete a car without purchased tires; an airline cannot keep its planes flying without purchased fuel; and a hospital cannot perform surgery without purchased IV (intravenous) solutions.

2. **Minimize inventory investment and loss.** One way to assure an uninterrupted material flow is to keep large inventory banks. But inventory assets require using capital that could be invested elsewhere; the cost of carrying inventory may be 24 to 36 percent of value per year. If purchasing can support operations with an inventory investment of $10 million instead of $20 million, at an annual inventory carrying cost of 30 percent, the $10 million reduction in inventory represents a saving of $3 million. Just-in-time purchasing systems, which have as their objective the selection of suppliers who will deliver a small quantity of purchased items of the specified quality precisely on schedule, enable an organization to substantially reduce inventory dollars.

3. **Meet or exceed quality standards.** To produce the desired product or service, a certain level of quality is required for each material input. Otherwise, the end product or service will not meet expectations or will result in higher-than-acceptable production costs. For example, if poor-quality computer storage discs are supplied to data processors, the data-input operation will be inefficient, and much of the work will have to be redone, increasing the total wage costs of the organization.

4. **Find or develop competent suppliers.** In the final analysis, the success of the purchasing department depends on its skill in locating or developing suppliers, analyzing their capabilities, and then selecting the appropriate source. Only if suppliers who are both responsive and responsible are selected will the firm obtain the items it needs at the lowest ultimate cost. For example, if a complex computer system is purchased from a supplier who later goes out of business and is not able to perform the long-term maintenance, modification, and updating of the system, the initial favorable price turns out to be extremely high because of the supplier's inability to make good on the original commitment.

5. **Standardize, where possible, the items bought.** From an overall company viewpoint, the best item possible for the intended application should be bought. If purchasing can buy a quantity of one item to do the job that two or three different items previously did, the organization may gain efficiency advantages through a lower initial price resulting from a quantity discount, lower total inventory investment (without lowering service levels), reduced personnel training and maintenance costs in the use of equipment, and increased competition.

6. **Maintain and improve the organization's competitive position.** An organization will be competitive only if it can control purchasing costs to protect profit margins; these costs are the largest single element in the operation of many organizations. Additionally, product design and manufacturing methods must change to keep pace with changing technology and production environments; the purchasing department can inform product design and manufacturing engineering about new products available and changes likely to occur in production technology. Finally, the purchasing department is responsible for assuring the smooth flow of materials necessary to produce goods and provide services as required to meet delivery commitments to customers; in the long run, the success of any organization depends upon its ability to create and maintain customers.

7. **Achieve harmonious, productive working relationships with other departments within the organization.** Purchasing actions cannot be effectively accomplished solely by the effort of the purchasing department; cooperation with several other departments and individuals within the firm is vital to success. For example, the departments requesting materials and the production control department must provide timely information on material requirements if purchasing is to have sufficient lead time to locate competent vendors and make advantageous purchase agreements. Engineering and production must be willing to consider the possible economic advantages of using substitute materials and different vendors. Purchasing must work closely with quality control in determining inspection procedures for incoming materials, in communicating to vendors the changes needed if quality problems are found, and assisting in evaluating the performance of current suppliers. To take advantage of payment discounts and to maintain good, long-term vendor relations, accounting must pay vendors on time. If there is a problem with the flow of information concerning payment to vendors, purchasing must correct the problem; the supplier deals directly with purchasing, not with accounting, receiving, or incoming inspection, and expects to be paid on schedule.

8. **Accomplish the purchasing objectives at the lowest possible level of administrative costs.** It takes resources to operate the purchasing department–salaries, telephone and postage expenses, supplies, travel costs, and accompanying overhead. If purchasing procedures are not efficient, purchasing administrative costs will be excessive. Because the objectives of purchasing should be achieved as efficiently and economically as possible, the purchasing manager continually must review the operation to assure that it is cost effective. If the firm is not realizing its purchasing objectives due to inadequate analysis and planning, perhaps additional personnel are needed. But the firm should be continually alert to possible improvements in purchasing methods, procedures, and techniques. Perhaps unneeded steps in processing purchasing paperwork could be eliminated; perhaps the computer could be used to make the storage and recall of necessary purchasing data more efficient.

Importance of the Purchasing Function

The key objectives of any organization are to provide a good or service needed by a customer and to do so effectively and efficiently in order to return adequate long-term rewards (profits) to the owners. The purchasing function plays an important role in achieving these key objectives.

Total Dollars Involved

Purchasing is the largest single dollar-control area with which most managers must deal. Obviously, the percentage of the sales or income dollar paid to suppliers will vary greatly from industry to industry. For example, in a hospital or bank, purchasing dollars as a percentage of operating income will be less than 25 percent since these industries are labor intensive rather than material intensive. But in the manufacturing sector, material dollars typically account for well over half the sales dollar. When an automobile producer sells a new car to a dealer for $10,000, it already has spent more than $5,000 (more than 50 percent) to buy the steel, tires, glass, paint, fabric, aluminum, copper, and electronic components necessary to build that car. When a soft-drink producer sells $1,000 of packaged beverages to the supermarket, close to $750 already has been paid to vendors for the liquid sugar, carbonation, flavoring, and containers necessary to produce the end product.

Table 5-1, which uses data collected by the U.S. Bureau of the Census for its *Annual Survey of Manufactures*, presents aggregate data for the entire U.S. manufacturing sector, broken down by type of industry. These figures show that, in the average manufacturing firm, materials account for 54 percent of the sales dollar; if expenditures for capital equipment are included, the figure goes up to 57 percent. This is one-and-a-half times the remaining 43 percent available to pay salaries, wages, other operating expenses, taxes, and dividends. In 1988, the 57 percent total purchase/sales ratio was about three times the 19 percent spent for all wages, salaries, and fringe benefits.

The material/sales ratio varies dramatically among industries. For example, in standard industrial classification (SIC) 38, "Instruments and related products," it is only 34 percent; but this industry includes firms making such items as the auto-pilot used on large commercial aircraft, which requires a higher percentage of engineering , quality control, and direct assembly labor. On the other hand, in SIC 20, "Food and kindred products," the material/sales ratio is 64 percent, almost twice as large. This category includes commercial bread bakeries and beverage producers whose production process is material intensive and requires a minimum amount of labor cost due to highly mechanized and automated manufacturing processes.

Table 5-1 shows that the average material/sales ratio in manufacturing has moved up from 53 percent in 1971 to 54 percent in 1988 because manufacturing processes have become more material and less labor intensive. The total purchase/sales ratio went from 56 to 57 percent in this same time period. Any function of the firm that accounts for the use of over half the firm's receipts certainly deserves a great deal of managerial attention.

Profit-Leverage Effect

If, through better purchasing, a firm saves $100,000 in the prices paid to vendors for needed materials, supplies, and services, that $100,000 savings goes directly to the bottom-line (before-tax) account on its profit-and-loss statement. If that same firm sells an additional $100,000 of product, the contribution to profit, assuming a 5 percent before-tax profit margin, would be only $5,000. Clearly, purchase dollars are high powered.

Perhaps an example, using a hypothetical manufacturer, will illustrate this:

• Gross sales	$1,000,000
• Purchases (assuming purchases account for 50% of the sales dollar)	500,000
• Profit (assuming a before-tax profit margin of 5%)	50,000

Now, assume this firm was able to reduce its overall purchase cost by 10 percent through better management of the function. This would be a $50,000 additional contribution to before-tax profits. To increase before-tax profits by $50,000 solely through increased sales would require an additional $1,000,000, or a doubling, of sales.

This is not to suggest that it would be easy to reduce overall purchase costs by 10 percent. In a firm that has given major attention to the purchasing function over the years, it would be difficult, and perhaps impossible, to do. But in a firm that has neglected purchasing, it would be a realistic objective. Because of the profit-leverage effect of purchasing, large savings are possible compared to the effort necessary to increase sales by the much larger percentage necessary to generate the same effect on the profit-and-loss statement. Since, in many firms, the sales function already has received much more attention, purchasing may be the last untapped "profit producer."

Table 5-1

Cost of materials—Value of Industry shipments ratios for manufacturing firms, 1988

Standard Industrial Code	Industry	Cost of Materials (millions)ᵃ	Capital Expenditures, New (millions)ᵇ	Total Material & Capital Expenditures (millions)	Value of Industry Shipments (millions)ᶜ	Material Sales Ratio	Total Purchase Sales Ratio
20	Food and kindred products	223,674	7,493	231,167	351,515	64	66
21	Tobacco products	6,691	410	7,101	23,832	28	30
22	Textile mill products	38,809	2,243	41,052	64,768	60	63
23	Apparel and other textile products	32,609	672	33,281	65,032	50	51
24	Lumber and wood products	43,310	1,732	45,042	72,065	60	63
25	Furniture and fixtures	18,523	936	19,459	39,226	47	50
26	Paper and allied products	65,749	7,211	72,960	122,556	54	60
27	Printing and publishing	50,350	5,008	55,358	143,907	35	39
28	Chemicals and allied products	123,937	10,858	134,795	259,699	48	52
29	Petroleum and coal products	105,306	2,614	107,920	131,415	80	82
30	Rubber, miscellaneous plastics products	48,209	3,559	51,768	94,200	51	55
31	Leather and leather products	5,184	100	5,284	9,664	54	55
32	Stone, clay, glass products	29,073	2,244	31,317	63,059	46	50
33	Primary metal industries	94,666	4,670	99,336	149,080	64	67
34	Fabricated metal products	80,035	4,169	84,204	158,834	50	53

35	Industrial machinery and equipment	116,829	6,855	123,684	243,261	48	51
36	Electronic, electric equipment	84,681	7,972	92,653	186,951	45	50
37	Transportation equipment	215,277	7,147	222,424	354,048	61	63
38	Instruments and related products	38,852	3,961	42,813	114,528	34	37
39	Miscellaneous manufacturing	16,037	715	16,752	34,869	46	48
	(1971)	356,016	20,940	376,956	670,970	53	56
	(1972)	407,418	24,072	431,490	756,534	54	57
	(1973)	478,169	26,978	505,147	875,443	55	58
	(1974)	581,580	35,696	617,276	1,017,873	57	61
	(1975)	597,327	37,262	634,589	1,039,377	57	61
	(1976)	681,194	40,545	721,739	1,185,695	57	61
All operating manufacturing establishments	(1977)	782,417	47,459	829,876	1,358,526	58	61
	(1978)	877,424	55,209	932,633	1,522,937	58	61
	(1979)	999,157	61,533	1,060,690	1,727,214	58	61
	(1980)	1,093,567	70,112	1,163,679	1,852,668	59	63
	(1981)	1,193,969	78,632	1,272,601	2,017,542	59	63
	(1982)	1,130,143	74,562	1,204,705	1,960,206	58	61
	(1983)	1,170,238	61,931	1,232,169	2,054,853	57	60
	(1984)	1,288,414	75,186	1,363,600	2,253,429	57	61
	(1985)	1,276,013	83,237	1,359,250	2,279,132	56	60
	(1986)	1,217,609	76,355	1,293,964	2,260,315	54	57
	(1987)	1,319,803	78,648	1,398,451	2,475,901	53	57
	(1988)	1,437,801	80,569	1,518,370	2,682,509	54	57

Table 5.1 (Continued)

[a]Refers to direct charges actually paid or payable for items consumed or put into production during the year, including freight charges and other direct charges incurred by the establishment in acquiring these materials. Manufacturers included the cost of materials or fuel consumed regardless of whether these items were purchased by the individual establishment from other companies transferred to it from other establishments of the same company, or withdrawn from inventory. It excludes the cost of services used such as materials, machinery, and equipment used in plant expansion or capitalized repairs which are chargeable to fixed assets accounts.

[b]Includes funds spent for permanent additions and major alterations to manufacturing establishments, and new machinery and equipment used for replacement purposes and additions to plant capacity if they are chargeable to a fixed asset account.

[c]The received or receivable net selling values, f.o.b. plant, after discounts and allowances, and excluding freight charges and excise taxes. However, where the products of an industry are customarily delivered by the manufacturing establishment, e.g., bakery products, the value of shipments is based on the delivered price of the goods.

Source: U.S. Bureau of the Census, 1988 Annual Survey of Manufactures (Washington, D.C.; U.S. Government Printing Office). Statistics for Industry Groups and Industries, M88 (AS)-1, pp. 1-5, 1-10, and Appendix.

Return-on-Assets Effect

Firms are increasingly more interested in return-on-assets (ROA) as a measure of performance. Figure 5-1 shows the standard ROA model, using the same figures as in the previous example and assuming, realistically, that inventory accounts for 30 percent of total assets. If purchase costs were reduced by 10 percent, the inventory asset base also would be reduced by 10 percent. The numbers in the boxes show the initial figures used in arriving at the 10 percent ROA performance. The numbers below each box are the figures resulting from a 10 percent overall purchase price reduction, and the end product is a new ROA of 20.6 percent. This is a highly feasible objective for many firms.

Effect on Efficiency

The effectiveness of the purchasing function shows up in other operating results. If the purchasing department selects a vendor who fails to deliver raw materials or parts that measure up to the agreed-upon quality standards, a higher scrap rate or costly rework, requiring excessive direct labor expenditures, may result. If the supplier selected does not meet the agreed-upon delivery schedule, the delay may require a costly rescheduling of production, decreasing overall production efficiency or, in the worst case, shutting down the production line while fixed costs continue, even though there is no output. Consider the effect, for example, on a fast-food restaurant if it runs out of buns; what if the payroll department does not have the blank checks needed to process the end-of-month payroll?

Effect on Competitive Position

A firm cannot be competitive unless it can deliver end products or services to its customers when they are wanted and at a price the customer considers fair. If purchasing doesn't do its job, the firm will not have the required materials when needed and at a price that keeps end-product costs under control.

Some years ago, a major automobile producer decided to buy all its auto glass from one firm (a single source). Some months into the supply agreement, it appeared that the forthcoming labor-contract negotiations might result in a deadlock and a long strike. To protect itself, the auto company built up a 90-day glass stockpile, even though the inventory carrying costs were high, and it had problems finding the physical storage facilities for that much glass. As anticipated, there was a strike in the glass industry, but the union struck only the glass firm supplying that auto

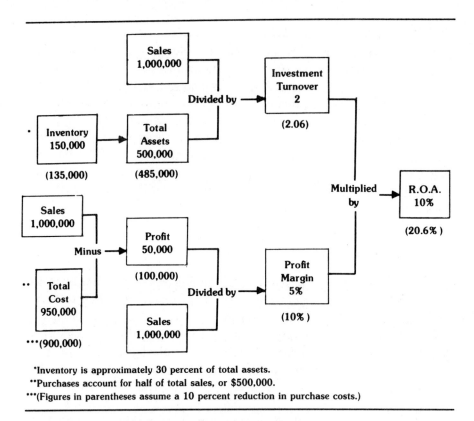

*Inventory is approximately 30 percent of total assets.
**Purchases account for half of total sales, or $500,000.
***(Figures in parentheses assume a 10 percent reduction in purchase costs.)

Figure 5-1. Return-on-Assets Factors

producer. The strike lasted 118 days, and the auto producer had to shut down its production lines for more than a month.

The auto company had a large net financial loss that year, since that sales loss dropped it below its break-even point. The president explained to the stockholders that the glass strike cost the company the sale of about 100,000 cars (a month's sales). Auto customers evidently were not willing to wait until the strike ended, and they went "across the street" to buy a car made by a competitor. The dealer can tell a customer, "Here's the car. Bring it back in a month, and we'll put the hubcaps on for you," and it will make the sale, but it's difficult to convince the customer to take the car now and bring it back later for the windshield! Actually, the producer probably lost closer to 500,000 auto sales: If a customer bought another maker's car when he or she couldn't get the car wanted and if he or she liked the different make, he or she probably returned to the new dealer to buy another car two or three years later, and then did so repeatedly.

Effect on Image

The actions of the purchasing department directly influence the public-relations image of a company. This is particularly true of a company making industrial products, because purchasing has many more outside contacts (with vendors and potential vendors) than the marketing department (which calls on only a limited number of customers). If actual and potential suppliers are not treated in a businesslike manner, they will form a poor opinion of the entire company and will communicate this to other firms. This poor image will adversely affect the purchasing firm's ability to get new business and to find new and better suppliers.

Training Ground

The purchasing professional, in performing his or her daily activities, interacts with all other areas of the organization. This provides a critical exposure to the needs and operation of the organization. The individual's ability and willingness to take risks and assume responsibility are scrutinized and evaluated when he or she makes decisions under pressure, in an environment of uncertainty and with potentially serious consequences. Many organizations include an assignment in the purchasing area as part of the formal job rotation plan for "fast-track" employees.

Information Source

The daily contacts of the buyer or purchasing manager provide a good deal of potentially useful information about the outside environment. What new products are being developed by competitors? What are the competitors' marketing strategies? What is the availability of new material? Is innovative technology being developed? What is the manufacturing strategy of competitors? Who are potential merger and acquisition candidates? What is the direction of the economy? Buyers are in a prime position to answer such questions and feed this intelligence to top corporate management, where it can be evaluated and used in developing and refining the organization's own objectives and strategies.

Organization of Purchasing/Materials Management

A proper organizational structure is necessary for effective performance. This enables the specialization, planning, coordination, communication, and control to make effective materials-acquisition decisions.

Centralization Versus Decentralization

If a firm purchases on a *decentralized* basis, each department manager will handle his or her own purchasing. The advantage to this approach is that the user knows what is needed better than anyone else. Also, it may be faster: When a department needs something, the manager simply picks up the phone and orders it.

But the advantages of *centralized* purchasing outweigh those of decentralized purchasing, and almost all but the smallest of firms are centralized. In centralized purchasing, a separate individual or department is given authority to make all purchases, except, perhaps, the very unusual buy, such as a new company aircraft. Centralized purchasing offers the following advantages:

1. It is easier to standardize the items bought if purchasing decisions go through one central control point.

2. It reduces administrative duplication. Instead of each department head writing a separate purchase order for light bulbs, the purchasing department writes only one order for the firm's total requirement.

3. By combining requirements from several departments, purchasing has the clout to go to a supplier and discuss an order quantity that is large enough to interest the vendor. Often the purchasing department can persuade the supplier to give concessions, such as faster delivery or a quantity discount. There also may be freight savings, because shipment now can be made in carload quantities.

4. In periods of materials shortage, one department does not compete with another department for the available supply and thus drive up the price.

5. It is administratively more efficient for the supplier, who does not need to call on several people within the company. Instead, the vendor makes a pitch to the purchasing manager.

6. It provides better control over purchase commitments. Since a large percentage of a firm's cash outflow goes for material purchases, a central control point is needed to monitor the aggregate commitment amount at any specific time. Also, purchasing decisions about placement of orders with vendors are sensitive: Kickbacks and bribery are possible if orders are issued to unscrupulous suppliers. It is easier to prevent such illegal and unethical practices if all decisions on the flow of purchase commitments go through one central funnel; this means the spotlight can be focused on the purchasing department, because purchase decisions are not scattered throughout the various departments of the firm.

7. It enables the development of specialization and expertise in purchase decisions and uses time more efficiently. When a department head also tries to be a purchasing agent, the time spent on purchasing probably could be better used in managing the department. Additionally, the department manager will not spend enough time in purchasing to develop any real expertise. A full-time buyer, who can devote undivided attention to purchasing, rapidly develops expert knowledge of purchasing techniques, sources of supply, available and new materials and manufacturing processes, markets, and prices. This development of expertise is the primary reason almost all firms have centralized the purchasing function.

A variation of centralized purchasing often exists in the multiplant organization. Here, the firm operates several different producing divisions, which often make different products requiring a different mix of purchased items. The firm often uses a profit-center management-motivation-and-control technique, in which the division manager is totally responsible for running the division, acts as president of an independent firm, and is judged by profits made by this division. Since material purchases are the largest single controllable cost of running a division and have a direct effect on the efficiency and competitive position of the division, the profit-center division manager insists on having direct authority over purchasing. It would be difficult to hold the division manager responsible for results if the manager lacked decision-making power over the major expenditure area.

This realization has led some firms to adopt decentralized-centralized purchasing, in which the purchasing function is centralized on a division or plant basis but decentralized on a corporate basis. Often a corporate purchasing organization operates in a staff capacity and assists the division purchasing departments in those tasks that are handled more effectively on a corporate basis: (1) establishment of policies, procedures, and controls; (2) recruiting and training of personnel; (3) coordinating the purchase of common-use items, where more clout is needed; and (4) auditing purchasing performance. Figure 5-2 presents a simplified organizational chart for a firm organized on a profit-center basis.

In the 1980s, there has been a gradual movement toward greater centralization of purchasing in the multiplant organization in order to gain the volume-buying advantages that lead to greater assurance of supply and closer control of purchase prices. *The Purchasing Function: From Strategy to Image,* a study published in 1982 by the Machinery and Allied Products Institute, found that 50 percent of the firms considered had further centralized their purchasing during the past decade; 65 percent predicted even more centralization in the next ten years.

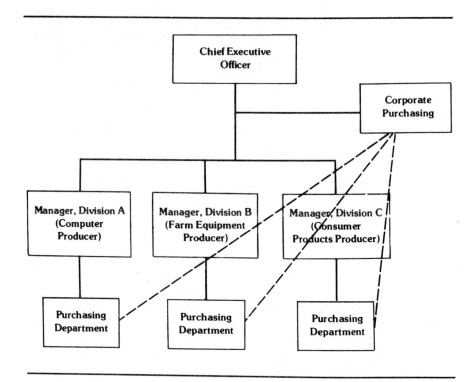

Figure 5-2. Multidivision Organization Structure for Purchasing

A 1988 study by the Center for Advanced Purchasing Studies, *Purchasing Organizational Relationships,* found that in 28 percent of the 297 large organizations, purchasing is centralized; all or most purchasing is done at one central location for the entire firm. In 13 percent of the firms it is decentralized; purchasing is done on a division or plant basis. But in 59 percent of the firms it is handled on a centralized-decentralized basis, in which some purchasing is done at corporate headquarters and purchasing also is done centrally at major operating divisions or plants. Evidently most organizations try to get the best of all possible worlds by mixing centralization and decentralization.

Changing Responsibilities

The 1988 study, *Purchasing Organizational Relationships,* also found that several new activity areas have been assigned to purchasing since 1980. Those activity areas newly assigned in at least 5 percent of the firms were personnel travel (14%), traffic/transportation (13%), countertrade/offset planning/execution (12%), strategic planning (9%), capital-equipment buys (7%), and providing economic forecasts/indicators (6%).

Several activity areas were indicated as ones in which purchasing has assumed an increased role or responsibility since 1980: strategic planning (in 43% of the firms), providing economic forecasts/indicators (41%), capital-equipment buys (37%), product development (31%), new-product evaluation (26%), traffic/transportation (23%), personnel travel (16%), countertrade/offset planning/execution (15%), and cash-flow planning (13%). Obviously, the purchasing function has assumed many increased responsibilities in the past decade, requiring more-talented, better-trained personnel to perform the function.

Materials Management

Some organizations have adopted the materials management organizational concept, whereby a single manager is responsible for planning, organizing, motivating, and controlling all those activities principally concerned with the flow of materials into a organization. Materials management views material flow as a system. Another way to look at materials management is to consider its major activities:

1. Anticipating material requirements

2. Sourcing and obtaining materials

3. Introducing materials into the organization

4. Monitoring the status of materials as a current asset

Figure 5-3 shows the specific functions that might be included in a materials management organization and their relations to other major functional areas of the firm. Not all eleven functions shown would have to report to the materials manager; production scheduling, in-plant materials movement, and incoming quality control often are excluded.

The materials management concept grew out of problems in the airframe industry during World War II. Production of an aircraft requires a large number of individual items, many of which are quite sophisticated and must meet stringent quality standards; these are procured from thousands of vendors located over a wide geographic area. Each item is vital to the total functioning of the end product. The objectives of materials management are solving materials problems from a total company viewpoint (optimize) by coordinating performance of the various materials functions; providing a communications network; and controlling materials flow. As the computer was introduced into organizations, it provided a further reason to adopt materials management: the materials functions have many common data needs and can share a common data base.

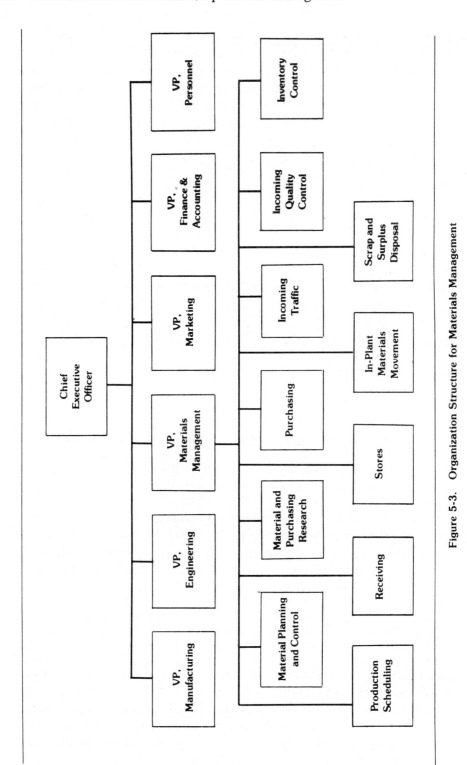

Figure 5-3.   Organization Structure for Materials Management

The single manager materials concept overcomes the shortcomings of the conventional organization, where the various materials functions are organizationally splintered. It recognizes (1) materials decisions as being additive and not independent of actions elsewhere, (2) the self-interest and potentially conflicting objectives of the individual materials functions, and (3) the need to concentrate authority and responsibility for materials decisions to avoid buck-passing. Materials management, in a formal organizational sense, is not needed in the small organization where the chief executive (normally the owner) makes all the materials decisions and provides the needed coordination and control.

The 1988 *Purchasing Organizational Relationships* study found that 70 percent of the organizations used the materials-management concept (defined as an organization in which at least three of the following functions–purchasing, inventory, production scheduling and control, inbound traffic, warehousing and stores, incoming quality control report to a single responsible individual). Materials management has become the typical form of organization in recent years.

Purchasing Prerogatives

If the purchasing department is to meet the objectives of good purchasing, it must have four key prerogatives:

1. Right to select the supplier. Purchasing should be the expert in knowing who is capable of producing needed items and in analyzing vendor reliability. If someone else selects the supplier, purchasing then is in a sole-source (no alternatives) situation and can do little to bargain for an advantageous purchase agreement.

2. Right to use whichever pricing method is appropriate and to determine the price and terms of the agreement. This is one of the main expertise areas of purchasing, which must have room to maneuver if it is to achieve the lowest possible price.

3. Right to question the specifications. Purchasing, which often can suggest substitute or alternate items that will do the same job, is responsible for bringing these items to the attention of the requisitioner. The user makes the final decision on accepting a substitute.

4. Right to control all contacts with potential suppliers. Communication with potential vendors must flow through purchasing. If users contact vendors directly, this encourages "backdoor selling," in which a potential supplier influences the specifications and creates a sole-source situation. Or, the requisitioner will make commitments to vendors

that prevent purchasing from reaching agreements that will give the buying firm the lowest ultimate price. If vendor technical personnel need to talk directly with personnel in the buyer's firm, purchasing will arrange for such discussions and will monitor their outcome.

The above purchasing prerogatives should be established as matters of company policy and approved by the chief executive officer.

The Standard Purchasing System

The standard purchasing procedure consists of nine steps: (1) recognition of need, (2) description of need, (3) source selection, (4) price determination, (5) purchase-order preparation, (6) follow-up and expediting, (7) receipt and inspection of goods, (8) invoice clearance and payment, and (9) maintenance of records. Performance of these steps varies from company to company, depending on such factors as the status of purchasing within the total organization, competence of purchasing personnel, and the extent to which electronic data processing is used.

Good management dictates that the procedures and policies of purchasing be written out to assure that the firm follows an approach consistent with its particular needs, to assure consistency and fairness in its purchasing actions, to provide guidance to both buyers and requisitioners in how purchasing is to be handled, and to establish the authority of the purchasing department. A well-managed firm will have a policy and procedure manual, which is the guidebook for those involved with purchasing. Policies should be established in areas such as authority to requisition, authority to purchase, use of competitive bids, maintenance of records, acceptance of gifts, use of local suppliers, disclosure of information to suppliers, purchasing for employees, adherence to federal and state laws and regulations, and actions to be taken in the event of discrepancies between the purchase agreement and actual vendor performance.

The key managerial tool used to determine the allocation of time and attention of buying personnel and to establish purchasing strategy is ABC analysis. If a firm arranges any given year's purchase history by listing the one item on which the largest total dollar expenditures were made and then listing in descending dollar value all other items down to the item on which the smallest total dollar expenditures were made, it generally would look like this:

- A items–those 5 percent of the purchased items accounting for 75 percent of the total dollars spent

- B items–those 10 percent of the purchased items accounting for 15 percent of the total dollars spent

- C items–those 85 percent of the purchased items accounting for 10 percent of the total dollars spent

The A items primarily will consist of raw materials and production parts. The B items also will be raw materials and production parts, but the usage amounts and values will be less than for A items. The C items primarily will be maintenance, repair, and operating (MRO) supplies. A given firm may have only 15 items in the A category, 30 items in the B category, and 255 items in the C category, out of a total of 300 items. Since the average annual dollars spent on each A item is 10 times greater than for each B item and about 128 times greater than for each C item, the A item has the largest profit leverage, and this is where most of the time and effort of the purchasing department should be concentrated. A 1 percent saving in the purchase of an A item will produce greater profits than a 99 percent saving on one of the C items. Obviously a 1 percent saving will be more easily attained than a 99 percent saving, which is almost an impossibility. One approach that might be productive is to aggregate several of the individual C items into a family of items (such as all hand tools), thereby moving the family of items into the B category where purchasing can afford to spend more time and effort. The multiple-item purchase agreement is called a systems contract.

This same ABC analysis technique also applies to other areas of purchasing. Purchase orders segregated by dollar value approximate the ABC breakdown, since most purchasing paperwork is for small-dollar orders. To reduce the quantity and cost of paperwork, a firm should develop a simpler system for processing the small-value, C orders, which require less control since the dollar risk is much lower. If dollars spent with various suppliers are arranged from highest amount by vendor to lowest amount, it also normally will approximate the ABC breakdown. The suppliers with whom purchasing does the most business are those on whom the most attention should be spent, because purchasing has the most clout with them and should cultivate good relations with them.

All the routine data collection, processing, and recording functions involved in the nine steps of the standard purchasing procedure can be handled through a computer system. During the past twenty years, the computer has made substantial inroads into purchasing, resulting in three major benefits: (1) reduction of clerical, manual effort; (2) closer control over purchase actions resulting from more accurate and more timely decision-making data; and (3) better decisions, resulting from the better data base. Significant changes, beginning in the early 1980s, can be attributed to desktop, personal-computer systems. The low cost and ready availability of these small, stand-alone systems are making comput-erization an integral part of the purchasing function in all organizations, large and small.

Recognition of Need

The purchasing process is triggered when someone within the organiza-tion recognizes that some material, supply, or service is needed and best can be obtained from sources outside the organization. Normally, a need is recognized by a user, such as production, which calculates its require-ment for a particular production part based upon its next month's pro-duction schedule; or by marketing, which anticipates a need for a new advertising brochure; or by the personnel department, which requires an additional typewriter. This step normally is not performed by purchasing, except in the case of standard, inventory items where purchasing may be responsible for inventory management and resupplying when the stock on hand reaches a preset order point.

In the case of production parts, many firms now use a computerized materials-requirements-planning (MRP) system (discussed in chapter 4) to notify the purchasing department of parts needed, quantities, and need dates.

Description of Need

If purchasing is to fill a recognized need, the user must notify purchasing of the specific characteristics of that need. A simple, two-part form called the purchase requisition generally is used; the original is sent to purchasing, and the requisitioner retains the carbon copy. The informa-tion on the requisition should include date prepared; department preparing and a signature of an individual who can authorize purchase action; description of the item needed; quantity needed; place where delivery is needed; and the date needed. A specific date (month and day) should be indicated; "rush" or "as soon as possible" is not precise enough to guide purchasing. "Rush" may be interpreted by purchasing as a real emergency, and they may pay a higher price to obtain next-day delivery, even though the item really isn't needed for two weeks and could be purchased by normal means and at a much lower price.

The requisitioner need not indicate "suggested price" or "suggested vendor," as purchasing has the expertise to determine the right price and appropriate vendor. If purchasing needs help in locating a vendor, it can ask the requisitioner. Also, if the requisitioner feels obliged to indicate a suggested vendor and price, he or she probably will contact the vendor directly, opening up the possibly for backdoor selling. If, after submitting the requisition, the requisitioner hears nothing from purchasing, it can be assumed that the needed item will arrive by the date specified. If purchasing runs into lead-time problems, they will be discussed with the requisitioner.

If the item is a one-time, immediate-use purchase, the quantity decision is straightforward: Purchasing buys the entire quantity for delivery by the needed date. If the item is an MRO item that normally is maintained in inventory or is an item needed over an extended time period, either inventory control or purchasing will make an economic order quantity calculation, as discussed in chapter 6.

If the item is an A category raw material, purchasing may wish to "buy to the market," based upon purchasing's long-term forecast of the supply-and-demand factors. If the item is forecast to be in a market oversupply situation, purchasing may decide to buy only enough to meet immediate needs (called "hand-to-mouth buying") and wait for the price to fall before making additional purchases. If the item is forecast to be in increasingly short supply, purchasing may decide to buy a several-month supply now, in anticipation of a price increase, and put most of it in inventory for later use. Called "forward buying," this decision to buy more than the immediate need is based on data and a realistic estimate of the situation; it is not speculation, which is gambling on price changes when the firm does not have a foreseeable need for the item and is attempting to make a profit from the buying and selling of materials.

The bill of materials (B/M) discussed in chapter 2, is used by firms that make standard, manufactured items over relatively long periods of time; it is a quick way to notifying purchasing of production needs. A B/M for a toaster made by an appliance manufacturer would list the total number or quantity, including an appropriate scrap allowance, of parts or material to make one end unit. Production scheduling then merely notifies purchasing that it has scheduled 18,000 of that model into production next month. Purchasing then will "explode" the B/M (normally by a computerized system) by multiplying through by 18,000 to determine the total quantity of material needed to meet next month's production schedule. Comparison of these numbers with quantities in inventory will give purchasing the "open to buy" figures. The B/M system simplifies the requisitioning process when a large number of frequently needed line items is involved.

The description of the item to be bought is important, because purchasing must understand the requirements if it is to select the most appropriate supplier and clearly communicate quality needs to that vendor. Purchasing's objective is to buy the least expensive item with the attributes needed for the job or application in question. Incoming quality control then will determine whether the item actually received from the supplier meets the specification on the purchase order.

There are several ways quality may be described to purchasing and then by purchasing to the supplier. Each has its peculiar advantages and disadvantages.

Brand or Trade Name

Specifying a product by brand name is a quick means of describing quality, and it is easy to determine whether the right item was delivered. It also gives some assurance that the quality will be consistent over time. Therefore, this is useful in specifying the C category of item, where simple purchase decisions are sought. However, a prime reason manufacturers brand their products is to build up customer loyalty; this permits manufacturers to charge higher prices than those charged for similar, and equally good, unbranded products. The marketing of aspirin is a good example of the price advantage available to a vendor who establishes a brand name in the mind of the buyer.

Market Grade

Many raw materials, such as agricultural and mineral products, have an established grading system that can be used to specify quality. Lumber is a good example. Market grade is a quick and easy method of description if the established grading system classifies quality in sufficiently specific intervals to meet a firm's production needs.

Word Picture

This is a complete, written word picture of the characteristics the needed item must possess. Although these can be very exact, they are difficult to compose so that the vendor understands exactly what is requested.

Blueprint

This is a dimensional specification normally used in the purchase of production parts. It is the most exact type of description, but the buyer is responsible for any errors on the print. Blueprints are costly to prepare.

Sample

Why not give vendors samples and ask for duplicates? This is often done when purchasing repair parts, where age or use makes it difficult to locate the original manufacturer. Samples also frequently are used to describe printed matter, such as forms. Sometimes, however, the printer and the buyer disagree about whether the newly delivered printing complies with the sample, particularly when color is involved.

Performance Specification

When purchasing equipment from a vendor who is familiar with the purchaser's needs, it may be enough to tell the vendor what job the needed equipment must perform. For example, a commercial baker might specify a piece of breadwrapping equipment by indicating the variations in loaf size it must be able to handle, the number of loaves to be wrapped per hour, and the various types of wrap (cellophane, plastic, waxed paper, or plain paper) the machine must use.

Source Selection

One key to good purchasing is the selection of responsible, cooperative suppliers. This is perhaps the most important step in the purchasing system, for all else depends on it. The care taken in selecting vendors will depend on the item involved and the dollar risk. Greater care will be taken in the purchase of a new item if it is hard to locate and crucial to the performance of the end product or if it is an A item in which the dollar risk from quality problems or delivery interruption is high. In purchasing a routine, C-category item, purchasing cannot afford to spend much time, since the risk is small and the savings potential is low.

In some instances, a firm is faced with a make-or-buy decision. For example, instead of buying printed forms, we may decide to purchase the needed equipment and print our requirements in-house. Or, our existing print shop may have excess capacity, and we may decide to fill that capacity with our own needs. Another example would be the reusable hypodermic syringe and needles that are sterilized after use and returned to inventory in a hospital: Perhaps it would be more cost effective to buy disposables. Machined-parts requirements frequently can be made in-house on existing equipment, or they may be purchased from an outside vendor. The make-or-buy decision is based upon a combination of cost, quality, and delivery-service considerations. Purchasing also should provide much of the information for, and should participate in, the make-or-buy decision.

The purchase of a new A item will be handled in four steps, and the process may take several months, compared with selecting a supplier for a C item, on which purchasing may spend only five minutes.

Directory Stage

This is an attempt to make as long a list as possible of vendors considered capable of producing the needed item. The buyer wants several possible vendors on the list, since many will be eliminated later in the evaluation process. The buyer's past experience will be the starting point and probably will produce several vendor names. The buyer then may check with some purchasing counterparts in other purchasing departments, both inside and outside the company. Often, salespeople can provide good leads on available sources. Also, vendor directories list suppliers according to type of product; among these are the telephone book Yellow Pages, *McRae's Bluebook*, and the catalogs available for specific industries, such as suppliers to the chemical industry. Probably the most-used vendor directory is the *Thomas Register of American Manufacturers*, which claims to list all American manufacturers by type of product. The *Thomas Register* contains about 44,000 pages and lists more than 152,000 U.S.and Canadian companies, 50,000 products and services, and 112,000 brand names and trademarks. These directories, however, do not evaluate the quality or reliability of vendors. Also, buyers, by reading purchasing trade journals and journals in their own industry and by attending various trade shows, will gather general information about possible vendors.

In many firms, the purchasing department makes a concerted effort to find and develop minority vendors–that is, vendors in which at least half of the ownership and top management is by minority citizens such as Blacks, Native Americans, Orientals, or Hispanics. Some vendor directories, such as *Try Us '91*, list only minority vendors. Similar emphasis often is given to the use of small vendors (referred to in Public Law 95-507 as "disadvantaged"). Public Law 99-661, passed in 1986, requires that suppliers to the Department of Defense spend 5 percent of their purchase dollars on each contract with minority-owned suppliers. The conscious action by purchasing decision makers is a result of a combination of government pressures plus a realization that minority-owned firms and small businesses will only be part of the mainstream of American economic life if purchasing managers select them as suppliers to medium- and large-size buying firms.

Evaluation

Here the buyer gathers information to predict how well the supplier would perform if selected. Again, the amount of effort expended depends upon the importance of the item to be purchased. Obviously, the information the buyer gathers will be imperfect, and some of the vendors finally selected will not perform as predicted. The areas subject to evaluation are almost endless and will depend on the item to be bought. Some key areas to be evaluated are

1. **Reliability.** Will the vendor do what it says it will do?

2. **Quantity.** Can the vendor supply enough to meet our needs?

3. **Time element.** Can the vendor meet our delivery schedule?

4. **Service.** Will the vendor provide needed before-and-after-sale support?

5. **Quality and quality-control methods.** Will the vendor's quality be consistent and meet our requirements? Does the vendor use adequate quality-control methods?

6. **Research and development.** Is the vendor doing anything to improve its products and production process?

7. **Capacity.** If our requirements increase, can the vendor handle them?

8. **Financial capacity.** Is the vendor's financial situation adequate to assure it will be in business long enough to meet our requirements completely? Or will its internal financial situation force it to try to cut corners?

9. **Labor relations.** What has been the vendor's record of work stoppages? What is its future labor situation likely to be?

10. **Managerial ability.** Is the vendor's management competent and progressive?

11. **Warranties.** What types of guarantees are provided?

12. **Transportation facilities.** Does the vendor's transport situation match our needs?

The buyer has several possible means of gathering information to evaluate potential vendors and probably will use a combination of the following data sources to cross-check conclusions.

1. **Past experience.** If the buyer has done business with a particular vendor, the outcome of those agreements is a good indication of the future, unless there have been major changes in the vendor's management or operating situation. Certainly, if past dealings were unsatisfactory, the buyer will approach future dealings with that vendor very cautiously.

2. **Experience of others.** Through contacts with purchasing personnel in other firms, the buyer probably can find out how the vendor has performed on purchase agreements. Purchasing people normally are quite willing to exchange vendor-performance information, if there is no discussion of prices.

3. **Obtain a sample.** This helps verify a vendor's quality capability. Unless the sample was obtained on a totally random basis, however, its utility is questionable. If the vendor-furnished sample is satisfactory, it merely indicates that the vendor is capable of producing a satisfactory item; it doesn't ensure that subsequent production quality will be as good as the sample, for the sample probably represents the vendor's best effort. But if the sample is unsatisfactory, that vendor can be eliminated.

4. **Salespeople's statements.** The buyer will talk with sales representatives and managerial personnel in the vendor firm, asking pertinent questions about the vendor's ability. This free information source should be used, but the buyer knows the vendor has a tendency to say whatever is likely to obtain a purchase order.

5. **Plant visit.** The best source of information about a new supplier is a visit to the vendor's plant for a firsthand look at the facilities and operating situation and a discussion with vendor personnel. The visit should be planned, and the buyer should know specifically what questions to ask and what data to obtain. After the visit, the buyer should make a complete record of information obtained for later evaluation and comparison. As part of the visit, the buyer should follow the product, starting with the vendor's purchasing department; if the vendor has a poor purchasing system, this will show up later in product quality, delivery, and/or cost. In many firms, the purchasing department periodically visits every A category vendor to note changes and to maintain close supplier contacts.

6. **Public data.** The business press, such as *The Wall Street Journal* and *Business Week,* often contains much useful data on medium-to-large

vendors. The buyer may wish to consult *The Wall Street Journal Index* and the *Business Periodical Index* to locate such information. To evaluate a vendor's financial status, the buyer will get a Dun and Bradstreet Credit Report (subject to some error but containing useful information), a corporate annual report, and the Form 10-K and 10-Q reports filed with the Securities and Exchange Commission. In the case of a privately held firm, the buyer may insist on being furnished an audited financial statement.

Approved List

Based on the evaluation, many of the possible vendors probably will be eliminated for one reason or a combination of reasons. To encourage competition, the buyer should develop an approved list containing at least two firms; three or four would be even better. Being on the approved list does not mean that a vendor will receive an order; that depends on the prices and terms obtained.

Experience Rating

While technically this is not part of the source-selection process, good management dictates that current vendors should be evaluated as a basis for placing future business, dropping vendors, helping vendors improve, and improving the selection process. In many firms, this vendor-performance rating is based on intuition: The buyer simply rates each vendor's performance in categories of "excellent," "good," "needs improvement," or "unsatisfactory." But the intuitive method has two major weaknesses. First, the rating will be unduly influenced by the most recent happenings. If, for example, the vendor was late on this month's shipment, it probably will receive an unsatisfactory rating, even though performance was excellent in all other regards and this was the first time there were any delivery problems. Second, this method does not provide top management with any hard, factual evidence to support a decision to drop a vendor or place more business with that vendor.

As an alternative, some more sophisticated firms have developed a vendor point-rating system that systematically rates vendors on several factors, such as quality, price, and service, based on factual performance records maintained by purchasing and incoming quality control. The ratings are aggregated into a single-number overall rating that can be used to compare total performance among vendors. The individual factor ratings indicate where vendors can improve their performance. To establish such a system, the purchasing department must: (1) identify the important performance factors, (2) determine the relative weight of each factor, (3) assign points based on actual performance records, and (4) total the points.   This is a more defensible and useful vendor-performance-evaluation approach.   Those firms with a computerized purchasing data system can produce these rating reports easily as an almost-free by-product; such a system also can be maintained manually on the A items at a reasonable cost.

Determining Price

While price is only one aspect of the overall purchasing job, it is extremely important. Basically, the purchasing department exists to satisfy the firm's purchase requirements at a lower overall cost than could be accomplished through decentralized purchasing.   The purchasing department must be alert to different pricing methods, know when each is appropriate, and skillfully arrive at the price to be paid.

Certain federal and state laws regulate pricing practices. If there is any question of possible violation, the firm's legal counsel should be consulted. The two most important such laws are the Sherman Anti-Trust and the Robinson-Patman acts. The Sherman Anti-Trust Act of 1890 states that any combination, conspiracy, or collusion with the intent of restricting trade in interstate commerce is illegal. This means that it is illegal for vendors to get together to set prices (price fixing) or determine the terms and conditions under which they will sell. It also means that buyers cannot get together to set the prices they will pay.

The Robinson-Patman Act (Federal Anti-Price Discrimination Act of 1936), known as the "one-price law," says that a vendor must sell the same item, in the same quantity, to all customers, at the same price. Some exceptions are permitted, such as a lower price (1) for a larger purchase quantity, providing the seller can cost-justify the lower price through cost-accounting data; (2) to move "distress" or obsolete merchandise; or (3) to meet the lower price of local competition in a particular geographic area. The act also states that it shall be illegal for a buyer knowingly to induce or accept a discriminatory price. The courts have been realistic in their interpretation of the law, however, holding that it is the buyer's job to get the best possible price for his or her company; as long as the buyer does not intentionally mislead the seller into giving a more favorable price than is available to other buyers of the same item, the buyer is not violating the law.

There are basically six methods the buyer can use in establishing price. Each is useful under certain circumstances.

List Price

Most suppliers periodically publish a catalog of the items they routinely sell; this normally is accompanied by a price list. The list price is not necessarily the only price the vendor will accept; it is the "asking" price. If the quantity is large enough to make the sale really attractive to the vendor, the buyer normally can obtain concessions, such as a lower selling price, larger trade-in allowance, better cash discount, or free service, such as equipment maintenance. But in the purchase of a C-category item, the buyer does not have the time to pursue a lower price since a 10 or 20 percent reduction is not significant. The buyer probably should pay the list price and use the time saved to do a better job of analyzing and purchasing the A items, where the real profit leverage exists.

Unpriced Purchase Order

Here the buyer sends out the purchase order (PO) complete in all respects, except that no price is shown. What this PO says, basically, is "ship the item as specified and send an invoice at the vendor's normally determined price." Unpriced POs should be used sparingly, for one of the key parameters in any purchase decision should be price, which should be determined prior to placing the order.

In two instances, use of an unpriced PO may be appropriate. In an emergency, such as an equipment breakdown, time may be of greater value than money, and the buyer may wish to get the vendor started immediately, even though price has not been determined. Second, in the purchase of routine, standard items–for example, a gross of No. 2 lead pencils–from a vendor with whom the company does other business, the buyer may decide merely to say "ship." If the price charged on the invoice is out of line, it will be challenged before payment.

Salesperson's Quotation

A salesperson may quote the buyer a price while in the buyer's office, and the buyer may accept by issuing a PO. Probably there will be no problem, although legally the salesperson presumably doesn't have agency authority, and the offer made by the salesperson legally does not commit the selling company *until* it has been accepted by an officer of that company. If the buyer wishes to accept a salesperson's offer and to know that the offer is legally binding, he or she should ask the salesperson to furnish a letter signed by an officer of the selling company stating that the salesperson possesses the authority of a sales agent.

Market Prices

The reported market prices for many raw-material items are listed regularly in many of the trade and business journals, such as *Iron Age* and *The Wall Street Journal.* Such market prices are the reported list prices at which commodities were offered for sale in the past. They are not offers to sell but indications of price levels. They may be used by purchasing as a general gauge of prices, although the astute buyer probably can obtain a better price.

Competitive Bids

This is the most effective means of obtaining a fair price for items bought; the forces of competition are used to assure that the price paid is barely enough to allow the seller to cover costs, plus make a minimum profit. Prospective vendors are sent a request-for-quotation form, which lists all aspects of the needed purchase (specifications, quantity, required date, terms, and conditions). These vendors are asked to respond with the minimum price at which each would be willing to supply this requirement. Each vendor knows that others also are being asked to bid and that the vendor with the lowest quote will get the order. Therefore, the vendor who wants the order should give the buyer an attractive quote. This places considerable pressure on the vendor.

For the bid process to work efficiently, several conditions must be present:

1. There must be at least two, and preferably several , qualified vendors.

2. The vendors must want the business; competitive bidding works best in a buyer's market.

3. The specifications must be clear so that bidders know precisely what they are bidding on and so the buyer easily can compare the quotes received from various bidders.

4. There must be honest bidding and no collusion among the bidders.

Negotiation

This most sophisticated and costly means of price determination is used for the purchase of large-dollar items where competitive bidding is not appropriate because one or more of the required conditions is absent. Negotiation requires that the buyer sit down across the table from a vendor; through discussion, they arrive at a common understanding of the essentials of a purchase/sale contract, such as delivery, specifications, warranty, prices, and terms. Because of the interrelation of these factors and many others, negotiation is a difficult art and requires the exercise of judgment and tact. Negotiation is an attempt to reach an agreement that allows both parties to realize their objectives. It is used most often when the buyer is in a sole-source situation; in that case, both parties know that a purchase contract will be issued, and their task is to define a set of terms and conditions acceptable to both. Because of the expense and time involved, true negotiation normally will not be used unless the dollar amount is quite large, probably $50,000 or more.

The buyer normally requests the vendor to present a proposal, accompanied by a cost breakdown detailing the following:

1. Direct material costs

2. Direct labor costs

3. Burden or overhead rates and costs

4. Tooling charges

5. Engineering charges

6. General, administrative, and selling costs

7. Profit

The buyer then analyzes these costs (or, if the vendor will not supply a cost breakdown, does a cost buildup, which is quite difficult) and determines areas of disagreement with the vendor's figures. These differences are called negotiation issues, and the purpose of the negotiation session is to resolve these issues in a manner satisfactory to both parties. Success in negotiation depends upon which party is best able to collect, classify, and analyze pertinent data. Some purchasing organizations have full-time price or cost analysts, whose sole job is to provide good data so the buyer can negotiate from a position of strength (knowledge).

Negotiation often is used to determine the price and terms on both capital-equipment purchases and the purchase of major raw materials over an extended time (long-term contract). In both of these situations, the vendor probably will be expending resources over a long future time (perhaps five or ten years) and faces many uncertainties that could cause production costs to accelerate greatly. To protect both the vendor's profit and the buyer's need for assured delivery, the vendor and buyer may need to talk out the various changes in the business environment that might occur and make reasonable provisions for handling each. Often the final, negotiated purchase contract will provide for a price escalation-deescalation clause as a protection for both parties.

Preparation of the Purchase Agreement

Actual preparation of the purchase order (PO) is the least important part of the purchase process; after decisions have been made on specifications, delivery dates, quantity, price, and conditions, PO preparation is largely a clerical process. In many firms, it is done by a computer *after* the pertinent information has been entered into the purchase data base. Because the PO has the status of a legal agreement, it requires a record of an offer (either a PO or a vendor quote) and the corresponding acceptance (a signed vendor acknowledgment copy responding to the PO or a PO accepting the vendor's offer). However, since it is unlikely that legal action to force performance would be taken, except in the case of very large dollar amounts, some firms have eliminated the use of the acknowledgment copy on all but large-dollar POs ($5,000 or over) to cut down on paperwork costs.

To reduce administrative costs in PO preparation, many variations can be used. Two examples are blanket orders and blank-check POs. Some firms write a PO with a vendor to cover the entire quantity of a given item for the next year. Terms and conditions are determined at that time. Since it is assured business, the vendor may be willing to give an attractive price and terms. Then, whenever the firm needs additional quantities, it simply sends a "delivery release" to the vendor, quoting the particular blanket-order agreement. The release may even be issued by someone other than purchasing, such as inventory control or the user.

With a blank-check PO, the vendor is sent a check along with the PO. When the merchandise is shipped, the vendor enters the amount due on the check and cashes it. This system has certain built-in safeguards: The check can be deposited only to the vendor's account; it must be presented for deposit within 60 days; and the check clearly is marked "Not good for an amount over $1,000." The risk to the buyer is small under these restrictions, and it reduces paperwork on those low-dollar purchases, which typically account for about 90 percent of the paperwork involved in purchasing. Also, it has other major advantages: It saves postage; the buyer can negotiate a larger cash discount in return for instant payment; and it requires complete shipment (no back orders allowed), which reduces the number of receiving reports, inventory entries, and payments. Since the vendor is receiving immediate payment for items shipped, there is a real incentive to ship the order complete.

Follow-up and Expediting

After a PO has been issued to a vendor, the buyer may wish to follow up or expedite the order. When the order is issued, an appropriate follow-up date is indicated. In some firms, purchasing has full-time follow-up and expediting personnel.

Follow-up is the routine tracking of an order to assure that the vendor will be able to meet delivery promises. If problems of quality or delivery develop, the buyer needs to know this as soon as possible so that appropriate action can be taken. Follow-up requiring frequent inquiries to the vendor on progress and possibly a visit to the vendor's facility will be done only on large-dollar or long lead-time buys.

Expediting is the application of pressure to get the vendor either to meet an original delivery promise or to deliver ahead of schedule. It may involve the threat of order cancellation or withdrawal of future business if the vendor cannot meet the agreement. Expediting should be necessary on only a small percentage of the POs issued; if the buyer has done a good job of analyzing vendor capabilities, only reliable vendors who will perform according to the purchase agreement will be selected. And if the firm has done an adequate job of planning its material requirements, it should not need to ask a vendor to move up the delivery date except in unusual situations. Of course, in times of scarcity, the expediting activity assumes greater importance. The use of MRP systems (see chapter 4) allows purchasing to make more timely decisions on where and when expediting is needed and whether vendor deliveries should be stretched out.

Receipt and Inspection

When goods arrive, a check (normally a simple count) must be made to verify that the quantity received is as ordered. In addition, if it is a production raw material or an item for which precise specifications have been supplied to the vendor, verification of the quality of the goods delivered must be made. Chapter 7 discusses the importance of incoming quality levels and the methods for verification. International competition and the use of concepts such as just-in-time manufacturing systems have intensified the need to ensure that purchased materials meet the requisitioner's quality and quantity specifications. In the medium- to large-size organization, there typically are separate receiving and incoming inspection departments. In the smaller organization, the purchasing department may handle receipt and inspection, although this compromises the checks and balances needed for adequate control.

Invoice Clearance and Payment

The vendor must receive payment for the delivery of satisfactory items. If cash discounts are available–for example, 2 percent cash discount if payment is made within 10 days, net amount due in 30 days–the paperwork flow must be handled expeditiously. A 2 percent/10, net 30 cash discount term amounts to a real annual interest rate of approximately 36 percent.

Payment will be made by accounts payable. Purchasing could handle the invoice clearance, but the clerical nature of this task dictates that it be done in accounts payable, provided it has the pertinent data for the task. Basically, the purchase order, the receiving report (showing quantities delivered), the incoming inspection report (verifying quality), and the vendor invoice are compared. If all documents agree or are not out of agreement by more than a set amount, such as either 10 dollars or 5 percent of PO value, the vendor is paid. If the documents do not agree, then the whole transaction goes back to the buyer for resolution.

Some companies with a computerized data system in purchasing use an invoiceless payment system: The PO goes into the computer on release, and the receiving report and incoming inspection data also go into the computer daily. The computer merely cycles through all POs each night; whenever it finds one in which the PO, receiving report, and inspection report all agree, it triggers a check to be written within a set number of days after the material was received. If the documents do not agree, then the whole transaction goes to purchasing. The advantage of this system is that the handling of the invoice is eliminated. This system also makes it more difficult for vendors to escalate prices after they receive the purchase order, for the PO is the action document that determines the price to be paid.

Maintenance of Records

Before the purchase transaction can be filed away and closed, the records of the purchasing department should be updated so they will be timely and accurate for future use. These records can be maintained in either a computerized or a manual data base. Numerous records might be kept for evaluation, review, and control purposes. The following are the four most important.

1. **PO Log.** Purchase orders are registered and controlled by serial number. A look at the log will identify any particular PO and show its status. When the order is closed, the log is updated to show completion.

2. **Vendor file.** Records should be kept on performance and evaluation of capability of those relatively few vendors with whom purchasing does the majority of business. These data permit a vendor-performance evaluation for later decisions.

3. **Commodity file.** A purchase-history file should be maintained, by commodity, on all major purchased commodities. It should indicate purchase date, vendor, quantity, price and terms, and the current order status.

4. **Contract file.** This shows all national contracts, blanket orders, and annual agreements that have been established, and performance under the contracts. For example, if the annual agreement commits the firm to purchase a total quantity over the next twelve months, the firm must know its current status. Also, a central reference point is needed to determine exactly what purchase items are under contract and should not be handled on an individual basis.

Current and Future Developments

Changes in the environment, the competitive marketplace, and technology, coupled with top management's growing awareness of the profit potential of effective purchasing and materials management, are causing fundamental changes in purchasing. Additional changes, some predictable and some not currently identifiable, undoubtedly will occur, providing an exciting challenge to the professionals performing in this area. Nine of these developments are highlighted here.

Single Sourcing

Many items are available from several reliable sources; when a conscious decision is made to place *all* the requirement with only one vendor, this is called single sourcing. This gives the buyer the advantage of volume leverage, often resulting in a substantially lower ultimate purchase price. The potential problem is the risk of nondelivery caused by problems in the single-source supplier's plant or with the transportation system. For single sourcing to be effective, the buyer must do an extremely thorough job of analyzing the vendor's management and capabilities and of negotiating a complete contractual agreement, in which all contingencies are anticipated. Japanese industry has used this approach for years; indeed, it is a key element in the just-in-time production system (see chapters 4 and 6). U.S. manufacturers are incorporating single sourcing into their new systems for automobile production. For example, on the production of one of the new model cars, one exhaust-system manufacturer has been selected as a single source; truckload shipments of mufflers must arrive at the auto-assembly plant at regular intervals throughout each work shift.

Supplier Partnering/Strategic Alliances

Beginning in the mid-1980s, some firms began looking at developing a partnership with one, or a very-limited number, of their key suppliers. A partnership is a long-term relationship which has substantial benefits to both parties, but a degree of independence for each. If the buying firm has an investment interest in the supplier firm, that often is referred to as a strategic alliance. In a supplier partnership, the operations of the buying and supplying firms almost merge. Much planning is required to successfully partner, which is why a given firm probably will have only a handful of such agreements. Some of the characteristics of a successful partnership are: a high degree of mutual trust; shared goals and vision; top management "buy in"; sharing of technical and market information; elimination of buyer inspection; mutual user-friendly systems; open communication; risk and profit sharing; and a commitment to continuous improvement.

Public Purchasing

Government purchases of goods and services are big business, deserving a major amount of attention by government administrators. The federal government buys about $380 billion worth of goods and services annually (about 80 percent of which is for national defense); state and local government purchases are over $535 billion each year. The total from all government sources is more than $900 billion annually. Government purchases were only $538 billion in 1980; thus, they have increased more than 70 percent during the 1980s.

An overall reduction of 10 percent in prices paid would result in annual savings for taxpayers of some $90 billion. Starting in 1978 in California with the passage of Proposition 13, often referred to as "the taxpayers' revolt," and followed by the 1983 recommendation of the President's Private Sector Survey on Cost Control task force (called the Grace Commission), much attention has been focused on improving the purchasing practices of governmental units. These taxpayer studies and actions underscore two points: Government buying does not differ basically from private-sector purchasing, and governmental units should follow the principles and practices of efficient purchasing outlined in this chapter in order to obtain maximum value for each public dollar spent.

Purchasing Transportation Services

The total transportation cost in the United States for movement of goods is estimated at nearly 7 percent of gross national product, or over $270 billion per year. A large share of that amount (perhaps half, or $135 billion) is payment for moving goods from a vendor's facility to the point where the buyer needs them. Depending on the type of goods, transportation may account for as much as 40 percent of the total cost of an item, particularly if it is of low value and bulky, such as construction materials. Before the 1980s, decisions about the mode of transport (air, rail, water, pipeline, or truck), routing, and tariff (price) were primarily clerical. In the past ten years, however, Congress has deregulated almost all modes of transportation, and the effects of deregulation have made decisions on carrier selection and pricing far more complex and important today.

The 1977 Air Cargo Act deregulated air cargo; the 1978 Airline Deregulation Act began the deregulation of passenger air transportation, permitting the entry of new airlines, routes, and ticket-price competition. The 1980 Motor Carrier Act relaxed the Interstate Commerce Commission regulation of trucking, allowing easier entry of new firms, new routes and schedules, and flexibility in setting rates. The 1980 Staggers Rail Act gave railroads greater freedom to set rates and to enter into long-term contracts with shippers; piggyback service was completely deregulated. The 1982 Bus Regulatory Reform Act removed all regulation of package express after 1985.

As a result of deregulation, many large organizations have separate transportation departments, often reporting to purchasing or to the materials manager. In the medium-size or smaller organization, where the number of traffic decisions does not warrant a full-time traffic specialist, the buyer or purchasing manager makes traffic decisions. In any event, the buying company is paying for transportation services. The transport decision maker must be able to make value analyses of alternatives, conduct cost and price analyses, negotiate with carriers, consolidate freight and obtain volume discounts, evaluate carrier performance, explore the possibility of using different transport modes, and develop compatible working relationships with selected carriers.

Electronic Data Interchange (EDI)

The use of the microcomputer in purchasing allows the purchasing data base to tie directly into a supplier's data base through the telecommunications system, using a computer modem. This helps both buyer and supplier obtain much more timely and accurate information, permitting paperwork reduction and better purchasing decisions. The cost of such direct data communication has decreased rapidly over the past few years, putting this technology within reach of almost all firms. With such communication links with suppliers, the buyer can quickly obtain price quotes, determine availability of items in a supplier's stock, transmit a PO, obtain follow-up information, provide information about changes in purchase requirements caused by schedule revisions, obtain service information, and send letters and memos. EDI rapidly is becoming the preferred way of doing business. A simple example is the use of facsimile-transmission (FAX) machines to transmit documents (e.g., purchase orders, change orders, and blueprints) over phone lines in a matter of minutes.

Foreign Purchasing

The amount of purchases U.S. firms make from vendors outside North America has grown markedly in the 1980s. In the middle 1980s, U.S. buyers paid over $300 billion to foreign vendors each year. The reasons for specific foreign-sourcing decisions are many and varied and include lower overall costs from foreign sources; more consistent quality; unavailability of items, such as chrome ore, domestically; more predictable delivery schedules; advanced technology; and better technical service. In addition, when a sale of a U.S. made product—for example, an aircraft or a computer—is made in a foreign country, the foreign buyer may demand that the U.S. firm spend a specific percentage (often 50 to 100 percent) of the selling price with suppliers in that country. This is called countertrade, and it has become a common practice for many firms. Variations of countertrade are called barter/swaps, counterpurchase, buyback/compensation, switch trade, and offsets. At least 61 countries, including Canada, Switzerland, the U.K., and Israel, require countertrades. It is estimated that the value of world countertrade is over $150 billion per year, or about 8 percent of total world trade.

The 1991 study titled *Countertrade: Purchasing's Perceptions and Involvement* found that countertrade has been expanding in U.S. international trade over the past five years, both in terms of total dollar amount and percent of sales agreements. East Asia mandates countertrade more often than any other part of the world. However, it was in Western Europe that the value of countertrade obligations between American and foreign firms grew most sharply over the past five years. The study found that those companies which utilize countertrade enjoy increased sales and increased utilization of plant capacity.

As the world grows smaller commercially, the purchasing department is becoming involved in sourcing and pricing with vendors all over the world. This brings new problems and opportunities that require a sophisticated degree of purchasing analysis and professionalism: The location and evaluation of foreign suppliers; extended lead times; expediting; currency fluctuations; payment methods; tariffs and duties; and legal, linguistic, and cultural differences are all concerns of the purchasing professional engaged in foreign transactions.

Purchase of Services

As firms move to reduce the size of their internal staffs, it becomes necessary to buy many services formerly performed in-house from outside service suppliers. Examples of services often bought outside are in areas such as advertising, architecture, auditing, cafeteria, computer programming, customs brokerage, household moves, insurance, interior decorating, janitorial, landscaping, legal, maintenance, payroll, personnel travel, protection and security, research, telephone, temporary help, transport, and waste removal.

While the techniques of service purchasing are very similar to those used in goods purchasing, the difficulties in evaluating vendor capabilities are greater (e.g., How do you evaluate in advance the capabilities of a law firm?). Also, since services cannot be inventoried, the importance of making good purchasing decisions is heightened. Anyone who has sat through a boring conference speech can attest to that! Modern purchasing departments are becoming more involved in service purchasing and are developing the analytical techniques needed to improve their decision making.

Purchasing Performance Benchmarking

One of the vexing problems faced by purchasing professionals is how to evaluate performance. Probably the best way is to compare purchasing performance of one company against that of peer companies. Starting in 1989, the Center for Advanced Purchasing Studies began collecting data from firms to develop purchasing benchmarks, standards which can be used in measuring quality or value.

The data are collected and published for over 20 different industries, such as Petroleum, Steel, Aerospace, Chemical, Banking, Food Manufacture, and Pharmaceutical. Some of the specific benchmarks, or measures, available for each industry are: Purchase $ as a Percent of Sales $; Purchasing Head Count as Percent of Total Company Head

Count; Cost to Spend a $; $ of Purchases Per Purchasing Employee; $ of Purchases Per Professional in Purchasing; Number of Active Suppliers per Purchasing Professional; Cost to Operate the Purchasing Department Per Active Supplier; Percent Change in Number of Active Suppliers; Percent of Purchase $ Spent with Minority-Owned Suppliers; Percent of $ Processed through Electronic Data Interchange (EDI); and Percent of Total Services Purchases Handled by the Purchasing Department.

The benchmarks of purchasing performance enable comparison of a specific purchasing department with a standard that is the composite of a large group of purchasing departments in that industry. Comparisons also can be made with other industries. In addition, on any one benchmark, the data are available to identify the best performer and the worst performer (but not by company name).

Thus, benchmarking permits an answer to the question, "How are we doing, compared to other firms?" by providing averages and ranges for measures of purchasing performance. This should lead a company toward those changes needed for developing industry-best practices and, in turn, superior performance.

Purchasing/Materials Management Strategy

Over the past 80 years, the purchasing function has evolved from a clerical activity to one that uses complex processes to provide information for effective decision making by professional purchasing managers who perform the function in an asset-management context. This change has stimulated the development of strategies to maximize the effectiveness of purchasing/materials management and, thus, overall organizational effectiveness. A strategy looks at the long term future (often from five to twenty years) rather than simply reacting to the current situation and requirements.

The five major categories of purchasing strategies are (1) assurance of supply, to meet future supply needs effectively and economically; (2) supply support, to maximize the likelihood that the considerable knowledge and capabilities of suppliers are made available to the buying organization; (3) environmental change, to anticipate and recognize shifts in the total environment (economic, organizational, people, legal, governmental, and systems) so they can be turned to the long-term advantage of the buying organization; (4) cost reduction, to reduce the total cost of acquisition and use–life cycle cost; and (5) competitive edge, to exploit market opportunities and organizational strengths. Among the more promising strategic opportunities are developing new supply sources (supplier development); supplier partnering; foreign sourcing;

single sourcing; promoting vertical integration by buying out a supplier; buyer-supplier data sharing; using the futures market (hedging); systems contracting; risk sharing with suppliers on new products or projects; make/buy; and supplier quality assurance or certification programs. Integrating some of these substrategies into a viable, overall purchasing strategy is a difficult task but one that is imperative for the survival of many of our current organizations into the twenty-first century.

Key Concepts

Material/sales ratio	**ABC analysis**
Profit-leverage effect	**Supplier evaluation**
Return-on-assets effect	**Negotiation**
Centralized purchasing	**Single sourcing**
Materials management	**Services purchasing**
Prerogatives of purchasing	**Purchasing/materials management strategy**
Partnering	**Electronic Data Interchange (EDI)**
Countertrade	**Purchasing Performance Benchmarking**

References

Dobler, Donald W., Burt, David N., and Lee, Lamar, Jr. *Purchasing and Materials Management.* 5th ed. New York: McGraw-Hill, 1990.

Fearon, Harold E. *Purchasing Organizational Relationships.* Tempe, AZ: Center for Advanced Purchasing Studies/National Association of Purchasing Management, 1988.

Forker, Laura B. *Countertrade: Purchasing's Perceptions and Involvement.* Tempe, AZ: Center for Advanced Purchasing Studies/National Association of Purchasing Management, 1991.

Heinritz, Stuart, Farrell, Paul V., Giunipero, Larry C., and Kolchin, Michael G. *Purchasing: Principles and Applications.* 8th ed. Englewood Cliffs, N.J.: Prentice-Hall, 1991.

Leenders, Michiel R., and Blenkhorn, David L. *Reverse Marketing*. New York: The Free Press, 1988.

Leenders, Michiel R., Fearon, Harold E., and England, Wilbur B. *Purchasing and Materials Management*. 9th ed. Homewood, IL: Richard D. Irwin, 1989.

Purchasing Performance Benchmarks for the U.S. Chemical Industry. Tempe, AZ: Center for Advanced Purchasing Studies, 1990.

Discussion Questions

1. "The purchasing function is not profit making but, rather, profit taking, since its job is to spend company funds." Is this statement correct or incorrect? Explain.

2. What is the overall price objective of purchasing?

3. "The most important part of the complete purchasing procedure is the writing of the PO, for this determines the agreement between seller and buyer." Do you agree or disagree with this statement? Explain.

4. What are the various means of price determination? Give an example of an item you would buy using each method.

5. Why have most organizations centralized the purchasing function?

6. Which of the eight objectives of purchasing is most important? Why?

7. Should an organization expend resources on strategic materials planning? Under what conditions?

8. Will the purchasing function become more or less centralized over the next five years?

9. Is foreign purchasing a viable alternative for most U.S. firms? What are the problems of foreign purchasing, and how can they be handled?

10. What does the most-recent National Association of Purchasing Management (NAPM) "Report on Business" (ROB) say about the U.S. economy? (Look in *The Wall Street Journal* or the *New York Times* the 1st or 2nd business day of the month).

11. If a supplier bills the buying company with terms of 1/10, n/30, should the buying company take the cash discount? Under what conditions? When should payment be made?

Problems

1. A firm has $500,000 in sales with a before-tax profit margin of 7%. Purchases amount to 60% of the sales dollar.

   A. If overall purchase cost could be reduced by 10%, how much additional before-tax profit would be generated?

   B. What increase in sales would be necessary to generate the same amount of profit?

2. Suppose the firm described above had a profit margin of 4%. How would this change the answers to A and B? If the firm had a profit margin of 7% but purchases were 40% of sales, how would the answers to A and B change?

3. A manufacturing company has $1,500,000 in gross sales, purchase costs amount to 55% of sales, and the profit margin is 8%. Next year, the firm intends to increase its sales by 20% and, at the same time, reduce its overall purchase costs by 5% from what they would have been without the cost reduction effort.

   A. How much additional profit will be generated next year?

   B. What part of the profit increase is due to increased sales and how much is due to the increased effectiveness of purchasing?

4. An organization with $4,000,000 in sales is facing a declining market and expects to lose 5% of its sales next year. Purchased materials amount to 40% of their sales dollar and their profit margin has been 6%. If they are to make the same amount of total before-tax profit next year, how much will purchasing have to reduce total purchase costs from what they would have been? What percent improvement in purchasing effort does that represent?

5. A firm has sales of $3 million and total assets of $1 million of which 30% is in inventory. Its profit margin is 5% and purchases account for half of sales value.

   A. Using the framework of figure 5-1, calculate the return on assets (ROA).

   B. If purchasing can reduce overall purchase costs by 8%, what effect will this have on the ROA?

6. Consider the following information about a firm:

Sales	$6,000,000
Inventory	$1,500,000
Other Assets	$2,500,000
Total Costs	$5,600,000

A. If purchases account for 35% of sales, what is the ROA for this firm?

B. If purchasing can reduce overall costs by 10%, what is the effect on ROA?

C. Instead of trying to reduce total purchase costs, suppose the firm puts the same effort into achieving a 15% sales increase. Assume that inventory would also increase by 15% but other assets would remain the same, as would the profit margin. What is the effect of their sales increase effort on the ROA?

7. A company is spending $1,000,000 per year purchasing 150 different items that it has classified into the ABC system based on total value. Information on ten of the items is given below. For each item, tell whether it is likely to be in the A, B, or C category.

ITEM	ANNUAL USAGE	UNIT COST
P-331	100,000	$ 1.05
P-335	250,000	.03
P-432	5,000	.10
P-440	10,000	16.00
P-475	800	.50
P-502	10,000	1.00
P-581	150,000	.10
P-582	18,000	.35
P-585	100,000	.01
P-587	9,000	.09

CHAPTER
6

Inventory Management

Every organization must manage inventories of some kind. These inventories may be raw materials, purchased parts, partly completed products (work-in-process), finished products, or simply office supplies. The importance of each type of inventory, and the management attention it deserves, depends on the industry, firm, or process. For example, raw material (crude oil) is critical to the oil refiner; partly completed components and purchased parts are important inventories for an assembler of finished products. Rapid turnover of finished goods is a cornerstone to the successful retailer and having office supplies available when needed is important to the office manager. No one can ignore the challenges of inventory management.

Dramatic changes in inventory management have taken place in the recent past. In the 1970s and 1980s, the development and maturing of MRP, MRP II, and JIT approaches emphasized the reduction of inventory levels through a systems approach to shorter set-up times, better relationships with suppliers, more flexible production processes, and the elimination of inefficiencies that were previously hidden by excessive levels of stock. Firms found that streamlining their operations allowed them to save the costs from reduced inventories without losing competitive advantage from quick delivery and rapid response to changes in demand.

However, the underlying functions of inventory and the costs associated with them are still relevant in modern operations systems, so our discussion will begin with a review of traditional inventory concepts.

The Functions of Inventories

Physical stocks of material and products can provide: (1) decoupling of operations, (2) buffering from the effects of unpredictable events, (3) stable production plans by anticipating peaks in demand, and (4) manufacturing economies through lot sizing.

Decoupling Stocks

Decoupling means to separate parts of the operation by inventories of partially completed units that act as "shock absorbers" for irregularities in the process. For example, consider a furniture manufacturer simplified into three departments: wood parts fabrication, assembly, and finish application. Without decoupling inventories between stages, any problem at one stage will shut down the entire operation leaving workers and equipment idle until the problem is solved. If small stocks of material are placed between departments, then the fabrication department can schedule and work on jobs in the appropriate sequence and lot sizes that are most efficient without having to coordinate exactly with the assembly department schedule. Similarly, the assembly department has some flexibility; it could operate for one day with one worker absent without disrupting the operations that precede or follow.

If no decoupling inventories are established, the operation is likely to be too rigid and will suffer from the shocks of any irregularity or deviation. On the other hand, if decoupling is carried to an extreme by placing large inventories between each work station, the inventory cost will be great, cycle times will be extended, and, as we will see in a later discussion of JIT systems, the decoupling inventories will tend to hide many inefficiencies from detection and correction.

Buffer Stocks

Buffer or safety stocks are maintained as a hedge against many unpredictable events that can disrupt operations. For example, suppliers can be late delivering material or the material may be defective when it arrives. Equipment can breakdown at the most inconvenient time, employees can be absent and intermediate processes may produce defective parts. Customers may change their minds at the last minute and increase the size of the order. For these and many other reasons, buffer or safety stocks are held to balance the costs of being out of stock with the costs of carrying the additional inventory.

An alternative to buffer stocks is the elimination of the disrupting element. For example, Just-In-Time practices would promote selecting and developing highly reliable suppliers and thus reduce the need for significant raw material buffers. Efforts to create more flexible production systems allows quicker changeovers and efficient operations even when one material or part is out of stock temporarily. And more accurate forecasting techniques will cause fewer problems in anticipating customer demand.

While organizations should work to reduce causes of these disruptions, some natural variations will always be present. Properly placed buffers will effectively reduce the damage done by these deviations.

Anticipatory Stocks

Stable production levels can be maintained even when the market demand is highly seasonal by building anticipatory stocks during the low demand season for sale in times of peak demand. Manufacturing need not match its production rate to the widely fluctuating demand pattern. A steady production rate, as noted in chapter 4, supports stable employment and better utilization of facilities.

In the case of make-to-order products and services, anticipatory stocks are generally not possible. The need for anticipatory stocks can be reduced by smoothing demand with marketing techniques such as off-season promotions and counter-seasonal products or services. Alternatively, designing the organization for flexible output rates may reduce the negative aspects of highly variable production.

Cycle Stocks

Many products have large fixed cost components relative to the variable costs per unit produced or served. Consider the process of spray painting wooden furniture in different colors. Every time we change colors we have to clean the spray gun nozzle and feed system. If several pieces of the same color were painted before changing to another color, a significant time savings would occur and less wasted paint and cleaning solvents would go down the drain. This logic is the basis for the traditional economic lot size (ELS). More units produced per clean-up (or setup) results in an increase of inventory beyond immediate needs, but at the same time it spreads the fixed costs over more units.

Similarly, allocating the fixed costs per order over the number of units of raw material purchased is the basis for the economic order quantity (EOQ). Finding the appropriate balance of these costs is the subject of the lot sizing sections later in this chapter.

The resulting inventories are called cycle stocks because of the way on-hand inventory goes up and then gradually goes down as users consume the inventory. This cycle repeats over and over.

Economies of scale is another reason to have cycle stocks. Consider a batch blending process such as paint manufacturing. The technology appropriate for small batches, say 100 gallons, is not likely to be cost competitive with equipment that can produce batches of 5000 gallons. The larger batch may represent two months of sales and hence a significant cycle stock cost, but it might be justified by the manufacturing economies of a lower production cost per unit.

Economics of Inventory Management

The management of inventory focuses on the appropriate achievement of decoupling, buffering, production smoothing, and manufacturing economies by considering many strategic factors and the analysis of costs incurred in obtaining and carrying inventories. We will identify these costs before addressing management decisions that set the levels of inventories.

Ordering Costs

The purchasing process was developed in detail in chapter 5. Many of the necessary steps in the purchasing cycle incur costs regardless of the size of the ultimate order. For example, recognizing a need for replenishment will cost about the same whether we purchase one carton of file folders or several, one CAD system or several, or one load of steel or several. Similar fixed costs can be associated with the preparation of a purchase order, follow-up tasks, receiving paperwork, invoicing, processing a return, and expediting a late order.

Ordering costs are associated with the number of orders placed, not the number of units purchased. For example, if our annual demand is for twelve tons of steel, we may place one order for twelve tons and incur the order cost once per year. On the other hand, we might order one-half ton every two weeks and incur an order cost 24 times per year. If we order enough to meet our needs for a long time, then our order processing efforts will be reduced, but our cycle stocks will be high.

Whether or not fewer orders translate into actual cost savings depends on the use of the saved time. In the short run, fewer orders may only create idle time among the buyers in the purchasing department. However, in the longer run, larger, less frequent orders may lead to more productive use of purchasing resources.

Setup Cost

Every time a manufacturer shifts from producing one product to another, certain changeover costs occur. These may include the people and materials needed to change tooling and adjust equipment, removing leftover material from the previous production run, modifying the work stations, assigning new work crews, testing the new setup to assure that it performs properly, and scrap losses associated with start-up. These are costs that a traditional cost accounting system can detect. Like the order costs, these costs vary with the number of setups made, but not with the number of units produced after the setup has been done.

A less obvious cost is the *lost production capacity* represented by the time spent in setup. This loss of productive time may represent lost sales if the work center is a bottleneck operation and market demand exceeds our capacity to produce. A bottleneck represents the weak (slow) link in a series of operations leading to a completed product. Any lost time due to setups, breakdowns, or working on the wrong jobs in a bottleneck operation can be much more costly than the visible, traceable accounting costs would imply.

Both the direct and indirect setup costs can be reduced when we place a high priority on improvements in this area and study setups using work methods analysis. Setup time reduction is a key element in Just-In-Time (JIT) manufacturing strategies discussed in more depth later in this chapter.

Inventory Carrying Costs

There are two categories of carrying costs: (1) those that are proportional to the value of the inventory and (2) those that are proportional to the physical characteristics of the inventory. In either case, the costs of carrying inventory vary with the amount stocked.

Costs that vary with the dollar value in inventory are

1. Cost of capital tied up in stocks

2. Insurance premiums on inventories

3. Property taxes on inventories

4. Obsolescence, deterioration, and damage to stocks

5. Pilferage

Carrying costs that are proportional to the physical characteristics of the commodity are

1. Storage space

·2. Storage labor

These costs will increase as the amount stocked increases if space costs actually change with the storage required and if handling actually increases. These relationships are not always clear cut. For example, if excess warehouse space is available, then moderate increases in inventory will occupy only space that has little or no alternative use. In this case, the storage-space costs do not increase. If the space is rented on the basis of space actually used, however, then a storage-space cost is relevant. Similarly, if larger inventories lead to more rehandling and more time spent performing physical inventories, then the additional labor costs of carrying inventory are relevant.

Managing the Economic Trade-offs

To minimize inventory costs, it is necessary to find the order quantity or production run that spreads the ordering or setup costs over as many units as possible without incurring excessive carrying costs. The larger the order quantity, the lower the ordering cost per unit. The larger order quantity, however, leads to higher average and peak inventories. The higher average inventory results in high costs due to the dollar value in stock. The peak inventories can be particularly significant (and costly) if storage space is limited.

Finding the best balance between ordering and carrying costs requires a great deal of data collection. The data then can be analyzed and appropriate decisions made. Because data collection and analysis can be expensive, the firm should attempt to reduce the size of that task. One approach is to direct attention to those inventory items that have the most significant value in dollars and are, therefore, the most important inventory items.

The next several sections consider the variety of techniques used to determine when and how much to order under different operating conditions. We consider the conditions of constant demand, the single-period order-quantity problem, the discrete batch pattern associated with materials-requirements planning, and the repetitive manufacturing environment associated with just-in-time. We begin with the economic order quantity approach applied to the relatively constant demand we see for finished goods, such as bath soap in a retail outlet.

Economic Order Quantity Model

The economic order quantity (EOQ) model determines the number of units to purchase that will minimize the combined costs of ordering and carrying the inventory. To use the EOQ model, certain assumptions must be met.

1. The annual usage of the item is known and constant, or at least very close to constant, over the entire period.

2. Material, when received, comes in all at once.

3. The order-cost factor includes all those relevant costs incurred when an order is placed, and these costs are not influenced by the size of the order.

4. The carrying-cost factor includes all the relevant costs that vary proportional to the size of the order.

5. No quantity discounts are considered.

The first two assumptions are reflected in figure 6-1. The representation of line AB as a straight line is consistent with constant usage. The vertical line BC shows that replenishment of stock is received in one shipment and enters stock immediately upon receipt. Minor deviations from these assumptions, as illustrated by lines CD and DE, do not seriously affect the model. Line FG shows the effect of delayed resupply. The result would be negative inventory (a stock-out) if reserves (safety stock) were not available. Line HI illustrates the consequences of above-average usage during the resupply cycle. These issues are discussed in more detail later in this chapter.

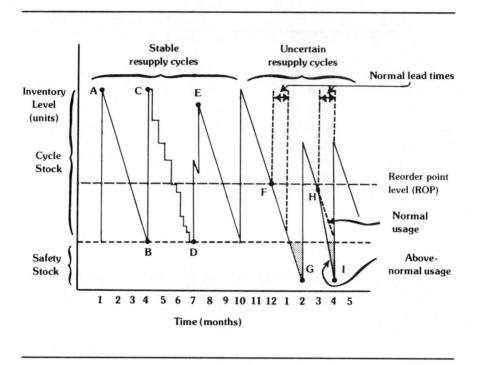

Figure 6-1. Inventory Levels Over Time

The Total Inventory cost Equation

The basic inventory-cost equation combines the ordering or setup costs for a year (or some other time period) with the carrying costs based on the average inventory level. To be complete, purchase cost also is included.

The number of orders per year is merely the annual demand divided by the number of units in each order. The result is the number of times the ordering costs are incurred. The ordering cost (S) is a constant and does not vary with order quantity (Q), thus incorporating assumption 3. The order quantity (Q) represents the cycle stock. If a zero safety stock is assumed, inventory will cycle from 0 units to Q units and back to 0 units. The assumption of uniform usage results in an average inventory of Q/2 units. This is the average inventory over the entire year, which is multiplied by the carrying cost per unit (IC) to get the annual carrying cost. As Q increases, the carrying cost increases, thus assumption 4 is incorporated into the following equation:

Total Cost = Ordering Costs + Carrying Costs + Purchase Cost

$$TC = \left(\frac{D}{Q}\right) S + IC \left(\frac{Q}{2}\right) + CD$$

where TC = total cost

D = annual demand (units) $\frac{D}{Q}$ = number of orders per year

S = ordering or setup cost

Q = order quantity (units)   IC = carrying cost per unit per year

I = carrying cost as a % of unit cost

C = item unit cost (purchase price) $\frac{Q}{2}$ = average inventory

EOQ Formula

Simple calculus is used to find the value of Q, which will minimize the total-cost equation. The resulting formula is:

$$EOQ = \sqrt{\frac{2DS}{IC}}$$

The EOQ quantity represents the optimum order size when the assumptions of the model are reasonably well met. One assumption that often is not met is that price is not affected by the order size. Another violation of the assumptions occurs when an order is received over a significant period of time. This situation will be considered later in this chapter in the discussion of economic lot sizes. The price issue is considered next.

EOQ with Discounts

Price discounts affect two components of the total-cost equation, the carrying cost and the purchase cost. Both costs are functions of the price. Price discounts lead to a family of cost curves, one curve for each price. Each curve applies to the range of order sizes for which the associated price is relevant. Figure 6-2 shows a contrast between the total-cost curve without discounts and the family of curves when there are three prices, based on two pricebreak points.

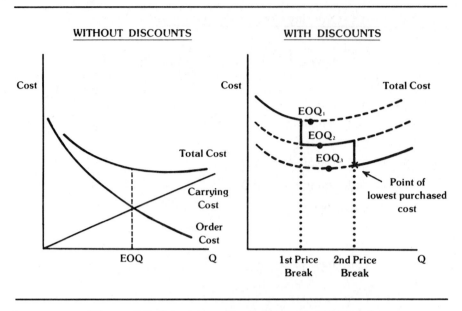

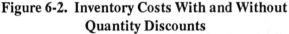

**Figure 6-2. Inventory Costs With and Without
Quantity Discounts**

An iterative process is required to find the optimum order quantity
when quantity discounts are available.

1. Compute the EOQ using the best price. If the result is large enough
    to obtain the best price, then this is the optimum, and the computa-
    tion stops. If this EOQ falls below the relevant price break, go to the
    next step.

2. Compute the EOQ using the next best price. Check the result to see
    if it falls in the relevant range. If EOQ is below the relevant price
    break, redo this step at the next lower price.

3. Once an EOQ has been found that is consistent with the price
    obtainable at the order quantity, the final step can be taken. This
    step is required to determine if an increase to one of the break points
    offers enough savings to offset the increased carrying costs.
    Therefore, it is necessary to compute the total cost at the valid EOQ
    point and at the price breaks above the EOQ point. The decision is
    made to order the quantity with the lowest total cost. Figure 6-2
    shows that EOQ(2) is in the relevant range but that the total cost at
    the second price break is lower and, therefore, is the optimum order
    quantity.

Economic Lot-Size (ELS) Formula

In the case of parts manufactured within the firm, the assumption of immediate, one-shipment replenishment often is unrealistic. The replenishment actually occurs over the period of the production run, which may be days or weeks. Figure 6-3 shows the basic pattern followed by the level of inventory on hand.

When the entire lot size is not delivered instantaneously, the peak inventory is lower. Specifically, it is lowered by the amount used during the time required to produce the lot. This period is equal to the lot size (100 units) divided by the production rate (50 units per week), or two weeks in this example. In figure 6-3, the usage during the production period is 10 units per week, or 20 units in total. Therefore, instead of 100 units (the lot size), the peak inventory is only 80 units. The average inventory carried is 40 units. Incorporating these changes into the total-cost equations and developing the optimum lot size (as done for EOQ) gives

$$TC = \frac{DS}{Q} + IC\left(1 - \frac{d}{p}\right)\frac{Q}{2}$$

$$ELS = \sqrt{\frac{2DS}{IC\left(1 - \frac{d}{p}\right)}}$$

where d = usage rate (units per time period)
     p = production rate (units per time period)
    D = annual demand
    S = setup costs
   IC = carrying cost per unit per year
   Q = lot size
ELS = economic lot size

With the exception of the replenishment modification, all the assumptions of the EOQ formula still apply.

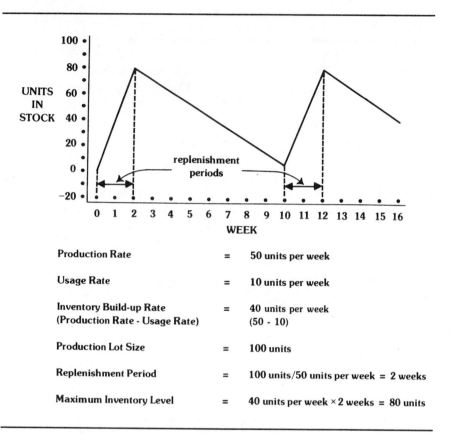

Production Rate	=	50 units per week
Usage Rate	=	10 units per week
Inventory Build-up Rate (Production Rate - Usage Rate)	=	40 units per week (50 - 10)
Production Lot Size	=	100 units
Replenishment Period	=	100 units/50 units per week = 2 weeks
Maximum Inventory Level	=	40 units per week × 2 weeks = 80 units

Figure 6-3. Inventory Levels with Replenishment Spread over Time

Periodic Review Model

It is sometimes more convenient to check inventory levels at regular intervals and order those items expected to run out before the next review is scheduled. By checking all inventory items or a class (for example, those items supplied by one vendor) at one time, the firm can combine all orders to a vendor and consolidate freight loads. Moreover, this approach does not require a perpetual inventory system–that is, one that keeps track of the inventory levels at all times. The other side of the coin reveals that more safety stock is required, and, if care is not taken, unbalanced work loads can be placed on inventory and purchasing personnel. Also, the review interval should reflect the economic order quantity. The desired interval for different items will vary, and this is in conflict with the consolidation advantages.

Assuming a review period of a month, the following procedure would apply:

1. Take a physical count of the items to be reviewed.

2. If the inventory balance of an item is less than a specified level, for example, (s) units, then order enough to raise the level to (S) units. Small (s) would be based on the demand over the review interval plus the normal lead time and the desired safety stock. Large (S) is the upper limit needed to cover the period between the current order and the next desired order review. If enough is on hand or on order, then do not place an order.

This approach results in unequal order quantities and requires more safety stock to obtain the same service level that would be needed if the EOQ model were used. However, simpler record keeping and consolidation advantages may make it desirable, particularly for class-C inventory items.

Sensitivity of EOQ and ELS

How accurate must the cost estimates and demand forecasts be? Figure 6-2 shows that the total-cost curve is quite flat in the area of the EOQ. This suggests that moderate departures from the EOQ will not be very costly. This observation is significant, considering how expensive it would be to develop extremely accurate estimates of all relevant costs. The insensitivity of the formulas permits the valid grouping of stock items and estimating the costs for groups as a whole. This approach, along with the ABC classification, can reduce substantially the cost of determining EOQ and ELS.

Safety Stocks and Uncertainty

If all the estimates and assumptions were realized in practice, then efficient inventory management would be relatively easy. But demand rarely is uniform and completely predictable, and stocks are not always replenished on time. The specific function of safety stocks is to reduce the risk of stock-outs due to unexpected demand, late resupply, or both. To set the level of safety stock, we must consider supply lead times, reorder points, and desired service levels.

Lead Times

Lead time refers to the time between the recognition of a need for and the receipt of the desired material. The purchasing lead time could consist of the requisition review time, the vendor-selection process, order preparation, mail-transit time, supplier-order processing time, supplier-setup and manufacturing time, shipment time, receiving time, and the time to make the item available from stock. If the time to perform some or all of these elements varies, then some additional stock will be needed. This situation is illustrated in figure 6-1 by line FG. The order placed in month 12, when the inventory was at level F, was expected to arrive in month 1. The order was a month late, arriving in month 2. Had there not been any safety stock, the organization would have run out of material when the inventory level crossed the dashed line representing the amount of safety stock.

Reorder Points

The inventory level that triggers the resupply process is called the reorder point. If everything were certain, then the reorder point would equal the normal usage during the normal lead time. But because of uncertainties in both usage and lead time, the reorder point (ROP) is equal to the safety stock (S) plus the normal demand during normal lead time (DNLT).

$$ROP = S + DNLT$$

In figure 6-1, the ROP illustrates a reorder point based on a safety stock of, say, 129 units and an average demand over normal lead time of 237 units, for example, or an ROP of 366 units. This means that whenever the inventory level gets down to 366, an order for the economic order quantity should be placed. On the average, the order will be received just as the inventory reaches 129 units, the safety stock.

Service Level

The inventory manager who is willing to have five stock-outs every 100 order cycles is expressing a 95% service level. Arriving at such a service-level policy requires judging the cost of a stockout.

The cost of a stock-out is difficult to define. Will the stock-out result in a lost sale or, worse, a customer lost forever? What is the cost of customer ill will? What are the costs of rescheduling production due to a stock-out? Clearly there is a heavy reliance on judgment in arriving at a service-level policy.

In some instances, such as supplies in a hospital operating room, service levels are set as close to 100% as possible. Other cases, however, might tolerate a very low service level (grape soda in the soft drink machine, for example might be set at 50%). Firms facing highly variable or unpredictable demand, inflexible production processes, and high costs per stock-out are forced to carry large safety stocks. To the extent that these factors can be changed, safety stocks can be lowered, but seldom eliminated completely.

With probability analysis, the amount of safety stock can be determined so that stock-outs are expected to be in a tolerable range. The use of past data on demand variations and delivery times can be helpful in estimating the safety-stock needed to achieve a given service-level.

One-Time Order Quantities

In cases in which items quickly become obsolete, the need will not remain long enough to require a reordering strategy. Unlike the previous models, this situation requires determining the best size of a single order. Imagine the problem faced by the newspaper kiosk owner; the apparel buyer estimating the order size of a seasonal, high-fashion item; or the grocery-store produce buyer. Each of these people must estimate the market and buy to cover a period of time; for the newspaper carrier, it is the day's demand; for the apparel buyer, the season's demand; and for the produce buyer, the week's demand. The trade-off they face is between not ordering enough, thus losing sales, and ordering too much and having to throw the excess away or sell it at distress prices.

These situations lend themselves to classical marginal analysis. If the marginal profit (MP) of adding one more unit to the order is greater than the marginal loss (ML), then the order should be increased. The same logic applies in the uncertain case when one increases the order by one if the expected MP exceeds the expected ML. If P is the probability of selling the next unit, then the probability of not selling the next unit is 1-P. Therefore, the decision to add one to the order depends on whether or not

$$P(MP) \geq = (1-P)(ML)$$

which simplifies to:

$$P \geq = \frac{(ML)}{(MP + ML)}$$

If one knows what the profit is when a sale is made and what the loss is if the sale is not made, it is an easy matter to compute the ratio

ML/(MP + ML), assuming MP and ML remain constant over the relevant sales volumes. The decision maker will increase the order size until the probability of selling the unit to be added is less than the computed ratio.

For example:

Sale Price = $5.00   Unit Cost = $3.00
Therefore:
MP = (5–3) = $2.00   ML = $3.00
Computed Ratio = 3/(2 + 3) = .60

nth Unit	Probability of Selling	
1	1.00	
2	.97	
3	.85	
4	.73	
5	.64	$\left\{\vphantom{\begin{array}{c}a\\b\end{array}}\right.$ Optimum order size is 5 since this
6	.54	is last item where P≥ .60
7	.25	
8	.05	
9 or more	.00	

MRP and Inventory Management

Materials requirements planning has grown well beyond an inventory-planning tool to include priority planning and a means of coordinating the planning of organizational, financial, human, and productive facilities. In chapter 4 we discussed the planning role of MRP. In this chapter we focus on the sizing of orders and safety stock issues.

Readers might want to review the MRP section in chapter 4. In summary, customer demand is called independent demand, since it is not controlled by the firm. Either customer orders or forecast estimates of the demand serve as the basis for a master production schedule. Remember, the master production schedule represents our strategy for meeting the customer demand. MRP translated the master production schedule into gross requirements for lower-level components that we refer to as dependent demand. When MRP detects a negative projected balance or a balance below a safety stock level, it plans an order. The size of the planned order depends on a lot-sizing decision which we assumed as given in chapter 4. We now address this question.

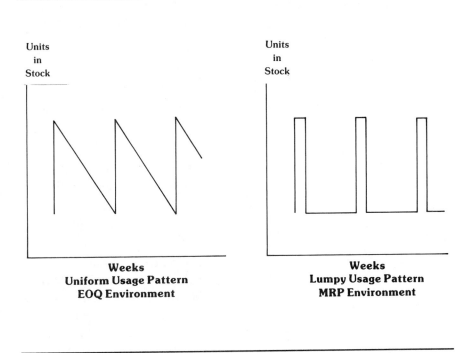

Figure 6-4. Contrast Between Uniform and Lumpy Demands on Inventory

Lot Sizing in a Material Requirements Planning Environment

The discrete batch approach common to many manufacturing firms does not meet the theoretical assumptions of steady production and usage rates required of the economic lot-sizing formulas. Figure 6-4 shows the contrast between the uniform usage appropriate to EOQ and the lumpy demand pattern typical of the MRP environment. Yet, the scheduler must choose some quantity to purchase and some lot size to produce. The setup costs (or order costs) associated with each batch (or purchase order) may justify sizable lot sizes and the associated inventory carrying costs, or it may prove more economical to make or purchase just what is required in the immediate schedule.

In MRP the lost sizing decision focuses on the net requirements portion of the time-phased inventory record developed in chapter 4. Figure 6-5 illustrates a set of net requirements for black picture frames and contains estimates of setup costs, inventory carrying costs, and annual demand. Let's consider a few ways of grouping these net requirements into production lots.

1. Lot-for-Lot	Limit the lot size to the requirements of one period
2. Economic Order Quantity (EOQ):	Balance setup and carrying costs ignoring the lumpy demand
3. Period Order Quantity (POQ):	Convert the EOQ into the average number of periods to be covered by an order.
4. Least Total Cost (LTC):	Add to the first net requirement the net requirements from subsequent periods until the carrying cost is about equal to the setup costs
5. Least Unit Cost (LUC):	Compute the carrying cost plus the setup cost divided by the size of the combined lot. As additional requirements are added, the cost per unit may go down. Eventually, stop when the increased carrying costs overwhelms the spreading of the setup cost.
6. Wagner-Whitin Algorithm:	An application of dynamic programming to inventory requirements of a specified period.

These techniques focus on only one level in the bill of materials. Lot sizing at one level affects the gross requirements at lower levels and can lead to excessively high inventories. This interdependency leads to a bias in favor of lot-for-lot to avoid small residuals and the buildup of inventory at lower levels.

Safety Stock and Safety Lead Time in MRP

MRP advocates discourage the use of safety stocks for dependent demand items. One of the goals is to reduce inventory and fractional lots of safety stock that will not support a full production run. Safety stock can serve as a protection against variations in quantity–for example, scrap losses or short shipments. Safety lead time, in the sense of producing or

PART NO. 101411002
10 x 14 Black Picture Frame

Setup Cost (S) = \$10 per order   Carrying Cost (IC) = \$6 per unit per year
or \$.12 per unit per week

Annual Demand = 2400 units

PERIOD (weeks)	1	2	3	4	5	6
NET REQUIREMENTS	0	50	75	0	50	100

LOT SIZING RULE

$EOQ = \sqrt{(2SD/IC)} = \sqrt{(2 \times 10 \times 2400)/6)} = 89$ or 90

Period:	1	2	3	4	5	6
EOQ Orders		90	90			95 *
Left over Units		40 **	55	55	5	0

* Here we interpret the EOQ as a minimum order quantity, rather than assume we have to order in multiple of 90 units.

** Note that the residual inventory carried from week 2 to week 3 did not save us a setup and therefore no net savings.

POQ = (EOQ/D) x Periods per Year = (90/2400) x 52 = 1.95 or 2 weeks.

Period:	1	2	3	4	5	6
EOQ Orders		125			150	
Left over Units		75	0	0	100	0

LTC   Trial order Q1:   125 units covering weeks 2 and 3
       carrying cost: (units carried over X carrying cost) = 75 x \$.12 = \$9

       Trial order Q2:   175 units covering weeks 2, 3, 4, and 5.
       carrying cost: \$9 + (50 x \$.12 x 3wks) = \$27

Order 125 units because the carrying cost of \$9 is the closest to the setup cost of \$10.

Figure 6-5 Different Lot-Sizing Techniques

The same procedure would lead to a second order of 150 units to cover weeks 5 and 6.

LUC   Trial order Q1:   50   Unit Cost = (S + Carrying Cost) /Q1
   = ($10 + 0) /50 = $.20

Trial order Q2:   125   Unit Cost = [$10 + (75 x $.12 x 1wk)] /125
   = ($10 + $9) /125 = $.15

Trial order Q3:   175   Unit Cost = [$10 + $9 + (50 x $.12 x 3wks)] /175
   = ($10 + $9 + $18) /175 = $.21

Order 1 will be 125 units because Q2 has the lowest unit cost ($.15). Purely by chance, this result is the same found using POQ and LTC.

Figure 6-5. (Continued)

bringing in a complete lot size early, is a hedge against timing problems, such as those caused by late deliveries or production delays. The Japanese approach would also discourage safety stock as well as safety time. The emphasis is on reducing the causes that lead to safety stocks, such as breakdowns, defective products, or production capacity expended on the wrong jobs due to invalid job priorities. If safety stock or safety lead times are used, those stocks should be made very clear to all so that priorities are not distorted. Generally, the firm should not be expediting a job to replace safety stock at the expense of efforts on jobs going to a customer.

Summary of MRP Benefits and Limitations

MRP makes a major contribution to the planning and acquisition of materials. In the short term, it tests the feasibility of the master production schedule when the component schedules and purchases are reviewed against available capacity and vendor lead times. MRP allows establishment of the valid priority of jobs, by highlighting which items should be expedited due to overdue situations and which items should be de-expedited due to decisions to delay orders. In the long term, MRP is useful in estimating capacity requirements through translating long-range market forecasts into specific capacity requirements.

The major limitations of MRP are associated with its demands for accurate data and extensive computer capacity. Since minimum inventory is one of the selling features of MRP, the system depends on the inventory records being very accurate (98 percent or better). Furthermore, if the bill of materials is not current and accurate, MRP

will translate higher-level demand into incorrect lower-level requirements. This could result in work stoppages, quality problems, or wasted
material. Therefore, it is imperative to maintain accurate stock-status
records and closely manage engineering changes that affect the bill of
materials. Many organizations have failed to achieve the accuracy levels
required, with resulting failure of the MRP system. The volume of
computations mandates the use of a computer, which brings many
changes into organizations that are not computerized. Even with computer facilities, major changes in inventory and engineering may be
required.

Finally, MRP is not equally applicable to all organizations. Since it
derives its value from coordinating the assembly of many components
into a final product in batches, the technique applies best to assembly and
batch manufacturing of multi-part products. On the other hand, fabrica-
tors often are dealing with one component, which negates MRP's
strength; and process industries are less batch oriented, which devalues
the replanning capability of MRP.

JIT: Just-In-Time Management System

JIT (Just-In-Time) concepts have gained a foothold in many U.S. industries as a result of global competition, particularly from the Japanese.
Faced with competitive pressures in price, quality, flexibility and responsiveness to customer needs, American managers have begun to study and
adopt the philosophy and techniques that comprise a JIT management
system.

As a philosophy, JIT focuses on organization-wide continuous improvement guided by a customer orientation. Everyone has a customer;
the sales force is concerned with the ultimate customer, but within the
firm, each individual, team, or department is both a user and a supplier of
products and services to other parts of the organization. For example,
the work team in a fabricating center is dependent on the raw materials
supplied to them by purchasing. The fabricating team, in turn, must meet
the needs of the assembly team who use the parts they produce. The
importance of these customer-supplier bonds is emphasized throughout
the material chain from the customer, through the firm, to the suppliers.

JIT is based on the fundamental principles of respect for people and
elimination of waste. Unlike the early work study efforts that sought to
simplify and standardize jobs, JIT emphasizes cross training and the
creation of multi-function employees to make the production system
more flexible and responsive. Elimination of waste, in a JIT system,
refers to the reduction of all inefficiencies in the production process such

as wasted time and motion, unnecessary operations, excess inventories, or ineffective distribution systems.

Many of the concepts, tools, and approaches contained under the JIT umbrella are not Japanese innovations; they have been practiced by American and European managers for decades. The unique contribution of JIT, therefore, is in linking together these ideas into a systems approach. Concepts like focused operations strategies, group technology, reduced setup times, preventive maintenance, uniform workload, purchasing partnerships, and total quality control are discussed elsewhere in this book. But it is appropriate here to see how these concepts are integrated in JIT.

Kanban: The Pull System

"Kanban" is a Japanese word that refers to the concept of "pulling" products through a production process based on customer purchases of end products rather than "pushing" products through based on production schedules derived from demand forecasts. In simple terms, the **pull system** says that when a unit of finished product is picked-up by a customer (internal or external), then a signal is sent to produce a replacement. Production is driven from the down-stream, customer end of the system.

If we visualize our desk as a work station with an In-Box and an Out-Box, then we would work in response to the "pull" from an empty Out-Box, not "pushed" by a full In-Box. When a customer (our boss) picks up a report from our Out-Box, we are authorized to complete the next high priority job and place it in the vacated Out-Box. Up-Stream, our "suppliers" are authorized to place more work in our In-Box only when it is empty. At any time, we should have one report in the In-Box, one report being worked on, and one completed report in the Out-Box ready to be picked up. If we finish the report we are working on and the Out-Box is not empty, we simply wait until it is.

This seems contradictory to some of the traditional principles of keeping everyone busy all of the time. The primary benefit, however, is that the system highlights bottlenecks, imbalanced workloads, quality problems, and other inefficiencies. If most workers are idle for long periods, the bottleneck is identified and additional capacity is added to that operation. Eventually, the process becomes more balanced and flows smoothly with a minimum of work in process waiting to be completed. Products spend less time in the system, so production cycle time is considerably reduced. Finally, all of the work that is being performed is in response to immediate customer need; there is less chance of producing products that will never be used.

This is significantly different from a **push system** which is driven from the up-stream side and takes the form of a overflowing In-Box. Under a push system we tend to have high work-in-process inventory and may be working on tasks that do not relate to the down-stream needs of the process or the ultimate customer. Products take a long time to produce because they spend so much time waiting for other jobs to be completed. In this environment, problems such as poor quality, inefficient operations, and equipment breakdowns do not appear urgent; with so many jobs and so much inventory in the process, the problems are hidden from view.

The objective of a JIT system is to uncover and solve problems to improve efficiency, quality, and responsiveness. It seeks to accomplish this through interrelated efforts to reduce setup times and lot sizes, reduce cycle times, and reduce overall inventory levels.

Reduce Setup Times and Lot Sizes

Someone once quipped that par on a Japanese golf course was 18 (a hole-in-one on every hole) implying that they strive for perfection–minimum or maximum–in everything they do. This is especially true in setup time reduction. In some instances, Japanese manufacturers have reduced the changing of dies on a complex press from two days to four hours and subsequently to twenty minutes. Their ultimate objective is to be able to set up any machine in one minute. They may not meet their goal, but they will continue to strive for it. The work study methods discussed in chapter 3 provide many clues for streamlining setup procedures.

Analysis of the ELS formula reveals that a shorter setup time and lower setup cost will yield a smaller production lot size. This allows the firm to produce small batches of that item very frequently rather than perhaps producing a six-month supply twice a year.

The implications of this change on the level of finished goods inventories and responsiveness to customer needs are dramatic. If all setups can be similarly reduced, the firm will attempt to develop a uniform workload and schedule to produce every product within a short time horizon (such as two weeks). As demand changes, the firm makes adjustments in lot sizes or frequency of producing a lot within the two-week period. Special orders can now be handled with a two-week lead time rather then the previous six month wait. Finished goods inventories previously contained an average three-months supply of every item (ranging from zero to six months) but now they average one week's usage; a reduction that may amount to millions of dollars in savings.

In addition to these benefits, the firm finds that its capacity has been greatly increased by spending more time producing products and less time making equipment changeovers. In the example cited earlier, the firm gained fifteen hours and forty minutes of productive capacity by reducing setup time from two days to twenty minutes.

If par on our golf course is to be 18, then our objective in the manufacturing process is to reduce setup times to one minute, reduce lot sizes to one unit, and reduce planning horizons to one day. Through the use of work study, group technology, cellular layouts, and automated but flexible equipment (see chapter 3) we are making progress toward this ideal in many industries.

Reduce Cycle Time

Production cycle time refers to the elapsed time from the receipt of a customer order (or the release of a production order to the shop) to the completion of the product ready to deliver. In many traditional batch production facilities, a job may spend as much as 90% or more of its time in the system waiting in line for other jobs to be completed. Only 5 - 10% of the time is productive work on the product. Thus a job that requires eight hours of work and could conceivably be completed in one day may have a cycle time of three months or more! Competitors who offer a few days lead time compared to your three months will put you out of business.

Reduction of setup times and lot sizes, as noted earlier, allows the job to pass through the system faster. If combined with a "pull" system, each job will spend a minimum of time waiting at overloaded work stations.

Cycle time reduction brings problems to the surface, so management must devote special attention to quality defects, equipment breakdowns, and work imbalance. For example, suppose one worker discovers defects in a batch, perhaps from the previous operation. Under a strict "pull" system, the entire process will stop until the problem is corrected. An immediate remedy for the defective product will be found, but the problem will not be considered solved until the root cause of the defects is identified and eliminated. In this way, the process is continually improved.

Similarly, equipment breakdowns would stop not only that operation, but the entire process. Preventive maintenance, therefore, takes on a very high priority. Work imbalances are resolved by shifting capacity or by increasing the efficiency of bottleneck operations. Since most employees in a JIT system are cross trained, it is relatively easy to temporarily assign one worker to help out another until the jobs are again flowing smoothly through the process.

Reduce Overall Inventory Levels

JIT seeks to continuously reduce inventory levels of raw materials, work in process, and finished goods. Lower levels of inventory means less space is required and there is a smaller chance of the product becoming spoiled, damaged, or obsolete. Materials handling of the lots is facilitated and often can be automated. An added side benefit of the inventory reduction is that operations can often be placed closer together thus enhancing communication and teamwork.

As noted earlier, finished goods inventories are reduced as a direct result of the shortened lead times and smaller, more frequent lots. Work-in-process inventories are significantly reduced as the firm implements a "pull" system and takes advantage of the associated production efficiencies that usually follow.

Reduction of raw materials is a key part of the JIT system that requires a special relationship with suppliers. If production delays are to be avoided, raw materials must arrive just before they are needed, they must be the right materials, and they must meet all quality specifications.

As described in chapter 5, JIT firms often reduce the number of suppliers and form "partnership" agreements with them. They share product designs, schedules, and quality specifications so that the supplier-buyer interface can be an integration of the two organizations providing a smooth flow of materials from one firm to the other. Suppliers know well in advance, from the product design and the buyer's production schedule, what materials will need to be shipped and when. The buyer is familiar with the performance record of the supplier and the quality control procedures employed. Often, the buyer accepts the documentation of quality tests by the supplier in lieu of incoming inspection of purchased materials. Built on mutual respect and trust, the relationship is beneficial to both organizations and allows each to operate more effectively and efficiently.

JIT Summary

JIT sounds like the solution to all production problems; it is not. It is a sound, integrated approach to making the firm meet all of its performance goals using a variety of tools, techniques, and approaches; but it is not a panacea. A JIT system is no better than the ability of the people in the system to identify and solve problems in their efforts to improve operational productivity.

JIT applies directly to a batch manufacturer making a relatively standard product to meet a stable demand. Other types of firms facing different market conditions will find JIT implementation more a process of adaption rather than adoption.

For example, a job shop, producing customized products to customer specifications, may have no control over the lot size (set by the size of the customer order) and will not be able to purchase raw material or schedule production until the order is received. It can, however, adapt many of the approaches with respect to quality, maintenance, setup reduction, and group technology to fit its unique circumstances. The same can be said for other types of manufacturing and, to some extent, to services.

In the future, JIT is likely to spread in scope and provide guiding principles for many organizations.

Physical Care of Inventories

The objective of warehousing (stock keeping) is to store items at a minimum cost and assure that they are available when needed. This requires finding the proper balance among the competing goals of efficient use of space, minimum handling of material, protection of the goods from damage or deterioration, avoidance of obsolescence through stock rotation, and on-time delivery of the goods to users. This section discusses two of the major issues associated with the physical control and care of inventory–storage methods and record keeping.

Storage and Material Handling

Traditionally, storage areas have been arranged with spaces or storage racks designated for a particular item. Although this makes goods easy to find and allows inventory clerks to see the entire stock of an item in one place, space utilization and flexibility were poor. On the average, the facility would be half empty, and a major reorganization of the material was necessary if the space needs for an item increased.

Recent developments in bar coding and automated material handling equipment have allowed a different system to be used. In many modern warehouses, items are received and placed in any available space; bar code tags on the item and on the rack space allow the computer to keep track of how many items are stored, their locations, and the date they were received. When items are needed, a pick list is generated and fed into the computer, often through hand-held remote units. The computer will then direct the stock picker to the location of the material needed.

In more advanced systems, the stock may be retrieved by automated equipment that can read the pick list and handle the material without human assistance. The system will assure that the oldest stock is used first and that the equipment will take the shortest path through the warehouse to fill the order. The equipment may even stop at the receiving dock and pick up a load of material to be stored while it is on its way to fill an order so that it minimizes the time it travels unloaded. All records of receipts and withdrawals from inventory are immediately fed into the computer record. The most advanced systems like this can actually operate in total darkness!

Inventory Record Keeping

Regardless of the storage system used, accurate inventory records are necessary. The inventory manager must be able to specify the location and quantities available for any item. Records must be kept on shipments received and storage locations, withdrawals from stock, transfers of material between departments, shipments of finished goods, and write-offs necessitated by scrap, damage, or obsolescence. Systems such as Materials Requirements Planning and JIT management depend heavily on accurate inventory records.

Errors in inventory records lead to wasted time looking for material, production interruptions due to stock outs, and inaccuracies in purchasing and scheduling production. To detect and eliminate errors, some firms conduct an annual inventory count of every item in the warehouse. Although the cost of an annual inventory is great, especially if production must be shut down during this time, it is justified by the need for accurate inventory records.

Many firms are opting to use cycle counting rather than an annual physical count. **Cycle counting** involves the physical count and justification of inventory records for some of the items each cycle (month or quarter, for example). Annual shut downs are avoided and a staff of inventory clerks are kept busy year-round checking inventory accuracy. Every item is counted at least once per year, but critical items may be checked more often to maintain closer control.

Inventory represents a major asset–and a substantial cost–for most business firms. Good decision making combined with proper physical care of inventories can help protect that asset and minimize those costs.

Key Concepts

Inventory Ordering Costs	Periodic Review Model
Setup Costs	Reorder Points
Inventory Carrying Costs	Service Level
Economic Order Quantity (EOQ)	Just-In-Time (JIT)
Cycle Stock	Cycle Counting
Decoupling Stock	Lot Sizing Rules
Buffer or Safety Stock	Kanban: Pull System
Anticipatory Stock	Cycle Time
Economic Lot Size (ELS)	

References

Chase, Richard B., and Aquilano, Nicholas J. *Production and Operations Management*. 5th ed. Homewood, IL: Richard D. Irwin, 1989.

Fogarty, Donald W., Blackstone, John H. Jr., and Hoffmann, Thomas. *Production & Inventory Management*. 2nd ed. South-Western Publishing Co., 1990.

Hall, Robert W. *Attaining Manufacturing Excellence*. Homewood, IL: Dow Jones-Irwin, 1987.

Orlicky, Joseph. *Materials Requirements Planning*. New York: McGraw-Hill Book Company, 1975.

Schonberger, Richard J., and Knod, Edward M., Jr. *Operations Management: Improving Customer Service*. 4th ed. Homewood, IL: Richard D. Irwin, 1991.

Vollmann, Thomas E., Berry, William L., and Whybark, D. Clay. *Manufacturing Planning and Control Systems*. 2d ed. Homewood, IL: Richard D. Irwin, 1988.

Wight, Oliver W. *MRP II: Unlocking America's Productivity Potential*. Boston: CBI Publishing, 1981.

Discussion Questions

1. What is meant by the decoupling function of inventories?

2. Discuss the cost trade-offs that are reflected in the EOQ and ELS formulas.

3. What happens to the ELS formula if p becomes very large relative to d? What if d = p? What real-world consequences might these outcomes have?

4. What are the assumptions of the traditional EOQ formula?

5. Describe the procedure for finding the best order quantity when price breaks are available.

6. Describe how the pursuit of minimum inventory is consistent with several just-in-time techniques or areas selected for improvement.

7. Why is the simple EOQ approach to lot sizing not appropriate in an MRP environment?

8. Under what circumstances is MRP most applicable, and what are some of the prerequisites of having a successful MRP system?

9. Discuss the pros and cons of different methods of storing goods.

10. Describe the concept of cycle counting, and indicate its advantages relative to traditional annual physical inventories.

Problems

1. Your company is offered the following price breaks on an electrical component of which it buys 1,000 per year.

Quantity	Price
0-200 pcs.	$12.50 each
201 & up	$10.00 each

   Your company has determined that it costs 10 percent of the purchase unit price to store an item for a year. Furthermore, your ordering costs amount to $15 per order. What is your best order quantity? Do not overlook the savings in overall purchase cost (the last term in the total-cost equation).

2. You are responsible for stocking the egg section of your grocery store once a week. Your supplier sells you the eggs for 60 cents per dozen. You price the eggs at 66 cents per dozen. At the end of the week you mark down whatever is left to 55 cents per dozen. This lower price has always cleared out the leftover inventory. Your past sales records support the following stable probability distribution of sales each week. What is your best stocking level each week? How would your decision change if you could get only 50 cents for the week-old eggs?

Demand (dozens)	Probability of Selling	Demand (dozens)	Probability of Selling
30	1.00	35	.57
31	.98	36	.37
32	.94	37	.19
33	.86	38	.07
34	.73	39	.01

3. Periodically you renegotiate a contract with your supplier of plastic beads for use in your injection-molding machines. You estimate that it cost you about $150 to negotiate and conclude the contract. Your company buys about 52,000 pounds of plastic per year at about $3.50 per pound. You use the plastic at a steady rate of 1,000 pounds per week. By agreement, your supplier will deliver a trailer load of 5,000 pounds a week until the order is completed. The last load may be a partial trailer load. It costs 90 cents to store a pound of plastic for one year. How much should you order, and what will be your annual inventory ordering and carrying costs? What would be the effect of an agreement to deliver at a rate of 2,000 pounds per week? What about an agreement to deliver reliably at a rate of 1,000 per week?

4. A lot size is to be determined which will cover the net requirements in week 1 at a minimum. The necessary data are provided below. Compute the size of the first order using:

A. Economic Order Quantity, EOQ

B. Period order Quantity, POQ

C. Least Total Cost, LTC

D. Least Unit Cost, LUC

Annual Demand (D) = 1350 units

Setup Costs (S) = $12.00 per setup

Carrying Cost (IC) = $7.80 per unit per year, or $.15 per unit per week.

	PERIOD (weeks)					
	1	2	3	4	5	Total
NET REQUIREMENTS	25	45	0	10	50	130

5. The JIT Implementation Leader has asked you to improve the setup time for a particular product fabricated in work center 35. The leader wants setups reduced to the point that a lot size of 12 can be justified by conventional EOQ analysis. The setup currently takes two hours and setup time is valued at $50 per hour. The annual demand for the product is 500 units and the carrying cost is $10 per unit per year.

A. How fast will the reduced setup time have to be?

B. What are the savings in annual setup and carrying costs?

C. What percent reduction has the Leader asked for?

D. What does this suggest about the importance of non-inventory cost issues in the justification of setup reduction?

C H A P T E R
7

Quality Management

Product quality has become a major competitive factor in determining the survival and success of manufacturing and service firms. With the proliferation of goods and services available, customers are demanding manufactured items that work properly the first time and every time during the expected product life. Services, too, are feeling pressures from competitors that provide more accurate bank statements, faster delivery of documents, and friendlier, more efficient and more helpful service in face-to-face situations.

Many firms are learning that higher quality does not have to mean higher costs; in fact, often the opposite is true. Intense foreign competition–first in goods and now in some services–has caused managers to reexamine their quality priorities and policies in an attempt to eliminate the *hidden factories* that spend time and resources to correct product defects that should not have occurred at all.

Most important, managers are moving from the concept of quality control to the broader concept of quality management. Although testing and statistical control methods will continue to play a major role in any production process, quality is now becoming part of the strategic focus of successful companies. The management of quality reaches every aspect of the production function.

To better understand quality in the production of goods and services, we must determine what quality is and what it is not—what the relevant costs of quality are, and how quality is produced or controlled. Furthermore, we should appreciate the importance of quality in products as more than just an economic concept. Quality has strong legal and social implications as well. It is inconvenient to buy an electrical appliance that doesn't work, but if things such as automobiles or health care are of poor quality, lives may be lost.

Many people equate *quality* with luxurious goods or lavish services. Expensive sports cars, grand hotels, exclusive clubs and restaurants, fur coats, and precious jewelry are typical examples of *quality* products. In truth, each may have high or low quality relative to its price, just as simpler items have varying degrees of quality.

Product Quality

Much of the following discussion concerns manufactured goods, since many of the pertinent quality techniques have been developed within and for manufacturing. Service firms recognize, however, that quality is no less important to their success and that many of the tools developed for goods can be applied to services as well. The concepts and tools must be adapted, of course, to fit the different nature of services and the process of service delivery.

As this chapter unfolds, consider how each topic may be applied to a service business, such as a bank, hospital, university, or insurance company. *Products* become checking accounts, surgical operations, undergraduate courses, and insurance policies. *Defects* may be translated into "errors"; *transportation* becomes "delivery of the service"; and so on. Not every concept will apply, but most will.

As noted in Chapter 1, many service firms produce a tangible product as well as a service. In a pizza parlor, for example, the quality of the food and the quality of the service can be separated; one can be excellent while the other is poor, and either can change from time to time. With firms that are more exclusively service oriented, defining the unit of output becomes difficult; legal counseling, consulting, teaching, and many government operations, such as parks and recreation or national defense, are examples. The closer the firm is to a pure service organization, the more difficult it is to define, measure, and control quality.

New methods are being developed, however, to measure quality characteristics and to identify countable errors in service industries. As these efforts continue, the establishment and use of quality-enhancement programs in service-oriented organizations are likely to increase as well.

The Meaning of Quality

To grasp the meaning of quality and its control, consider a business: Quality Doghouses, Inc. The basic product, a doghouse, is made from plywood and is spray painted. The deluxe model has a shingle roof, carpeting, and a chain that attaches to a clip next to a swinging door. The price of the deluxe model is twice the price of the standard model, but the deluxe model is not necessarily the *high-quality* model. Either model can be of high or low quality.

Quality Defined

Quality is a characteristic of a product, as is its size, shape, or composition. Specifically, it is a characteristic that determines a product's value in the market and how well it will perform the function for which it was designed. The quality of a product in general is expressed as a standard, and the quality of specific units of that product is measured in terms of the degree of conformance with the standard.

Thus, the definition of quality must include both the standard and conformance to the standard. Merely changing the standard does not change quality; quality must actually be built into the manufacture of a good or the provision of a service.

The standard may be set in a number of ways. First, customers may set standards by their past buying behavior; market research gives some idea of the quality level customers want and are willing to pay for. Second, top management may set a standard in terms of the policy or strategy the firm wants to implement; it can aim at the top, bottom, or middle of the quality market. Third, a design technician in the firm may set a tolerance that a certain part must meet if it is to fit properly with other parts. Ultimately, each of these standards must be translated into specific technical standards to guide the manufacture and assembly of the product.

These concepts can be illustrated with the doghouse example. The primary function of the doghouse is to protect the animal from the weather. To achieve this, the roof must not leak; this standard will be applied in a leak test as part of the manufacturing process. Another aspect of the doghouse is the finish. Runs in the paint will not affect the function of the doghouse, but they may affect its value in the market if the doghouse buyer considers it important. Another standard must be developed for the number and type of tolerable blemishes in the paint.

The following fundamental elements of control must be applied to the quality dimensions of the product:

1. Measure the quality characteristic.

2. Compare actual results to the standard.

3. Take corrective action when the deviation between actual results and the standard exceed tolerable limits.

4. If possible, determine the cause of the deviation and eliminate it.

Corrective action may consist of stopping the process or rejecting a shipment of materials. Units suspected of poor quality can then be screened, reworked, scrapped, or returned to the supplier depending on the circumstances.

Determining and eliminating the cause involves research into the nature of the deviation and how it occurred. A useful tool for performing this analysis is the **fishbone diagram**, illustrated in figure 7-1 for a problem of customer complaints of bad-tasting coffee on a catering truck. So named because of its shape, the fishbone diagram directs the analyst to explore the basic determinants of quality in an operation: Material, Employees, Measurement, Machines, and Methods. Some of the likely causes are listed on the diagram. Each of these will be explored to determine if it is the primary cause, and then corrections will be made as needed.

Dimensions of Quality

Quality is not a single characteristic; it is multidimensional. Some organizations may separate some of these dimensions from their definition of quality, but they are related so closely that they should be included as part of the total quality concept.

1. **Functionality.** This refers to whether the product performs its function at the end of the manufacturing process or when it is first put to use. Functionality can be measured on a yes-or-no basis–either the light bulb works or its doesn't–or as a continuous measure–in terms of how many footcandles of light the bulb emits.

2. **Reliability.** Reliability may have several different meanings:

   A. How long will the product function (durational reliability) under normal operating conditions?

   B. Does the product function every time it is used (functional reliability) or does it fail intermittently?

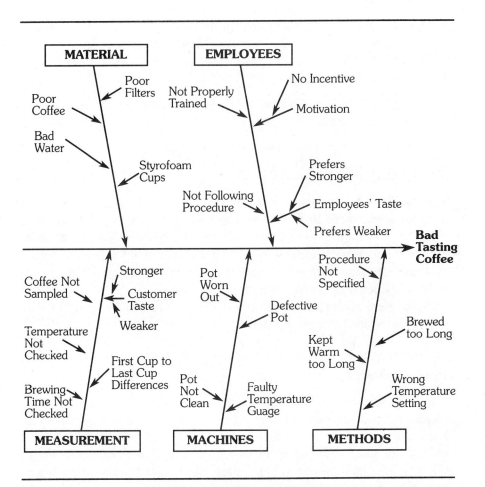

Figure 7-1. Fishbone Diagram

C. If a product is assembled from components that each have a given probability of failure, what is the probability of failure (system reliability) of the completed product?

D. How consistent is the level of quality (process reliability) in successive units produced by a process?

3. **Durability.** How well and how long will the product function under adverse conditions? Can the product withstand shock, vibration, heat, cold, dust, and other conditions that it reasonably might be expected to encounter?

4. **Esthetic characteristics.** This refers to the appearance of the product and is not necessarily related to its function. The smoothness of the surface, the symmetry of decorative designs, and the absence of chips, dents, or scratches illustrate this dimension.

5. **Safety.** Will the product perform its function without unnecessarily endangering the user? Electrical appliances should not produce electrical shocks during normal use; lawn-mower blades should stay attached to the spindle.

A high-quality doghouse cannot be produced unless all these aspects have been considered.

Total Quality Management

The quality-control function in an organization often is viewed as sort of a police department that checks outgoing products and gives tickets to offenders. A total quality program, however, must include much more than just an inspection function. Quality cannot be *inspected* into a product: It must be *designed* and *built* into the product. And quality control assures that this has been done.

There are several areas within the firm where quality (good or bad) can be introduced into the product.

Product Design

The end product probably will be no better than its design. Design engineers must consider not only the functionality of the early prototypes but also the ease with which the elements of the product can be produced in quantity and assembled into final units. The choices of screws versus rivets, tongue-and-groove versus miter joints, and braces or no braces determine whether the product will withstand the quality tests of the consumer. Designers may have to revise their basic design several times to fit the needs and constraints of later stages of development and manufacture.

Process Design

To manufacture the doghouse, certain machines, such as saws, sanders, spray painters, and hand tools, are needed. The choice of machines will affect the quality of output; more expensive saws may make a cleaner cut and give a closer fit of parts in final assembly.

The effect of other aspects of process design on quality is less obvious but nonetheless important. The layout employed, materials-handling and storage methods used, sequencing of operations, and even maintenance policies can influence the number of defective units produced.

Raw Materials

Generally, the better the quality of the raw materials, the better the quality of the finished product. Plywood, for example, comes in several grades, which indicate the smoothness of the surface. Cheaper grades of wood could be used, but to maintain the standard, much of this material would have to be filled, sanded, or discarded. Purchased parts, such as hinges or chains, also must meet specifications, even though the firm does not manufacture these items.

The problem of obtaining raw materials of proper quality can be subdivided into several steps. First, the proper material must be selected. Should it be plywood, particle board, or masonite? Second, the appropriate supplier must be selected. Third, incoming raw material receipts should be monitored to assure that the quality standard is met throughout the manufacturing period. Failure to consider any of these three steps may jeopardize the quality of the end product.

Employees

In addition to materials and equipment, the third major input category is people. To achieve the quality goals, employees must be trained properly in the quality aspects of the task they are to perform, and they must be motivated to produce at the level of desired quality. Selection and training policies should consider the level of quality that workers are expected to achieve. It is incorrect to assume that workers naturally will produce at the right quality level. And it is unwise, and often costly, to rely on inspection to police the employees' work.

Operation of the Production Process

The doghouse manufacturer might have the best design, the best equipment, the best raw materials, and the best employees, but if it fails to *manage* the quality function in its day-to-day operations, it may not produce an acceptable product. The maintenance policy for equipment may be sound but not implemented carefully. Housekeeping could be lax, resulting in damage to the product during manufacturing. Supervisory styles, communications, scheduling, stores control, wage and salary policies, and many other operating policies, rules, and procedures can determine whether the firm produces at or below its quality capability. Seemingly insignificant decisions such as the scheduling of coffee breaks often can have a pronounced impact on quality.

Packaging

Many firms incorrectly assume that their quality responsibilities end when the item comes off the assembly line. If it passes *final inspection,* then a quality product has been produced. The customer, however, does the *final* inspection. If a product fails to meet the customer's quality criteria when it is put to use, then it is a defective unit. Packaging is the first of several activities between the assembly line and the point of purchase that can influence the quality of the product.

If the doghouse is sent out with no packaging at all, it will end up with scratches, dents, missing parts, and a variety of other defects unacceptable to the customer. It could be put in a plastic bag to protect it from dirt or in a cardboard box to reduce the effects of rough handling. Ultimately, the firm could construct a packing crate more costly than the doghouse itself to assure that the item arrives in the same condition as it left the plant. Packaging that it is cost effective and commensurate with the characteristics of the product must be selected.

Transporting

Among the alternatives for shipping the doghouse to market are truck, air, rail, and boat. The type of transportation chosen will influence not only the costs but also the quality of the product. Air cargo is subject to extreme pressure and temperature. Rail and truck shipments may involve vibration and exposure to the weather, as well as several loading and unloading operations. Company-owned vehicles may be specifically adapted to the size and weight of the cargo, but cost effectiveness also must be considered.

Obviously, the packaging used and the transportation method chosen are interdependent. Items shipped by commercial carrier may need more protection, but air shipments should minimize the package-weight required. Whatever combination of packaging and transportation is chosen, the decision should be tempered by the effect on the quality of the product and should fit with the firm's overall quality policy.

Storage

An area often overlooked as a quality determinant is storage. The doghouses will be kept in warehouses, stockrooms, and other storage facilities for weeks, months, or years before they are sold. This product is fairly durable, but there are limits to how high it should be stacked, how far it can be dropped, and what environmental conditions it can withstand. A more delicate product might have severe restrictions on allowable temperature, humidity, dust, or light. Perishable products–those with a *shelf life*–should be rotated to assure freshness.

Packaging also is interdependent with storing: The more protective the packaging, the less likely the product is to deteriorate during storage. Also, packaging materials can be marked with storing instructions that help assure that the product will be in an acceptable condition when needed.

After all the effort that is put into the design and manufacture of a quality product, it is unfortunate to lose it through careless storage and handling.

Total Quality Management and the Baldrige Award

Since the introduction of the term Total Quality Control (TQC) in the early 1950s, some firms began to see quality as more than just inspection. Today, many firms are adopting a Total Quality Management (TQM) approach that recognizes quality as a top competitive priority and coordinates all activities toward this goal. TQM makes quality a part of everyone's job and emphasizes prevention rather than detection and correction.

In 1988 the Federal Government established the Malcolm Baldrige National Quality Award to be administered by the Department of Commerce, the American Society for Quality Control, and the American Productivity and Quality Center. Named for the late secretary of the Department of Commerce, the purpose of the award was to recognize outstanding quality achievements by U.S. firms in manufacturing, service, and small business categories. Applicants for the award are evaluated by a board of examiners, site visits are conducted for finalists, and recommendations are made to a panel of judges for a final decision. Recipients of the award include Motorola, Globe Metallurgical, Westinghouse, Milliken, Xerox, IBM, Cadillac, and Federal Express.

Criteria for the award are:

1. **Leadership:** Senior executive involvement in quality and their role in instilling quality, managing quality, and carrying out public responsibility.

2. **Information and Analysis:** The scope, analysis, and management of quality data and the ability to effectively use competitive comparisons and benchmarks.

3. **Strategic Quality Planning:** Managing the strategic quality planning process including the establishment of quality goals and plans.

4. **Human Resource Utilization:** Managing human resources toward quality goals including employee involvement, training, recognition, performance measurement, and morale.

5. **Quality Assurance of Products and Services:** Designing and managing a continuous improvement process for assuring high quality levels in materials, production processes, and support functions.

6. **Quality Results:** The actual results of quality performance in products, processes, support services, and suppliers.

7. **Customer Satisfaction:** Assuring high customer satisfaction through determining customer requirements, setting customer service standards, verifying customer satisfaction results, and displaying a true commitment to the customer.

Together, these criteria provide guidelines for a total quality management effort and form a basis for self-assessment by all organizations pursuing quality excellence.

Factors Affecting Quality

A total quality management (TQM) approach requires an understanding of the stages of production in which quality is affected: product design, process design, raw materials, and so on. If TQM is to lead to improved quality, however, managers also must understand the organizational factors that influence quality levels. Figure 7-2 is a useful conceptual framework for organizing these factors. Furthermore, it shows that inspection and testing do not improve the quality level. They can only catch some defects before products reach the customer and provide information to managers about problems that need correction.

Behavioral and Technical Factors Affecting Quality

The actual quality of the product (good or service) when it reaches the customer is determined by a multitude of factors involved in the creation and delivery of the output. Generally, these can be divided into behavioral factors (those that relate to the people in the process) and technical factors (the characteristics of the tools, equipment, materials, and processes).

Some behavioral factors, such as the amount of training an employee has received, will determine the potential for achieving high quality. A poorly trained employee simply is not as capable of high-quality work as a well-trained one. Similarly, technical factors, such as the capabilities of

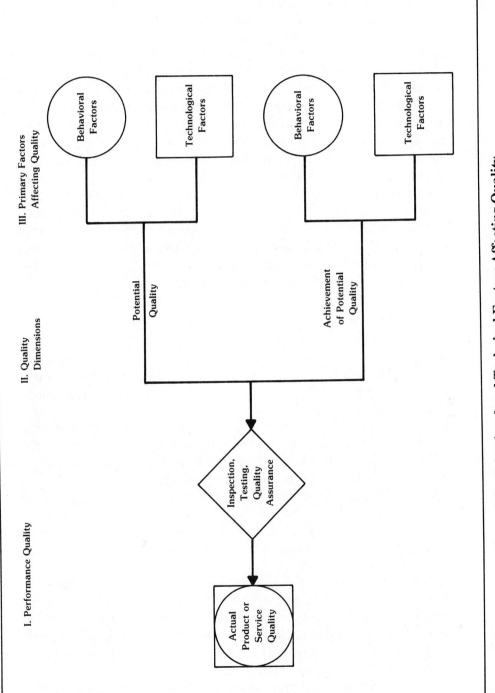

Figure 7-2. Behavioral and Technical Factors Affecting Quality

the equipment or the specifications of the raw material, determine the potential quality level of the process.

On the other hand, some behavioral and technical factors influence the quality levels in day-to-day operations. That is, they determine whether or not the potential quality level of the process is achieved. For example, employees may be properly trained and capable of doing high-quality work, but if they are poorly motivated due to inadequate rewards, they may fail to work up to their quality potential. Similarly, machines that are poorly maintained or materials that are handled improperly can introduce defects into a process that has been well designed but badly managed. If quality expectations are not being met, management must determine the reason by attempting to isolate the specific problem. Obviously, it would make no sense to try to increase employees' motivation toward higher quality if employees already are doing their best with the poor tools and materials with which they have to work. On the other hand, it is useless to invest in better equipment if employees lack the motivation to produce proper levels of quality.

Quality Programs

Many companies have established quality programs aimed more at the behavioral factors than at the technical factors affecting quality. These programs range from simple motivational efforts using posters, meetings, and perhaps incentives for quality improvement to elaborate programs intended to change the culture of the company with respect to quality. Some of the programs have met with limited success, but others have become so successful that they have developed a standard format applicable to a variety of companies in different industries.

One example is *quality circles*, a technique developed in Japan in the 1950s. Some credit the quality circle approach with moving Japanese industry from the image of *cheap junk* to becoming one of the world's leading producers of high-quality, sophisticated electronic and mechanical products.

A quality circle is a group of workers who meet together weekly to discuss problems of quality, or other factors, and develop solutions. Employees who are close to the work on a daily basis often can find answers not apparent to engineers and analysts. If possible, solutions are implemented immediately, and the result is a higher-quality product and workers who feel they have made a positive contribution to that product.

Quality circles are no longer unique to Japan. American companies such as Westinghouse, Techtronics, Motorola, and many others have reported using them, with excellent results. Quality circles also have been successfully implemented in government operations such as the Naval Shipyard at Norfolk, Virginia. Based upon past results, the potential for quality improvement in products and services through the implementation of quality circles is enormous.

Another example is *Zero Defects*, which is applicable in service, office, and manufacturing operations. Designed primarily to raise the level of awareness of every employee to quality problems, this program promotes the goal of defect-free performance by isolating the cause of every error and tracing it to the source. If the root cause of defects can be identified and removed, then the goal of zero defects can be achieved.

Many adaptations of these ideas have been incorporated into quality programs for organizations of all types. Their success rate depends on many factors, but key among them is the degree to which the top management of the firm places quality in a high priority and supports efforts to make changes that will improve quality performance.

Quality Costs

Some managers state their objective as "producing the highest-quality product at the lowest possible cost," whereas others argue that higher quality costs more, so one must choose between the two. The crux of the argument lies in the differing definitions of quality. As stated earlier, quality is not the same as luxury. A Rolls Royce and a Volkswagen differ in many respects, but are they the same or different in quality? It may be difficult to decide which is the better value in terms of a quality/cost ratio.

It may be useful to differentiate between low quality and poor quality. A firm may choose to compete at the low end of the market for quality and price, but it cannot survive if it produces shoddy products that fail to give good value. For example, some airlines provide no-frills service by eliminating meals, preassigned seats, and other amenities in an effort to provide the lowest fare in the market. Yet they must still do proper maintenance on the aircraft and maintain an acceptable on-time record if they are to compete at any price. Similarly, disposable pens, cigarette lighters, and razors may be inexpensive, but they must perform their function well and meet the customer's expectation for reliability and durability.

The challenge in managing quality costs is similar to the challenge in many areas of operations management: Seek the lowest total cost of quality. To reach this goal, the operations manager must find the proper balance of four costs of quality (see exhibit 7-1).

Exhibit 7-1

Costs of Quality

COSTS OF CONTROL		COSTS OF FAILURE	
Prevention	Appraisal	Internal Failure	External Failure
- Quality planning and administration - Process analysis and improvement - Design and development of quality information equipment - Quality training and work-force development - Product design verification - Systems development and management	- Test and inspection of purchased materials - Laboratory acceptance testing and other measurement services - In-process inspection and testing - Checking quality by direct labor - Test and inspection equipment and material; setup; maintenance - Quality audits - Field testing	- Scrap (labor + material) - Rework (labor + material) - Additional material-procurement costs - Disposal costs - Product and production engineering time spent on quality problems - Production disruption, downtime, and rescheduling	- Warranty costs - Complaints out of warranty - Service cost to correct defects - Product liability - Product recall - Product returns - Loss of reputation, sales, and profits

Appraisal Costs

When raw materials are purchased and received, they normally are inspected and tested before being placed in inventory or released to production. Inspection of incoming materials requires inspection labor, test equipment, facilities space, and time to perform the tests. In some tests, part of the material must be destroyed before its quality can be properly checked. Test equipment must be maintained and periodically calibrated to assure accuracy. Finally, record keeping must be maintained to analyze quality histories on vendors and to perform quality audits.

Similarly, inspections and tests are performed at various stages in the process of manufacturing a product or producing a service. Sometimes these quality checks are performed by inspectors; often they are done by the worker doing the task. Inspections and tests throughout the process, including final inspection, incur more of the same costs described for incoming quality control. Together, these appraisal costs are incurred to determine whether the incoming material and the products produced meet quality standards.

Internal Failure Costs

If an unacceptable number of defects are found in incoming materials or in a batch of partially completed units, the batch will be rejected. Rejected lots may be returned to the vendor, screened to eliminate defective items, reworked to correct defects, or disposed of as scrap. Rejected lots must somehow be replaced; either new material must be ordered, or employees will need to work overtime to catch up to production schedules. If items are being produced repetitively rather than in batches, quality problems may necessitate stopping the process to correct the cause of defects.

All this lost material and disruption to the production schedule incurs additional costs for the firm. Internal failures, by definition, never reach the customer, but internal failures raise the cost per unit of the good items that are sold.

In services, examples of internal failure include finding too much salt in the soup before it is served, or finding a misrouted package in time to correct the error and still deliver it on time. However, since services usually involve the customer in the process of producing the service, most failures are external rather than internal.

External Failure Costs

Inevitably, some defects pass final inspection, and other defects may be created in the operations of packaging, material handling, transporting, storing, displaying, installing, and other postproduction activities. Defects that reach the customer (industrial or consumer) are called external failures. The costs of servicing warranties and guarantees as well as servicing out of warranty can be substantial. If an item fails, it may require return, repair, or replacement. If serious defects, such as design flaws, are found, a product recall may be necessary. In some cases, an external failure can result in a costly lawsuit under product-liability laws. Finally, too many external failures begin to erode the company's reputation and consequently affect its sales and profits.

Whereas manufactured goods usually can be returned and corrected, often services cannot. Poor service in a restaurant or a late-delivered package cannot be redone. Recently a patient had an operation to remove a malfunctioning kidney. The surgeon made an error and removed the good kidney. Compensation through a malpractice suit is the only remedy.

Prevention Costs

Rather than emphasizing detection and correction of defects, many firms today are placing more effort on preventing defects. The quality management approach examines the design of the product or service, the process and equipment used, the capabilities of the work force, and the planning and administration of all information systems in an effort to eliminate the cause of defects. No system can be error free, but if quality carries a high priority for the firm, sufficient attention will be given to preproduction planning activities and day-to-day operations to effect significant increases in quality levels.

It takes time and costs money to carefully review a product design for defects in the design itself or for defects that easily might be introduced during its manufacture. Perhaps Ford Motor Company should have spent more time reviewing the design of the Pinto. Very likely, that is one of the reasons Ford now has a corporate quality strategy.

Services, again, are subject to the same conditions. Many computer programmers and systems analysts have learned the hard way that additional time spent debugging the system prior to installation is less costly than dealing with errors after the system is implemented.

Minimum Total Quality Cost

It seems obvious that the way to reduce the costs of appraisal and failure is to prevent the defects and errors from being made. If causes of failure are reduced, less appraisal is needed and fewer corrections are required.

However, this is a classic cost trade-off problem, in which precise cost-benefit calculations for quality are difficult to obtain by traditional accounting systems. Most quality experts agree, however, that the total cost of quality is much higher than most executives would estimate and that far too little is spent on prevention rather than on appraisal or failure.

Conceptually, quality costs can be depicted as a cost-optimization problem (Figure 7-3). As more emphasis is placed on prevention activities, their costs rise. Correspondingly, the need for appraisal is reduced and the number of internal and external failures falls so these three costs go down. Somewhere in between is the optimal quality program. Although these costs cannot yet be precisely measured, a firm is more likely to be to the left of optimum than to the right.

Toyota provides an example of this concept. In many of its assembly plants, a cord is hung above the line similar to the emergency cord on a train that signals the engineer to stop. If any production worker spots a quality or safety problem, the cord is pulled and the line immediately stops.

Since downtime costs hundreds of dollars per minute, this grabs the attention of supervisors, managers, and engineers who immediately converge on the line. The problem is corrected and the line restarted; but, more important, the cause of the problem is analyzed and eliminated if possible. No one wants it to happen again. If it is an operator error, that worker does not want everyone in the plant to know about the foul-up. If it is an equipment or material problem, the appropriate person will follow up to see if this type of error can be prevented in the future.

At first, U.S. auto executives discarded this idea as too costly. Yet they were tolerating vast numbers of internal and external failures. Warranty costs were high and, at times, acres of parking lots were filled with cars awaiting rework after they had failed final inspection. Recently, some U.S. automobile manufacturers have implemented this new approach to quality improvement.

Although this cost analysis implies that there is an optimum between too high and too low a quality level, many firms are finding that the optimum lies at or very near zero defects. Motorola, competing in the volatile international electronics market, has instituted a program that they label "Six Sigma" meaning that their goal is to produce no more than two defects per billion units produced! Competition in this industry, as

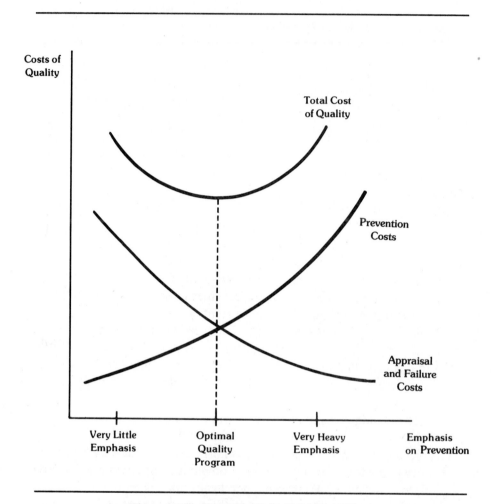

Figure 7-3. Quality-Cost Relationships

well as others such as health care, air transportation, and nuclear power generation, demand near perfection.

Statistical Quality Control

As indicated, a total quality program involves much more than simply inspecting the product; yet applications of statistical quality control to inspection and testing can be the key to *ensuring* that the quality program meets its goals. In fact, many firms have dropped the term "quality control" in favor of a more descriptive term, such as quality assurance, quality evaluation, customer assurance, or product integrity.

Inspection and testing can be causal or sophisticated. Some items can be inspected visually by the worker or an inspector to assure that no parts are missing and that the product "looks okay." In other applications, such as in pharmaceuticals, elaborate tests are employed against rigid standards for purity, weight, and content. Inspection points sometimes are placed throughout the process to monitor progress at each stage of completion. In still other instances, only a final inspection is performed.

Some defects are dichotomous; that is, the item is either good or bad. For example, a light bulb either lights or doesn't, and a packet of washers contains the right number of units or it doesn't. This situation is referred to as quality by **attributes.**

In other instances, quality can be measured by some continuous gauge. A can of coffee rarely contains *exactly* 1 pound. An acceptable range for this measure might be 15.3 to 16.7 ounces; a container with less than 15.3 ounces or more than 16.7 ounces is considered a "defective" unit. Other examples would be in the diameter of a rod, the temperature of a mixture, or the percentage of fat in hamburger. Quality in these cases is measured by **variables.**

Inspection and testing are performed for two basic reasons: (1) to remove all or most of the defective items, which is done by 100 percent inspection or *screening,* and (2) to predict the number of defects present, in which a small sample of items is checked by acceptance sampling.

Screening

Screening is performed when the cost from a defect is relatively high and the cost of inspection is relatively low. Screening also is indicated when many defects are believed present.

Consider a simple test for an electronic part that goes into a TV set. The test costs an average of 80 cents per unit for the inspector's time, equipment, supplies, and overhead. If a bad part is assembled into the set, the set will not work and will be rejected by the final inspection at the end of the assembly line. Rejected sets then are examined by a technician who must find the problem, remove the bad part, and replace it with a good part. This procedure costs the company 20 dollars for each defective set.

If only 3 percent of the parts are defective, then 3 percent of the assembled TV sets will incur the 20 dollar repair cost, or an average of 60 cents per set. But inspecting every part increases the cost of each set by 80 cents. In this instance, the firm would not perform the test because it would be more economical to repair the sets after assembly. If however, 5 percent of the parts were bad, it would pay to do the inspection. The 80 cent inspection cost per unit would be lower than the average repair cost of 5 percent times 20 dollars, or 1 dollar per set. The indifference point is

4 percent, where the cost of inspection and the cost of repair would be the same.

The same analysis can be applied to defective items that reach the customer, but the costs usually are not as well defined. Defects that reach the customer cost the firm in return, repair, customer dissatisfaction, and, occasionally, lawsuits. These costs must be balanced against the costs of testing and inspection before the product is sold.

One hundred percent inspection or screening does not guarantee freedom from defects; no inspection is perfect. Items can be inspected three, four, or even ten times and still malfunction. The defect may not show up in the test. It may have been overlooked, or it may have been introduced between the time of inspection and use of the product.

Acceptance Sampling

Acceptance sampling applies statistical analysis to a small sample of items to predict the number of defects present. It can be divided into the major categories of batch sampling and process sampling.

Batch sampling by attributes. Suppose the electronic parts mentioned above were purchased from a supplier in lots of 1,000 units. If the batch contained 4 percent or fewer defects, the firm would want to accept it and use it in production. If the batch contained 5 percent or more defects, it would be best to reject it and either return it to the manufacturer or screen it before use. The challenge is to predict the number of defects in the batch through statistical analysis of a sample.

If a firm is sampling by attributes (the part is either good or bad), a sample is drawn, the number of defects in the sample is counted, and then the lot is accepted or rejected based upon the results of the sample.

A sample plan contains two elements: a sample size and an acceptance number. Charts and tables are available for determining the proper sample plan, but to use these effectively, the underlying theory of sampling must be understood.

For example, take a sample of 50 units, with an acceptance number of two. This plan says to count the number of defects in the sample and accept the lot if there are zero, one, or two defects; three or more defects in the sample indicate the lot should be rejected. Sampling does not give perfect information; two types of errors can be made, as illustrated in figure 7-4.

In the example, a "good lot" is one with 4 percent or fewer defects; a "bad lot" is one with more than 4 percent defective items. With a sample of 50, it would be possible to get three or more defective items even though the lot contains less than 4 percent defective (less than 40 out of

	Accept	Reject
Good **Lot**	No Error	Type 1 Error (Alpha)
Bad **Lot**	Type II Error (Beta)	No Error

Figure 7-4. Sampling Errors

1,000). The sample then would indicate rejection of the lot, which would be a Type I error. Usually, however, the sample would be correct, and the lot would be accepted.

With probability theory, the chance of accepting or rejecting a lot with a given percentage defective can be calculated. Calculating the probability of acceptance for each different lot percent defective produces an operating-characteristics curve like the one in figure 7-5.

The operating-characteristics curve indicates that lots with 2 percent defective items will be accepted 85 percent of the time; 15 percent of the time they will be rejected. This 15 percent is α (alpha) and often is called the *producer's risk,* because even though a good lot was produced, by chance it was rejected. Similarly, a lot with 7 percent defective would, with this sample plan, be accepted 20 percent of the time. This probability is labeled β (beta) and is called the *consumer's risk,* because the consumer runs a 20 percent chance of accepting this lot that really should be rejected.

A sample plan is set by choosing values for four variables. First is the specification, in terms of percent defective, of a really good lot, one that very often should be accepted. The percent defective specified is called the acceptable quality level (AQL), and the probability associated with "very often" is alpha. In this example, lots with an AQL of 2 percent will be accepted 85 percent of the time, but the plan will reject them 15 percent of the time. Next, a really bad lot, one that should be accepted infrequently, must be specified. The bad lot percent defective is called the lot tolerance percent defective (LTPD), and it is accepted with a probability of 20 percent (beta). These four coordinates define one, and

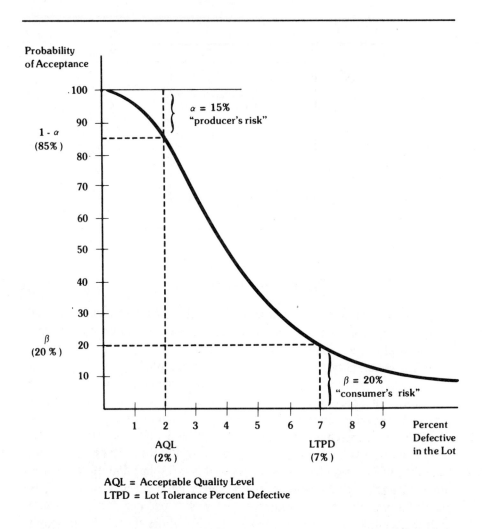

AQL = Acceptable Quality Level
LTPD = Lot Tolerance Percent Defective

Figure 7-5. Operating-Characteristics Curve

only one, operating-characteristics curve that is associated with only one sample plan made up of a sample size and a given acceptance number.

To make fewer errors, or if the firm is willing to make more errors, a different sample plan must be used. The problem is one of balancing a Type I error (alpha) against a Type II error (beta) and then balancing the cost of these errors against the cost of sampling. Figure 7-6 illustrates the relationship of the acceptance number to the types of errors when the sample size remains the same. A *tighter* plan (n, sample size = 50; c, acceptance number = 1) will make more Type I errors but fewer Type II errors. Fewer lots of any percent defective will by accepted, meaning that

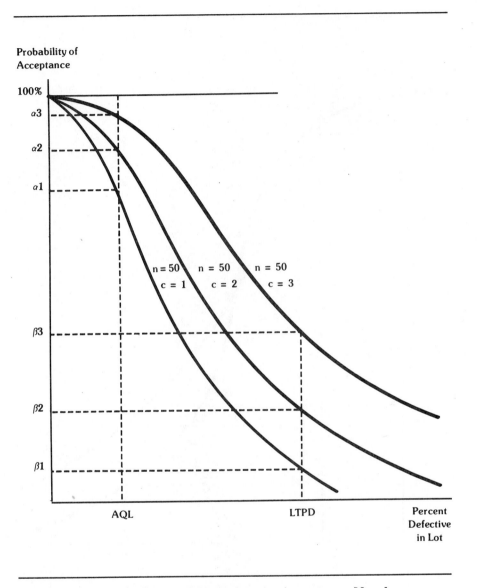

Figure 7-6. Effect of Changing the Acceptance Number

more good lots will be rejected, but fewer bad ones will be accepted. A *looser* sample plan (n = 50; c = 3) would do the opposite.

To make fewer errors of both types, the firm must go to a larger, more accurate sample. Figure 7-7 illustrates the effect of a larger sample size using the same relative acceptance number. The larger sample will lead to fewer errors but will be more costly.

The operating-characteristics curve illustrates the theory behind batch sampling for attributes. To find an appropriate sample plan,

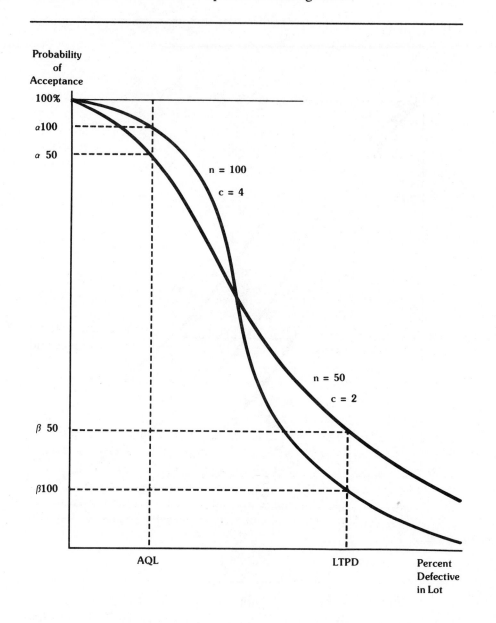

Figure 7-7. Effect of Changing the Samples Size

however, the decision maker needs only to set levels for the AQL, LTPD, alpha, and beta and use the charts established for this purpose.

Batch sampling by variables. If the quality characteristic being inspected, such as weight, temperature, or thickness, is measured on a continuous scale, tolerance limits must be set to distinguish good from bad items. For example, one type of automobile tire may be considered acceptable if it will last 25,000 miles, plus or minus 3,000 miles. A sample of several tires from the batch could be drawn and tested, and the average mileage in the sample would be used to estimate the percent of tires in the lot that would last 22,000 to 28,000 miles. The lot then would be accepted or rejected based upon that estimate.

Process Control

If the item being inspected is manufactured repetitively rather than in batches, the problem involves monitoring the process to assure that standards are being met. Periodic random samples are taken and plotted on a chart to determine whether the process is "in control" and should continue or is "out of control" and requires corrective action.

Control charts have a line of central tendency (average) and both an upper and lower control limit. These limits generally are set at plus and minus three standard deviations from the mean.

A **P-Chart** (figure 7-8) is used for **process sampling by attributes,** thus the central line is the average percent defective for the process when it is operating under normal conditions. Samples taken from the process are inspected and the percent defective in each sample is plotted on the chart. To determine if the process is in control, upper and lower control limits are needed.

Although the underlying distribution for drawing a sample from a dichotomous process is binomial, the central limit theorem tells us that estimates of the population percent defective will tend to be normal with a standard deviation of

$$\sigma_p = \sqrt{\frac{\bar{p}(1-\bar{p})}{n}}$$

where n is the sample size and $\bar{p}$ is the average percent defective for the process. Upper and lower control limits are generally set at three standard deviations from the mean, thus

$$\text{UCL} = \bar{p} + 3\sigma_p \quad \text{and} \quad \text{LCL} = \bar{p} - 3\sigma_p$$

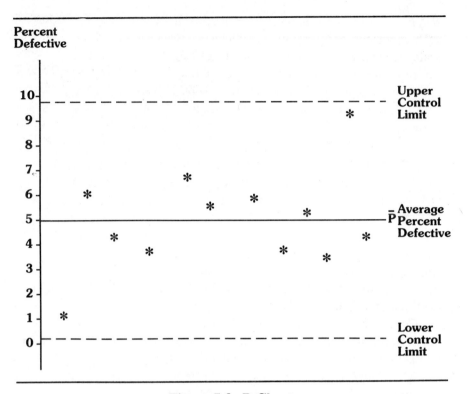

Figure 7-8. P-Chart

For example, consider a process with a long-term average of 5 percent defective (0.05) from which we plan to take periodic samples of 200 units. The standard deviation would be

$$\sigma_p = \sqrt{\frac{(0.05)\ (0.95)}{200}} = 0.015$$

and the control limits would be

$$UCL = 0.05 + 3(0.015) = 0.095 \text{ and}$$
$$LCL = 0.05 - 3(0.015) = 0.005$$

Data plotted on the p-chart in figure 7-8 for the first twelve days of operation indicate that the process appears to be in control.

Process sampling by variables requires monitoring both the mean and the variance of the quality characteristic. The mean of the sample (average weight, for example) is plotted on an $\bar{X}$ ("x-bar") **chart,** illustrated in figure 7-9. Samples outside the control limits indicate that the average weight of the units has probably shifted (too heavy or too light)

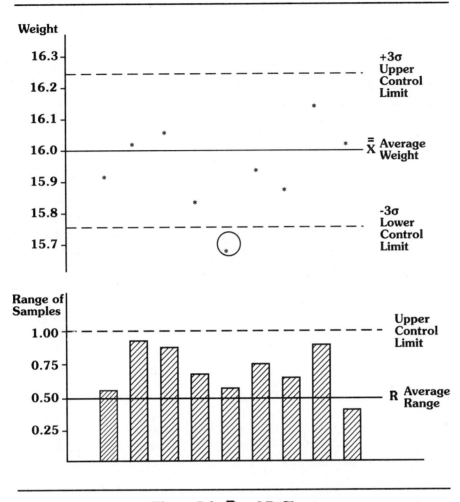

Figure 7-9. X̄ and R-Chart

and a machine adjustment is necessary. Below the X̄-chart, the range of the weights of the units sampled is plotted on an R-chart to indicate the variance of the process. A sample outside the control limits on this chart would indicate that some units are too heavy and others too light, even though the average is still in acceptable limits.

If the process mean and standard deviation are not known, the analyst can assure that the process is operating properly ("in control") and then take successive samples calculating the mean and range of each. The average of the means, X̄̄, is used as the line of central tendency on the X̄-chart. The average range of the samples, R̄, is an estimate of the variance of the process and, therefore, can be used to calculate the control limits of the X̄-chart using the A_2 factor from table 7-1. Factors in

Table 7-1

Factors for Control Charts

n	A_2	d_2	D_3	D_4
2	1.880	1.128	0	3.267
3	1.023	1.693	0	2.575
4	0.729	2.059	0	2.282
5	0.577	2.326	0	2.115
6	0.483	2.534	0	2.004
7	0.419	2.704	0.076	1.924
8	0.373	2.847	0.136	1.864
9	0.337	2.970	0.184	1.816
10	0.308	3.078	0.223	1.777
11	0.285	3.173	0.256	1.744
12	0.266	3.258	0.284	1.716
13	0.249	3.336	0.308	1.692
14	0.235	3.407	0.329	1.671
15	0.223	3.472	0.348	1.652
16	0.212	3.532	0.364	1.636
17	0.203	3.588	0.379	1.621
18	0.194	3.640	0.392	1.608
19	0.187	3.689	0.404	1.596
20	0.180	3.735	0.414	1.586
21	0.173	3.778	0.425	1.575
22	0.167	3.819	0.434	1.566
23	0.162	3.858	0.443	1.557
24	0.157	3.895	0.452	1.548
25	0.153	3.931	0.459	1.541

Source: Reproduced with permission from Table B2 of the A.S.T.M. Manual on Quality Control of Materials, 1951, p.115.

this table are constants that adjust for the difference between the range and the variance of a distribution.

The control limits for the $\bar{X}$-chart are then found with the formulas:

$$UCL_{\bar{X}} = \bar{\bar{X}} + A_2\bar{R} \qquad \text{and} \qquad LCL_{\bar{X}} = \bar{\bar{X}} - A_2\bar{R}$$

In the coffee filling example, analysis of past samples have revealed an average mean, $\bar{\bar{X}}$, of 16.0 ounces with an average range, $\bar{R}$, of 0.52 based on samples of size six. The $\bar{X}$-chart has a central line of 16.0 and control limits of

$$UCL = 16.0 + 0.483\,(0.52) = 16.25 \text{ and}$$
$$LCL = 16.0 - 0.483\,(0.52) = 15.75$$

The R-chart can be displayed in the same format as the $\bar{X}$-chart or it can be plotted as a bar graph as shown here in figure 7-9. (The $\bar{X}$-chart and the R-chart are always shown together because they track two parameters of the process–mean and standard deviation–with each sample.) $\bar{R}$ is the line of central tendency and the control limits are found with the following formulas using the factors from table 7-1.

$$UCL_R = D_4\bar{R} \qquad \text{and} \qquad LCL_R = D_3\bar{R}$$

The R-chart for the coffee filling example has a central line of 0.52 with control limits of

$$UCL_R = 2.004\,(0.52) = 1.042 \text{ and}$$
$$LCL_R = 0\,(0.52) = 0$$

Examination of the charts in figure 7-9 reveals that the fifth sample fell outside of the lower control limit of the $\bar{X}$-chart indicating that there may be a problem with the filling equipment or the consistency of the coffee. Although none of the samples fell outside of the control limits of the R-chart, there may still be a problem indicated. If the process were in control, one would expect approximately half of the sample ranges to fall above the central line and half below. For this period, most of the samples fell above the central line indicating that there is a high probability that the process variance is out of control. In addition to looking for points outside the control limits, astute analysts look for patterns on the charts that indicate problems.

Patterns on Process Control Charts

Results of samples drawn from a process population are governed by the laws of probability, in this case based on the normal distribution. Although aberrations can occasionally occur, patterns that deviate from these statistical expectations indicate probable problems with the process provided that the samples were taken randomly. For example, based on the normal distribution, over two-thirds of the samples should fall within $\pm$ one standard deviation of the mean and approximately 96 percent should be contained within two standard deviations about the mean. Runs, such as five or six sample statistics going consistently up or down are extremely unlikely and give a strong indication that the process is going out of control. Figure 7-10 contains several patterns that should catch the analyst's attention.

Process Capability

A process is in control if it is set up and operating properly within the limits of its capability. That does not mean that the product from this process will meet the specifications or tolerances set by the design engineer, the customer, or, in some cases, government regulations. **Process capability** is the relationship of the normal variance of the process (plus and minus three standard deviations) to the tolerance limits set for the product. It can be calculated using the **process capability index:**

$$C_p = \frac{UTL - LTL}{6\sigma}$$

where

$$UTL = \text{upper tolerance limit}$$
$$LTL = \text{lower tolerance limit}$$
$$\sigma = \text{standard deviation of the process}$$

In the coffee filling example, the tolerances are 15.3 to 16.7 ounces. The standard deviation of the process can be estimated from the range using the formula $\sigma = R/d_2$ where d_2 is a factor from table 7-1. Our

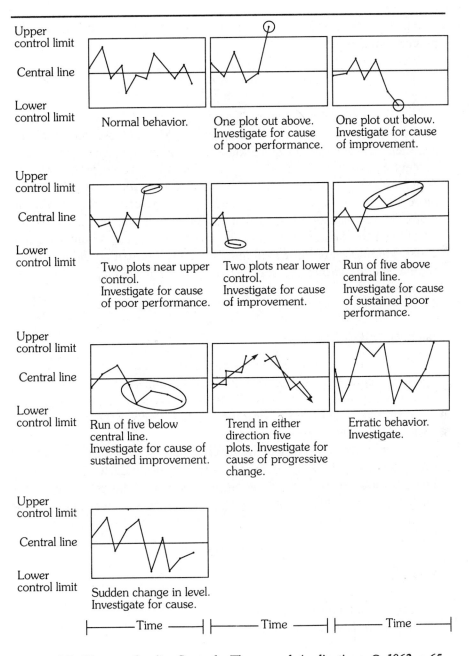

Upper control limit

Central line

Lower control limit

Normal behavior.

One plot out above. Investigate for cause of poor performance.

One plot out below. Investigate for cause of improvement.

Upper control limit

Central line

Lower control limit

Two plots near upper control. Investigate for cause of poor performance.

Two plots near lower control. Investigate for cause of improvement.

Run of five above central line. Investigate for cause of sustained poor performance.

Upper control limit

Central line

Lower control limit

Run of five below central line. Investigate for cause of sustained improvement.

Trend in either direction five plots. Investigate for cause of progressive change.

Erratic behavior. Investigate.

Upper control limit

Central line

Lower control limit

Sudden change in level. Investigate for cause.

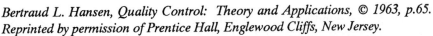

├——— Time ———┤├——— Time ———┤├——— Time ———┤

Bertraud L. Hansen, Quality Control: Theory and Applications, © 1963, p.65. Reprinted by permission of Prentice Hall, Englewood Cliffs, New Jersey.

Figure 7-10. Control Chart Patterns

estimate of the standard deviation is $\sigma = 0.52/2.534 = 0.205$ and the process capability, therefore is

$$C_p = \frac{16.7 - 15.3}{6\,(0.205)} = 1.138$$

A process capability of 1.0 means that if the process is perfectly centered between the specifications, it would produce less than three percent defects, but if the process shifted at all, it would produce more. A process capability less than one means that the process would produce more than three percent defects under the best of conditions, and an index greater than one means that the process is capable of remaining well within the tolerances even if the mean of the process shifts slightly. These conditions are illustrated in figure 7-11. Our coffee filling process should operate within the specified tolerances if no major shift in the process mean occurs.

System Reliability

One of the several meanings of reliability given earlier is system reliability, defined as the probability that the finished product will function properly given that it is assembled from components which are less than perfect. Calculation of system reliability involves the application of basic probability concepts.

For example, suppose a manufacturer is assembling a lamp composed of a plug, a switch, and a bulb (plus other parts). Each of the components must work properly if the lamp is to light. The reliability of the lamp (the probability it will work when assembled) is determined by the formula:

$$R_S = R_1\,R_2\ldots R_n$$

where

R_S = reliability of the system
R_n = reliability of the nth component

In our example, if each component contains five percent defective units (95 percent reliable) the reliability of the lamp is:

$R_S = (0.95)\,(0.95)\,(0.95) = 0.857$

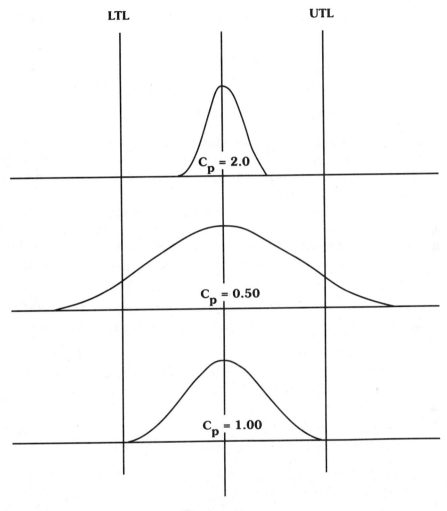

Reprinted by permission from The Management and Control of Quality, James R. Evans and William M. Lindsay. Copyright © 1989 by West Publishing Company. All rights reserved.

Figure 7-11. Process Capability Index

Thus less than 86 percent of the lamps will work properly; about fourteen percent $(1 - 0.857)$ will fail.

This does not mean that the company will ship fourteen percent defective items. A final inspection will catch all lamps that fail. Defective items will be checked to see which component is at fault and that component will be replaced. This process of "rework" costs $50.00 per defect for labor and materials and therefore adds $(1 - 0.857)$ $(\$50) = \$7.15$ to the unit cost of all items produced. This is the "hidden factory" referred to earlier.

Suppose a new supplier can be found that will furnish plugs that cost $1.50 more per unit but are guaranteed to be no more than one percent defective. Is this a wise purchase? the new system reliability would be:

$$R_S = (0.99)\ (0.95)\ (0.95)\ =\ 0.893$$

and with $1 - 0.893 = 0.107$ (10.7 percent) defects, the failure cost would be $(0.107)\ (\$50) = \$5.35$ for a savings of $1.80 per unit produced. Compared to the purchase price increase of the plug of $1.50, the firm would save a net $.30 per lamp.

The reliability of complex systems drops rapidly as the number of components increases. For example, a system assembled from only ten components which are five percent defective yields a system reliability less than 60 percent. To combat this problem, firms use three primary strategies.

1. **Foolproof designs** for products and processes reduce or eliminate the possibility of introducing a defect in the manufacture of the product.

2. **Reliable components** increase system reliability directly; in some industries "five nines" (0.99999) reliability standards for components are common.

3. **Redundancy** adds back-up components to the system so that if a component fails, the back-up prevents system failure.

The reliability of a system with a redundant component can be calculated by first determining the reliability of the redundant component and then following the standard procedure for determining system reliability. For example, the system diagramed below has four components with a back-up for component two. The reliability of each component is shown. Since both elements of component two must fail to cause system failure, the probability of this happening is $(1 - 0.90)\ (1 - 0.90) = 0.01$ so the reliability of this component is $1 - 0.01 = 0.99$. The system reliability is then $R_S = (0.96)\ (0.99)\ (0.98)\ (0.98) = 0.912$.

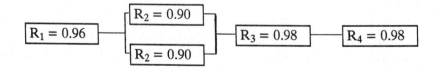

Systems reliability applies to services in much the same way is does to manufactured products. The components of a service delivery system—

people, equipment and materials–must be present and functioning properly for the service to be successfully accomplished, and the same strategies are employed to improve reliability. For example, many service firms build redundancy into their system in the form of stand-by equipment or extra employees to hedge against equipment breakdown or absenteeism.

The Growing Importance of Quality

Quality always has been an important factor in the production of goods and services, but recent developments have added emphasis and urgency. It is likely that the quality dimension of output will grow in relative importance as firms adjust to changing times.

Consumer advocacy, typified by the work of Ralph Nader, tells organizational leaders what consumers expect. They are tired of products that break, appliances that do not function, and services that are superficial and shoddy. Through both the marketplace and the media, united groups of citizens have found that even the largest organization can be influenced to change the quality of its output.

Consumers also are gaining more strength through new legislation and interpretations of existing legislation relating to product and service liability. Million-dollar lawsuits, which used to be rare, are becoming much more common. The cost of a defect should be weighted against the cost of quality-control efforts to prevent it. Product-liability suits have the effect of pushing up the cost of a defect. Rational decision makers within the firm respond by redoubling their efforts to assure that million-dollar liability defects do not leave the plant. Automobile recalls, food and drug prohibitions, malpractice suits, and scandals in financial institutions indicate that all forms of businesses, private and public, are feeling the pressures.

Increasing foreign and domestic competition merely intensifies the problem. Detroit automobile makers are painfully aware of the quality as well as the cost and style differences between their products and those from Japan or Europe. The U.S. Postal Service is losing business to private delivery services that can provide better service in some urban areas.

In response to these pressures and in anticipation of increasing emphasis in the future, some consumer-product firms have created a new corporate-level executive with the title of vice president of product integrity. The job involves not only monitoring the manufacture of many products but also working with designers, chemists, industrial engineers, and others who have an impact on the quality of the product. The executive conducts extensive environmental tests on all products and has the power to recall any item considered unsafe, unreliable, or unfair to the consumer.

Emphasis on quality is just one indicator of the recognition of its importance in the ever-changing production function.

Key Concepts

Definition of Quality	**Sample Plan**
Dimensions of Quality	**Operating Characteristics Curve**
Total Quality Management (TQM)	**Type I/Type II Errors**
Behavioral and Technical Factors Affecting Quality	**Consumer's Risk/Producer's Risk**
Quality Costs	**AQL/LTPD**
Attributes/Variables	**Process Sampling**
Batch Sampling	**X-Bar and R-Chart**
Process Control	**System Reliability**
P-Chart	**Redundancy**
Process Capability	**Fishbone Diagram**
Control Chart Patterns	**Baldrige Award**

References

Crosby, Philip B. *Quality Is Free.* New York: McGraw-Hill, 1979.

Deming, W. Edwards. "Improvement of Quality and Productivity through Action by Management." *National Productivity Review* 1 (Winter, 1981–1982): 12–22.

Deming, W. Edwards. *Quality, Productivity, and Competitive Position,* Boston: MIT Center for Advanced Engineering, 1982.

Feigenbaum, Armand V. *Total Quality Control.* 3d ed. New York: McGraw-Hill, 1983.

Garvin, David A. "Quality on the Line." *Harvard Business Review* 61 (September–October) 1983): 64–75.

Garvin, David A. *Managing Quality,* New York: The Free Press, 1988.

Gitlow, Howard S., and Gitlow, Shelly J. *The Deming Guide to Quality and Competitive Position.* Englewood Cliffs, NJ: Prentice-Hall, 1987.

Grant, E. L., and Leavenworth, R. S. *Statistical Quality Control.* 6th ed. New York: McGraw-Hill, 1988.

Hostage, B. M. "Quality Control in a Service Business." *Harvard Business Review* 53 (July–August 1975): 98–106.

Juran, J. M. *Juran on Planning for Quality,* New York: The Free Press, 1988.

Leonard, Frank S., and Sasser, Earl. "The Incline of Quality." *Harvard Business Review* 60 (September–October 1982): 163–171.

Shingo, Shigeo. *Zero Quality Control,* Stamford, CT: Productivity Press, 1986.

Zeithaml, Valerie A., Parasuraman, A., and Berry, Leonard A. *Delivering Quality Service,* New York: The Free Press, 1990.

Discussion Questions

1. An optimal quality-control policy balances opposing costs. What are the costs involved and the problems of finding the optimal balance in each of the following:

   a. McDonald's hamburgers?

   b. Grant County Blood Bank?

   c. Southwestern Publishing Company–textbook division?

   d. Gaines Petfood Division?

   e. American Airlines–maintenance division?

2. Your company is planning to introduce a super-deluxe doghouse with lights, air conditioning, windows, and an automatic food and water dispenser. What quality problems would you anticipate?

3. You are the president of a company in a meeting with several of your department heads. The marketing vice president says that company salespeople have received customer complaints that the quality of the product is not up to that of competitors. Also attending the meeting are the following:

a. Purchasing manager–responsible for acquisition of all raw materials and supplies

b. Personnel Manager–responsible for recruiting, selecting, and training all workers

c. Plant Engineer–responsible for equipment installation, layout, maintenance, and repair

e. Quality-Control Manager–responsible for all incoming, in-process, and final testing and inspection

What would you tell each of these department heads? Are there others who should be in this meeting? What additional information do you need?

4. Alice wants to take a random sample of the product her department is making to assess its quality. Because she is busy with other things, she decides that the easiest strategy is to take four samples: one the first thing in the morning, one before she goes to lunch, one when she returns from lunch, and one just before she goes home. What problems do you see with this plan?

5. A customer complained that the switch on the lawn edger your company produces is faulty. The salesperson explained that the switch is a purchased part; since your company does not manufacture it, you cannot control its quality. The customer, not satisfied with that answer, wrote a formal letter of complaint to you, the company president. What letter would you write in response?

6. Five dimensions of quality were discussed in this chapter. Do any or all of these dimensions apply to a service business, as a car wash or a pizza parlor? Explain.

7. Carefully explain the difference between the tolerance limits for a product set by the design engineer and the control limits on the process chart for that product.

8. Which is more important in affecting quality: technical factors or behavioral factors? Concisely explain the relationship between the two.

9. The various costs associated with quality tend to change as the environment changes. Which of these costs is likely to increase in the future, and which is likely to decline? What effect will this have on the optimal quality program?

10. If you were buying a bicycle and had a choice between one that cost $50 but fell apart at the end of one year, and a different model that

cost $200 but lasted five to ten years, which one would you buy? Which one is of the higher quality?

Problems

1. An inspector took thirty samples of eight items and found $\bar{\bar{X}} = 520$ and $\bar{R} = 36$. Determine the control limits for the $\bar{X}$-chart and the R-chart. What is your estimate of the standard deviation of the process?

2. Twenty-four samples of six items produced an $\bar{\bar{X}}$ of 8.25 and an $\bar{R}$ of 3.5. Determine the control limits for the $\bar{X}$- and R-charts.

3. The following data was taken from a new process using samples of n = 4. Use this data to determine the central line and control limits for an $\bar{X}$-chart and an R-chart.

SAMPLE	X	R	SAMPLE	X	R
1	25.44	0.55	11	24.95	0.80
2	25.31	0.67	12	25.21	0.50
3	24.90	1.10	13	25.75	0.44
4	25.83	0.73	14	25.30	0.78
5	24.98	0.58	15	25.64	1.05
6	25.23	0.85	16	25.22	0.75
7	26.03	0.64	17	25.60	0.90
8	25.54	0.88	18	25.48	0.82
9	25.60	0.71	19	25.77	1.02
10	25.39	0.97	20	25.86	0.66

4. A process has a mean of $\bar{\bar{X}} = 120.0$ and an $\bar{R} = 26.5$ based on fifty samples of ten. Construct the $\bar{X}$-chart and R-charts and then plot the following recent samples on the charts. Interpret the results.

SAMPLE	$\bar{X}$	R	SAMPLE	$\bar{X}$	R
1	126	28.0	6	117	31.5
2	119	22.5	7	121	28.0
3	121	26.0	8	124	18.0
4	123	15.0	9	125	35.5
5	116	19.5	10	127	24.5

5. To develop a control chart for attributes, an inspector took twenty-four samples of eighty items each. The average percent defective was 3%. Determine the upper and lower control limits for the chart.

6. Over the past month fifty samples of 350 units from a process yielded a total of 263 defects. Construct the control chart for this process.

7. If $p = 0.025$ and $\sigma_p = 0.008$, construct a p-chart and plot the following data. Interpret the results. Should any action be taken?

SAMPLE	SIZE	DEFECTS
1	150	3
2	150	6
3	150	4
4	150	5
5	150	3

8. If a product is composed of seven interdependent parts, four of which are 95% reliable and the other three are 99%, 92%, and 98% reliable, what is the system reliability of the product?

9. In the example above, if one of the 95% reliable components were made redundant with a backup, how much would the system reliability of the product change?

10. A product currently has four components with reliabilities of 98%, 97%, 90%, and 96%. The cost of a failure in the product is $100. How much would the firm be willing to pay to provide a backup for the third (90%) component? How much for the first (98%) component?

Glossary

ABC Analysis: Arrangement of activities–for example, total dollars spent for purchase of particular items–in descending dollar value, so that resources (time) can be allocated according to the relative importance of each activity.

Absentee Service: A category of service in which no physical product is involved and the customer does not have to be present; custodial service is an example.

Acceptable Quality Level (AQL): The percentage of defects in a lot that would be acceptable most of the time.

Acceptance Number: The maximum number of defects allowed in a sample for acceptance of a lot.

Acceptance Sampling: Inspection of a sample in order to predict the number of defects present in the entire lot. (*See* Batch Sampling and Process Sampling.)

Alpha Error: In quality control, for a given sample plan, the percentage of times a good lot is rejected. (*See* Type I Error.)

Anticipatory Stocks: Items produced and stored to meet high demand in a later period.

Appraisal Costs: Costs incurred in efforts to inspect and detect defects in incoming material or within production processes.

Approved List: List of those vendors who have been evaluated and estimated to be capable of satisfactory performance.

Assembly Chart: A chart showing the components and subassemblies of a product and the sequence of assembly.

Attributes Sampling: Quality sampling in which the characteristic is measured on a dichotomous basis, such as "good/bad."

Attributes: In quality control, refers to dichotomous characteristics that make each unit either good or bad (defective); *See* also variables.

Automated Batch Manufacturing Systems (ABMS): A system of several individual machines that process parts into finished units while carried through the system attached to pallets.

Baldrige Award: An award presented annually by the U.S. Department of Commerce to a manufacturing, service, and/or small business firm for exceptional quality performance.

Batch Production: Producing items periodically in batches (lots) to meet demand.

Batch Sampling: Inspection of a sample from a lot in order to accept or reject the entire lot.

Behavioral Factors: Characteristics of the worker, such as knowledge, skills, and motivation, that affect the quality of the product produced.

Benchmarking: Comparisons of organizational performance, such as quality, purchasing effectiveness, or productivity, to the best organizations in the world.

Beta Error: In quality control, for a given sample plan, the percentage of times a bad lot is accepted (*See* Type II Error.)

Bill of Materials: A list of all parts and materials, including the quantities of each, that are required to produce one unit of a finished product.

Blank-Check Purchase Order: Purchase agreement in which vendor is sent a signed, blank check. (After shipment, the vendor enters amount due on the check and deposits it.)

Blanket Order: Purchase agreement with a vendor to provide the supply of an item for a fixed time period, normally one year.

Break-Even Analysis: Determination of production volume where sales revenue equals the total of variable and fixed costs, or where costs from two processes intersect.

Break-Even Time: A model for evaluating research and development which determines the time for the operating profit for a product to cover all development costs.

Breakdown Repair: Maintenance work undertaken only after the equipment malfunctions or breaks down.

Buffer Stock: *See* Safety Stock.

Capacity Requirements Planning (CRP): A process that translates manufacturing plans into labor hours and machine processing hours required in each time period (e.g., one week) for the time covered by the planning process.

Carrying Costs: Those costs incurred because something is being stored and not currently used. (The cost is proportional to the number or quantity of the item stored. Typical carrying costs reflect the value of the space occupied by the stored item, the value of the funds tied up in the stock, and insurance costs to protect the stock).

Cash Discount: Discount, normally 2 percent, granted if payment is made to vendor within a limited time, normally ten days.

Cellular Layout: Arrangement of several machines into a cell or group to produce a family of related products.

Centralized Purchasing: System in which all purchase decisions must be made, and all purchase orders released, by the purchasing agent or department.

Chase Production Strategy: *See* Flexible Production Strategy.

Competitive Bid: Offer to sell, at a price, made by a vendor.

Components of Variation: Types of variation in a time series that must be considered in making forecasts; *See* Cyclical, Random, Seasonal, and Trend Components.

Computer Integrated Manufacturing (CIM): Integrating planning, scheduling, and production control with computer methods that link together automated manufacturing equipment.

Computer-Aided Design (CAD): A design technique in which the computer is used to instantaneously draw pictures on a television screen of what an engineer has designed.

Computer-Aided Manufacturing (CAM): Use of a preprogrammed tool path to provide direct numerical control in the operation of equipment.

Consumer's Risk: *See* Beta Error.

Control Chart Patterns: Patterns of sample statistics, such as runs or erratic behavior, that indicate a process is likely out of control even though samples are within control limits.

Countertrade: An agreement to buy a certain percentage (often 50 to 100 percent of sales) in foreign goods from a country that is buying U.S. goods.

CPM: Acronym for the critical path method, a network modeling technique used to plan and control large-scale projects.

Cross-Functional Teams: Teams made up of members from engineering, production, marketing, purchasing, and other functions to do product design, production planning, or some other activity.

Cycle Counting: A method of checking inventory levels and records on a routine basis–for example, verifying 2 percent of all stock items each week, with some important items being checked more than once a year. (This approach avoids the disruptive effects of the annual "physical" inventory).

Cycle Stock: The active portion of inventory–that is, the quantity that is depleted, resupplied, depleted, and resupplied again and again. (Cycle stock does not include the quantity known as safety stock.)

Cycle Time: The time required, including normal delays, to manufacture a product or produce a service from the release of the order to its completion.

Cyclical Component: Time-series variations that are periodic in nature, extending over a period of years; important in forecasting demand.

Decoupling Stock: That inventory used to isolate sequential operations or departments from one another so that they can perform independently.

Dependent Demand: Demand derived from the demand for a final product or other item; also called internal demand.

Detailed Scheduling: Matching the job and resource flows required to meet the master schedule requirements on a time scale.

Durability: The ability of a product to function under adverse conditions.

Economic Lot Size (ELS): The number of units produced at one time to minimize the combined costs of setups and carrying inventory over a specified planning period, usually a year.

Economic Order Quantity (EOQ): The number of units purchased at one time to minimize the combined costs of ordering material and storing the inventory over a specified planning period, usually a year.

Effectiveness: The degree to which the organization's objectives or purposes are achieved.

Efficiency: The relative amount of resources and time consumed in the production of output.

Electronic Data Interchange (EDI): Transmission of data between a firm's purchasing data base and a supplier's data base through a telecommunications system to facilitate purchasing.

Element: A subdivision of a task. (Elements are used in the analysis of work.)

Energy Management Program (EMP): A program designed to control and reduce energy requirements.

Escalation/Deescalation: Purchase contract clause in a long-term agreement which provides that price automatically increases or decreases if a specific economic change occurs (e.g., basic steel price increases).

Expediting: In purchasing, putting pressure on a vendor to assure that the original delivery promise is met or to get earlier delivery. In production, it means changing the priority of a problem job so that it or other jobs may progress more smoothly through subsequent operations.

Exploding: Multiplying the number of end items to be produced by the bill of materials to determine the components and materials needed.

Exponential Smoothing: A mathematical forecasting model that uses past forecasts and forecast errors to make a new forecast.

External Demand: *See* Independent Demand.

External Failure Costs: Costs associated with a defect that reaches the customer; includes returns, warranty costs, lawsuits, and customer dissatisfaction.

Extrinsic Models: Forecasting techniques that determine how variables external to the organization (e.g., new building permits issued) help predict variables internal to the organization (e.g., lumber sales).

Factory of the Future: The concept of a highly automated computer-controlled factory that can produce large or small lots efficiently and respond to changes quickly.

Finite Loading: Assigning jobs to a work center not to exceed its capacity.

Fishbone Diagram: A schematic tool that outlines the possible causes of a problem; organized by employees, machines, methods, measurement, and materials.

Fixed Path Equipment: Relatively inflexible equipment (conveyors, chutes, cranes, and hoists) that handles materials in large volume, normally in a continuous flow.

Fixed-Position Layout: Due to weight or bulk of the product being manufactured, the product remains in one position while workers, tools, and materials move to it.

Flexible Manufacturing System (FMS): Processes that are easily adaptable to different products and lot sizes with minimal changeover time.

Flexible Production Strategy: Planning production to meet the highs and lows of current demand; also called a "chase" strategy.

Flow Diagram: Symbols connected by arrows on a floor plan to depict the flow of the work process.

Flow-process production: Continuous-flow manufacturing, where the output is not in discrete units. Petroleum refining is an example of flow-process production.

Follow-up of Purchase Order: Routine checking on the status of a purchase to determine whether the vendor will be able to meet the required delivery date.

Forecast Horizon: The time period over which the forecast is to be developed.

Foreign Purchasing: Purchase by U.S. firms of goods from vendors outside North America.

Forward Buying: Purchase of a larger-than-normal quantity, due to anticipated shortage or price increase.

Functionality: The degree to which a product or service performs the function for which it was designed.

Group Layout: *See* Cellular Layout.

Group Technology: An approach to manufacturing that groups families of related products to gain planning and manufacturing economies.

Hand-to-Mouth Buying: Purchase of a smaller-than-normal quantity, due to anticipated market oversupply or price decrease.

Heuristic: A rule-of-thumb approach developed and utilized as a guide to solving problems and making decisions.

Independent Demand: Demand originating from external sources such as direct customer orders; also called external demand.

Infinite Loading: Assigning jobs to a work center without regard to its capacity.

Internal Demand: *See* Dependent Demand.

Internal Failure Costs: Costs associated with defects found before they reach the customer; includes scrap, rework, materials returned to the vendor, and production disruptions.

Intrinsic Models: Forecasting techniques that use only the history of the variable to be projected; commonly called time-series models.

JIT (Just-In-Time) Management System: An integrated combination of techniques designed to improve performance through reduced set-up times, smaller lot sizes, shorter cycle times, and lower overall inventory levels.

Job Shop: Production of many products in small lot sizes, usually to a customer order, such as a print shop.

Judgmental Models: Forecasting techniques that use expert opinion regarding anticipated happenings to predict future occurrences.

Kanban: A specific form of the "pull" system of production in which cards are used to signal reorders of materials or the performance of production activities at work centers.

Layout: The arrangement of machines, equipment, materials handling, aisles, service areas, storage areas, and work stations within the facility.

Lead time: The time required from the recognition of a need to the replenishment of stock through ordering from a vendor or through manufacturing the item; *See* also Cycle Time.

Level Production Strategy: Planning production to be as consistent as possible; excess production from periods of low demand are carried in inventory to cover needs in periods of high demand.

Line Balancing: Arranging each step in the process within a product type layout to provide equal capacity so that material flow will be uninterrupted.

Loading: Assigning jobs to a work center, usually in terms of the labor content of the jobs relative to the labor capacity of the work center.

Lot Sizing: Determining the number of units to purchase or manufacture at one time. (*See* Economic Lot Size and Economic Order Quantity.)

Lot Tolerance Percent Defective (LTPD): The percent of defects in a lot that would make it unacceptable most of the time.

Lower Control Limit: The line on a quality control chart (generally three standard deviations below the mean) that indicates, from a sample statistic, that the process has likely shifted downward.

Make or Buy: Consideration of cost, quality, and delivery time and reliability factors to determine whether a particular item should be made in-house or purchased from a vendor.

Mass Production: *See* Repetitive Production.

Master Schedule: A plan indicating the necessary timing and quantities of finished products or assemblies to be produced.

Material/Sales Ratio: Percentage of the sales dollar spent for materials, supplies, and services needed to build a product or create a service.

Materials Management: Organizational concept in which a single manager has authority and responsibility for all activities principally concerned with the flow of materials into an organization. (Purchasing, production planning and scheduling, incoming traffic, inventory control, receiving, and stores normally are included.)

Materials Requirements Planning: *See* MRP.

Methodology (of Transformation): Management principles and techniques, such as planning, forecasting, scheduling, and controlling, involved in transforming inputs into outputs; *See* also Technology.

Minority Vendor Program: Conscious action by the purchasing department to locate, develop, and buy from firms owned by minority citizens.

Modular Design: Design of products with easily detachable sections, or modules.

MRO: Maintenance, repair, and operating supplies (as distinguished from raw material or capital equipment).

MRP: Acronym for materials requirements planning, a technique providing an integrated approach to scheduling.

Multiple-Activity Chart: Depicts against a time scale the respective activity of one or more persons operating one or more machines.

Multiplicative Model: A forecasting model that accounts for trends, seasonal, and cyclical components by multiplying initial forecasts by adjusting factors.

Negotiation: Arriving at an agreement on the essentials of a purchase contract, through discussion between buyer and seller.

Netting: Subtracting the on-hand inventory from gross requirements for an item to determine the net amount needed to order or produce.

Nine-Box Model: A model that contains calculations of productivity, price recovery, and profitability for the organization.

Numerical Control (N/C) Machines: Equipment preprogrammed to follow a cycle of operations repetitively without human intervention.

Office Process Flow Chart: Depicts the chronological flow of multiple copies and accompanying operations in paperwork systems.

Operating Characteristics Curve: For each quality control sample plan, the curve that shows the probability of acceptance of a lot relative to the percent defective in the lot.

Operation Chart: Uses symbols to depict how a worker uses each hand during the work cycle at an individual work station.

Operations Research: The use of quantitative tools–for example, simulation–to structure and analyze a problem in order to reach a mathematically optimal solution.

Operations Strategy: Guidelines for integrating the elements of POM into a consistent production plan.

Ordering Costs: Those fixed costs associated with placing a purchase order, regardless of the dollars or number of units represented in the order.

P-Chart: Plots the percent defective (attributes) of samples taken from a continuous process.

Partial Productivity Measure: The ratio of total outputs to only one or some part of the resources required.

Partnering: A long-term relationship between a supplier and a buyer that involves a sharing of plans, schedules, product specifications, quality data, and other information.

Performance Rating: Evaluation of the employee effort or pace against normal performance or normal pace (100 percent).

Periodic Review Model: A method of inventory reordering in which stock is checked at periodic intervals and the amount needed is ordered.

Personal Service: A category of services in which no physical product is involved but the customer generally must be present; counseling is an example.

PERT: Acronym for the program evaluation and review technique; a network modeling technique used to plan and control large-scale projects; *See* also CPM.

Pilot Production Run: A trial run of a manufacturing or service process for a new product under simulated normal production conditions to determine any product defects or process inefficiencies that may still exist.

Plant Visit: Inspection and evaluation of a vendor's facility, normally done prior to purchase of the vendor's products.

Prevention Costs: Costs associated with efforts to prevent defects in the process; includes improved product designs, better process design and operation, and increased capabilities of the workers.

Preventive Maintenance (PM): A program of scheduled maintenance designed to reduce the likelihood of equipment breakdown.

Price Recovery: The ratio of output prices to input prices; indicates the percent of resource price increases that are passed on to the customer in the form of higher product prices.

Process Capability: The ability of a process to produce items that meet technical specifications; measured as the ratio of the tolerance limits to the variance of the process.

Process Chart: Use of standard symbols to chart the sequence, distance, and time involved in the flow of work.

Process Focus: Organization of the firm based on processes in terms of strategies, layouts, production planning, and other decisions.

Process Layout: Arrangement of work facilities based on grouping together similar types of equipment.

Process Sampling: Inspection of a sample from an ongoing process to see if corrective actions are needed.

Producer's Risk: *See* Alpha Error.

Product Delivery: A category of services in which a physical product is involved and the customer does not have to be present; transportation is an example.

Product Focus: Organization of the firm based on products in terms of strategies, layouts, production planning, and other decisions.

Product Layout: Arrangement of work and equipment so that material flows according to the progressive steps by which the product is made.

Product Life Cycle: The five steps through which a product passes during its life: introduction, growth, maturity, saturation, and decline.

Product: The output of the production process including manufactured goods or services.

Production Function: The process of transforming inputs (material, equipment, effort, energy) into outputs (goods and services).

Production Planning: Specification of the products to produce and the resources needed within a time period; *See* also Level and Flexible production strategies.

Production Scheduling: Determination of the sequence and timing of production activities.

Production Strategy: *See* Operations Strategy.

Productivity: The ratio of outputs (goods and services) to inputs (labor, material, capital, and energy); indicates how well an individual, a business firm, or a national economy utilizes resources to produce products.

Profit-Leverage Effect of Purchasing: A dollar saved by better purchasing has the same effect on profits as a sales increase of many (ten to twenty) times that amount.

Profitability: The ratio of total revenue to total costs; indicates the percent of revenue that covers the costs of resources and the percent that goes to profit.

Progress Control: Constant monitoring of jobs, as they pass through a facility, to assure that all manufacturing requirements are being met. Also called Shop Floor Control.

Project Production: Manufacture of items when only one or a very few complex units are produced. (Shipbuilding is an example of project production.)

Pseudomanufacturing: A category of services in which a physical product is involved and the customer generally is present; a restaurant is an example.

Pull System: A system, such as Kanban, in which production is driven by customer purchases and products are "pulled" through the process with little inventory between stages.

Purchase Order: Legal document that spells out the quantity, quality, delivery date, price, and conditions of the purchase of items from a vendor.

Purchasing/Materials Management Strategy: Long-term (5 to 20 years) planning of purchase actions.

Push System: A traditional system in which production is driven by forecasts of demand; products are "pushed" through the system by schedules which may cause build-ups at bottleneck operations.

Quality Circle: A group of workers who meet together weekly to discuss problems of quality, or other factors, and develop solutions.

Quality Costs: Costs associated with the detection, correction, and prevention of defects; *See* costs of appraisal, internal failure, external failure, and prevention.

Quality: Characteristics of a product or service that determine its value in the marketplace and how well it performs the function for which it was designed.

R-Chart: Plots the range of a sample characteristic (variable) taken from a continuous process; *See* also X-bar Chart.

Random Component: Variations in time-series data that have no regular pattern or change over brief periods of time; also called irregular or noise influences; important in forecasting demand.

Receipt and Inspection of Goods: Verification that quantity and quality of items received from a vendor agree with the purchase specifications.

Redundancy: Providing a back-up component in a product to reduce the chance of failure; providing back-up equipment or workers in a process to reduce the effects of production disruptions.

Reliability: A quality characteristic that may refer to how long or how often the product will function, its probability of failure, or the consistency of a process to produce defect-free products.

Reorder Point: Stock level that signals the inventory controller to start the reordering process because there is only enough stock to meet normal needs during the resupply lead time and still have the desired safety stock available.

Repetitive Production: Manufacturing of many units of the same product with a unit moving through each state of the process as that operation is completed–for example, an automobile assembly line.

Research and Development: Those activities principally concerned with investigation directed toward discovering new scientific knowledge (research) and translating this new knowledge into marketable goods and services (development).

Responsiveness: The ability of a firm to react quickly to changes in demand, product innovations, competition, or other market forces.

Return-on-Assets: Measurement of the productivity of assets employed by a firm; computed by multiplying investment turnover times profit margin.

Robinson-Patman Act: Federal law requiring that a vendor charge all buyers the same price for the same item purchased in the same quantity.

Robot: Equipment that is computer controlled and designed to replace the human operator.

Route Sheet: Lists the sequence of operations necessary to start from material inputs (shown in the bill of materials) through production of the finished product.

Safety Stock: That inventory used to protect against running out of supplies because of late delivery from suppliers or unusually high usage during the resupply period.

Sample Plan: The number of units to be sampled from a lot, and the number of defects that determines acceptance or rejection.

Sample Size: The number of units sampled from a lot of material.

Sampling: *See* Work Sampling, Acceptance Sampling, Batch Sampling, and Process Sampling.

Screening: Inspection of every unit in a lot.

Seasonal Component: Time-series variations that are periodic and can be expected to recur regularly within a certain period, usually one year or less; important in forecasting demand.

Seasonal Inventories: *See* Anticipatory Stocks.

Service Level: The percentage of time that an item will be in stock.

Service: Something intangible that satisfies a customer's need in addition to or instead of providing that customer with a tangible product.

Setup Costs: Incurred when a system is rearranged to perform a different task–for example, changing a TV studio set in preparation for taping a different series. (The cost is independent of the number of times the new arrangement will be used.)

Sherman Anti-Trust Act: Makes illegal any combination, collusion, or conspiracy by sellers or buyers to set price or restrict trade.

Single Sourcing: Purchase of all requirements of a given item from only one vendor, even though several vendors could supply it.

Specifications: The detailed description of a product, usually including a list of measurable characteristics, the different parts or materials that go into a product, and often a detailed set of directions about how to assemble the unit or properly perform the service.

Standardization: The process of establishing agreement on uniform identifications for certain characteristics of quality, design, performance, quantity, and service. (An agreed-upon uniform identification is called a standard.)

Statistical Quality Control (SQC): The use of probability theory and statistical principles to determine quality-sampling procedures.

Stockout: Demand in excess of current stock on hand.

Strategic Material Planning: Long-term forecast of demand, supply, and price of key raw materials to identify potential problems. Forecast results are used to formulate alternative action courses.

Subfunctions of POM: The functions that comprise the field of production/operations management: product design and development, facilities location, capital equipment, facilities layout, work design and measurement, forecasting, planning, scheduling, purchasing/materials management, inventory management, and quality management.

System Reliability: The probability that a system or product will function properly given the reliability (defect rate) of each of the components.

Technical Factors: Characteristics of the process, such as the capability of the equipment, the layout, and the material specifications, that affect the quality of the product produced.

Technology (of Transformation): Scientific principles applied to convert inputs into outputs, such as the chemistry and physics involved in petroleum refining; *See* also Methodology.

Therblig: A fundamental movement or action–for example, transport, load, grasp, or hold–used in constructing detailed motion charts for the analysis of hand movements.

Thomas Register of American Manufacturers: Widely used directory listing United States manufacturers by type of item produced.

Time Standard: *See* Standard Time.

Time Study: Work measurement technique that normally uses a stopwatch to determine the time required to do a job. (The analyst then uses a performance rating and allows for normal delays to determine a standard time.)

Time-Series Models: *See* Intrinsic Models.

Tolerances: Upper and lower specifications, generally set by the design engineer, that define an acceptable product.

Total Productivity Measure: The ratio of total outputs to the total of all resources required.

Total Quality Management (TQM): An organizational approach to the strategic management of quality in all phases of the design and manufacturing process.

Transportation Deregulation: Removal of restrictions regarding service and rates for movement of goods by carriers.

Trend Component: The tendency of a variable to have a long-term increase or a long-term decrease; important in forecasting demand.

Type I Error: Rejecting a lot that should have been accepted; also called an "alpha error" or "producer's risk."

Type II Error: Accepting a lot that should have been rejected; also called a "beta error" or "consumer's risk."

Types of Services: Categories of services defined by the presence or absence of the customer when the service is performed and whether there is a physical product involved; *See* absentee service, personal service, product delivery, and pseudomanufacturing.

Upper Control Limit: The line on a quality control chart (generally three standard deviations above the mean) that indicates, from the sample statistic, that the process has likely shifted upward.

Value Analysis: The organized and systematic study of every element of cost in a material, part, or service to ensure that it fulfills its function at the lowest total cost.

Variables Sampling: Quality sampling in which the characteristic is measured on a continuous scale such as length, temperature, or weight.

Variables: In quality control, characteristics measured on a continuous scale, such as temperature, length, or color; *See* also Attributes.

Varied Path Equipment: Flexible equipment (such as a forklift truck) that normally handles equipment in lots.

Vendor Directory: Volume that lists vendors and their addresses, arranged by product.

Vendor Point Rating System: Method of evaluating vendor performance in which points are assigned to how well the vendor performed on several factors, such as quality, delivery, and price.

Vendor: An outside supplier of raw materials, supplies, or services needed in the operation of an organization.

Work Design: Systematic approach to finding the most effective and efficient method of doing a job; also known as methods study or motion study.

Work Measurement: Determination of how long it should take a qualified and trained employee working at a normal pace to do a specific task or operation, with due allowances for fatigue and personal and unavoidable delays; also known as time study.

Work Sampling: The application of probability theory involving random observations to determine the time distribution within a given work activity.

Work Study: Analyzing the people, equipment, materials, and product requirements to determine the most efficient methods and flow of work for a new or existing process.

X-bar Chart: Plots the mean of a characteristic (variable) for a sample taken from a continuous process; *See* also R-Chart.

Index

ABC analysis, 182
Acceptable quality level (AQL), 261
Acceptance sampling, 260
Acquisition of inputs, 7
Activity based accounting, 36
Air Cargo Act, 1977, 201
Airline Deregulation Act, 1978, 201
American Express, 2, 97
American Production and Inventory
    Control Society (APICS), 41
American Society for Quality Control
    (ASQC), 41, 249
American Society of Mechanical
    Engineers (ASME), 99
Anheuser-Busch, 54
Annual Survey of Manufactures, 168
Anticipatory stocks, 211
Assembly chart, 103
Assembly lines, early, 13
Automated batch manufacturing
    systems (ABMS), 95
Automatic storage and retrieval
    systems (AS/RS), 94

Babbage, Charles, 13
Backdoor selling, 185

Baldrige Award, 249
Basic Motion Time Study (BMT),
    105, 110
Batch sampling, 260
Bic Pen Corporation, 51
Bids, competitive, 194
Bill of materials (B/M), 64, 141, 143,
    185
Blank-check purchase order, 196
Blanket orders, 196
Blueprint, 186
Booz, Allen, and Hamilton, 152
Brand or trade name, 186
Break-even
    after release (BEAR), 70
    analysis, 66
    time, 69
Buffer stocks, 210
Bus Regulatory Reform Act, 1982,
    201
Business Periodical Index, 191
Business plan, 136
Business Week, 190

Cadillac, 249
Capacity requirements planning
    (CRP), 147

Capital equipment, 23
Careers in production/operations
    management, 39
Causal models, 131
Cellular layout, 90
Center for Advanced Purchasing
    Studies, 163, 178, 203
Centralized purchasing
    centralization versus
        decentralization, 176
Certification programs, 39
"Chase" strategy, 138
Commodity file, 199
Competitive bids, 194
Computer applications, 14
Computer-aided design (CAD), 15,
    58, 95
Computer-aided manufacturing
    (CAM), 15, 95
Computer-integrated manufacturing
    (CIM), 15
Consumer's risk, 261
Consumer-opinion surveys, 127
Contract file, 199
Contribution to profit, 37
Conversion process, 10
Coors, 51
Countertrade, 202
Critical path method (CPM), 152
    event times, 154
    network diagramming, 153
    the critical path, 157
Cycle stocks, 211

Decentralized purchasing
    centralization versus
        decentralization, 176
Decoupling stocks, 210
Delphi technique, 127
Department of Commerce, 249
Dependent demand, 126, 224
Disney, 2
Dodge, H. F., 14
Durability, 245

Ecology, 18
Economic lot size (ELS), 211, 219
Economic order quantity (EOQ),
    212, 215, 226
Effectiveness, 33

Efficiency, 33
Electronic Data Interchange (EDI),
    201
Energy management, 97
Environment, business, 11
Environmental responsibility, 38
EOQ
    formula, 217
    with discounts, 217
Equipment
    capital, 23
    selection, 94
Expediting, 196
Exploding, 64, 143
Exponential smoothing, 130
Extrinsic models of forecasting, 131

Facilities layout, 23
    cost comparisons, 92
    CRAFT, 92
    fixed-position layout, 90
    group or cellular layout, 90
    layout analysis, 92
    manufacturing layout, 88
    marketing layout, 90
    objectives of, 86
    office layout, 90
    process layout, 88
    product or line layout, 89
    service layout, 91
    storage layout, 90
    yard layout, 90
Facilities location, 22
    analysis methods, 82
    break-even analysis, 83
    key factors, 80
    linear programming, 85
    simulation, 83
    transportation method, 85
    weighted factor method, 82
Factories, early, 14
Factory of the future, 16
Federal Anti-Price Discrimination
    Act of 1936, 192
Federal Express, 249
Finite loading, 147
Firestone Tire and Rubber Company,
    61
Fishbone diagram, 244
Fixed costs, 67

Flexibility, 38
Flexible manufacturing systems
    (FMS), 16
Flexible production strategy, 138
Flow diagram, 102
Flow-process production, 28
Foolproof designs, 274
Ford Motor Company, 256
Ford, Henry, 13
Forecast horizon, 126
Forecasting, 24
    demand, 125
    exponential smoothing, 130
    extrinsic models, 131
    intrinsic models, 127
    judgmental methods, 127
    linear regression, 130
    mean absolute deviation (MAD),
        135
    methods of, 127
    multiplicative model, 131
    running sum of the forecast errors
        (RSFE), 135
    simple moving average, 128
    simple weighted average, 128
    time-series models, 127
Foreign purchasing, 202
Forward buying, 185
Functionality, 244

Gantt charts, 149
General business strategy, 31
General Motors (GM), 7
General objectives, 33
Gilbreth, Frank and Lillian, 13, 105
Gillette, 51
Globe Metallurgical, 249
Goldratt, Eliyahu, 150
Grace Commission, 200
Gross domestic product (GDP), 20
Group layout, 90

Hand-to-mouth buying, 185
Harris, F. W., 14
Hewlett Packard, 69
History of production/operations
    management, 13

IBM, 249
Independent demand, 126, 224

Infinite loading, 147
Innovation, 38
Inputs, 7
Interstate Commerce Commission,
    201
Intrinsic models for forecasting, 127
Inventories
    carrying costs, 213
    functions of, 210
    physical care of, 234
Inventory management, 25, 209
    carrying costs, 213
    cycle counting, 235
    economic lot size (ELS), 211
    economic lot-size (ELS) formula,
        219
    economic order quantity (EOQ),
        212
    economics of, 212
    JIT (Just-In-Time) management
        system, 229
    lead times, 222
    lot sizing, 225
    one-time order quantities, 223
    ordering costs, 212
    periodic review model, 220
    record keeping, 235
    reorder points (ROP), 222
    safety stock, 221, 226
    service level, 222
    setup cost, 213
    storage and material handling, 234
    total cost, 216
Inventory status, 141
Iron Age, 194
Islands of automation, 15

JIT (Just-In-Time) management
    system, 229
    cycle time, 232
    inventory levels, 233
    kanban, 230
    lot sizes, 231
    setup times, 231
Job sequencing, 148
Job-shop
    production, 27
    scheduling, 149
Judgmental methods of forecasting,
    127

Jumbled shops, 31
Jungle, The, 14
Just-in-time (JIT), 14, 151

Kanban, 151, 230

Lead times, 222
Least total cost (LTC), 226
Least unit cost (LUC), 226
Level of product, 50
Level production strategy, 138
"Lights out" factory, 16
Line balancing, 93
Linear programming, transportation
    problem, 85
Linear regression, 130
List price, 193
Location decision making, 82
Lockheed Aircraft Corporation, 152
Lot tolerance percent defective
    (LTPD), 261
Lot-for-Lot (L4L), 226

Machinery and Allied Products
    Institute, 177
Maintenance, 96
    breakdown repair, 96
    custodial services, 96
    group replacement, 96
    millwright, 96
    preventive maintenance (PM), 96
    repair, and operating (MRO), 183
    standby equipment, 96
Malcolm Baldrige National Quality
    Award, 249
Manufacturing
    layout, 88
Market
    grade, 186
    prices, 194
    research, 59
    surveys, 127
Mass production, early, 13
Master production schedule, 143
Master schedule, 139
Material requirements planning
    (MRP), 14, 141, 184, 224
    economic order quantity (EOQ),
        226
    least total cost (LTC), 226

least unit cost (LUC), 226
lot sizing, 225
lot-for-lot (L4L), 226
    period order quantity (POQ), 226
safety lead time, 226
Wagner-Whitin Algorithm, 226
Materials handling, 93
Materials management, 179
McDonalds, 2, 38
McRae's Bluebook, 188
Mean absolute deviation (MAD), 135
Methods Time Measurement
    (MTM), 105, 110
Microprocessors, 15
Milliken, 249
Minicomputers, 15
Mission statement, 30
Modular design, 58
Motor Carrier Act, 1980, 201
Motorola, 16, 249, 252, 257
Multiple-activity chart, 104
Multiplicative model, 131

Nader, Ralph, 275
National Association of Purchasing
    Management (NAPM), 41, 164
Naval Shipyard at Norfolk, Virginia,
    253
Netting process, 143
Nine-Box Model, 119
Numerical-control (N/C), 95

Operating-characteristics curve, 261
Operation chart, 105
Operations
    definition of, 5
    research (OR), 14
    strategy, 33
Ordering costs, 212
Outputs, 10

P-chart, 265
Packaging, 248
Performance specification, 187
Period order quantity (POQ), 226
Periodic review model, 220
Pilot production run, 62
Planning
    business plan, 136
    controlling projects, 152

planning for production, 136
production, 136
production plan, 138
scheduling, 24
Polaroid, 50
Preparation of the purchase
    agreement, 196
Price negotiation, 194
Price recovery, 116
Process
    capability, 270
    charts, 99
    control, 265
    design, 246
    focus, 31
Producer's risk, 261
Product
    availability, 51
    definition of, 6
    definitions of, 1
    description, 63
    focus, 31
    level of, 50
    life cycle, 48
    line, 51
    research and development, 52
    specifications, 63
    strategy, 50
    testing, 61
Product design and development, 22,
    47, 246
    computer-aided design (CAD), 58
    market research, 59
    material, 55
    modular design, 58
    organizing for, 71
    pilot production run, 62
    resources, 60
    standardization, 57
    testing, 61
    value analysis/value engineering,
        55
Production
    forecasting, 24
    function, 7
    planning and scheduling, 24
    production plan, 138
    scheduling production, 139

Production/operations management
    and other business functions, 11
    careers in, 39
    definitions of, 1, 2
    functions of, 21
    history of, 13
    reasons for study, 6
    the future of, 16
Productivity, 19, 37, 112
    firm, 115
    individual, 115
    partial productivity, 112
    productivity ratios, 114
    total productivity, 112, 116
Profit-leverage effect, 169
Profitability, 116
Program evaluation and review
    technique (PERT), 152
    event times, 154
    network diagramming, 153
    the critical path, 157
Progress control, 150
Project production, 27
Public purchasing, 200
Purchase order
    log, 198
    unpriced, 193
Purchasing
    Center for Advanced Purchasing
        Studies, 163
    foreign, 202
    services, 203
Purchasing/materials management,
    25, 163
    centralization versus
        decentralization, 176
    effect on competitive position, 173
    effect on efficiency, 173
    importance of, 167
    maintenance of records, 198
    material/sales ratio, 169
    objectives of, 165
    organization of, 175
    performance benchmarking, 203
    profit-leverage effect, 169
    purchasing prerogatives, 181
    return-on-assets effect, 173
    standard purchasing system, 182
    strategy, 204

Pure Food and Drug Act, 14

Quality
    acceptance sampling, 260
    appraisal costs, 255
    as a competitive factor, 37
    attributes, 259
    Baldrige Award, 249
    batch sampling, 260
    consumer's risk, 261
    costs, 253
    definition, 243
    dimensions of, 244
    external failure costs, 256
    factors affecting, 250
    prevention costs, 256
    producer's risk, 261
    product quality, 242
    quality circles, 252
    screening, 259
    six sigma, 257
    statistical quality control (SQC),
        258
    variables, 259
    zero defects, 253
Quality management, 26, 241
Quotation
    salesperson's, 193

R-chart, 267
Radio Shack, 51
Raw materials, 247
Redundancy, 274
Reliability, 244
    system, 272
Reorder points (ROP), 222
Repetitive production, 28, 111
Research and development
    evaluating, 69
    product, 52
Resources, 60
Responsiveness, 38
Return-on-assets effect, 173
Robinson-Patman Act, 192
Romig, H. G., 14
Route sheet, 66
Running sum of the forecast errors
    (RSFE), 135

Safety, 246

Safety stocks, 221
Salesperson's quotation, 193
Scheduling production, 139
Screening, 259
Securities and Exchange
    Commission, 191
Sequencing jobs, 148
Services
    designing, 62
    purchasing of, 203
    types of, 29
Setup cost, 213
Sherman Anti-Trust Act of 1980, 192
Shewhart, W. A., 14
Shop-floor control, 150
Simple moving average, 128
Simple weighted average, 128
Single sourcing, 199
Six sigma, 257
Small Parts, Inc., 8
Smith, Adam, 13
Source selection, 187
Staggers Rail Act, 1980, 201
Standardization, 57
Statistical quality control, 258
    control limits, 265
    process capability index, 270
    process control, 265
    system reliability, 272
Stopwatch time study, 108
Storage, 248
Strategy, 33
    product, 50
Supplier partnering/strategic
    alliances, 200

Taylor, Frederick W., 13
Techtronics, 252
Testing, 61
The Wall Street Journal, 194
Therbligs, 105, 110
Thomas Register of American
    Manufacturers, 188
Time phasing, 143
Time-and-motion study, 109
Time-based competition, 38, 72
Time-series models for forecasting,
    127
Total quality management (TQM),
    246

Toyota, 257
Transformation
    technology of vs. methodology of,
        10
Transportation problem, linear
    programming, 85
Transporting (or transportation), 248
Try Us '91, 188
Types of manufacturing, 26
Types of services, 29

U.S. Bureau of the Census, 168, 172
U.S. Navy Special Projects Office,
    152
U.S. Postal Service, 275
Unit cost, 36
Unpriced purchase order, 193
Upton Sinclair, 14

Value analysis/value engineering
    (VA/VE), 56
Variable costs, 67
Vendor
    approved list, 191
    directories, 188
    evaluation, 189

experience rating, 191
file, 199
minority, 188
selection, 187

Wagner-Whitin Algorithm, 226
Waiting-line theory, 14
Wall Street Journal, 190
Wealth of Nations, The, 13
Westinghouse, 249, 252
Word picture, 186
Work
    design and measurement, 24
    Factor, 105, 110
    measurement, 105
    sampling, 110
    study, 97
    study charts, 99

$\overline{X}$ chart, 266
Xerox, 249

Young, John, 70

Zero defects, 253